CAIRO
SINCE 1900
An Architectural Guide

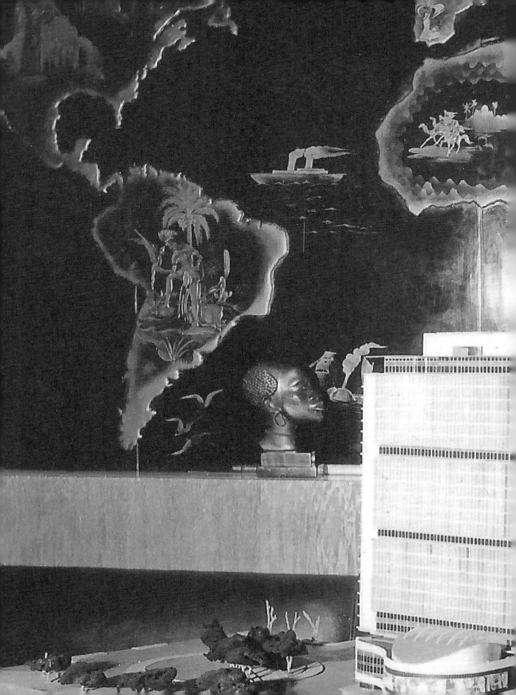

CAIRO
SINCE 1900
An Architectural Guide

MOHAMED ELSHAHED
Foreword by Mercedes Volait

The American University in Cairo Press
Cairo · New York

Pages 2–3
Architects at the office of Mahmoud Riad looking over a maquette of the League of Arab States building (#11, completed 1955). Courtesy RiadArchitecture.

Pages 4–5
Architects putting the finishing touches on a maquette of the 1949 Industrial and Agricultural Exhibition, which took place at the Exhibition Grounds (#131). Private collection.

Pages 6–7
Architect Sayed Karim pictured in the 1950s at his home office in his villa (#207), with a maquette of an unbuilt mixed-use tower. Private collection.

Page 8
The main stairs at Villa Sayed Karim (#207, built 1948) with the three-story neon light pendant in the center. Courtesy RBSCL, AUC.

First published in 2020 by
The American University in Cairo Press
113 Sharia Kasr el Aini, Cairo, Egypt
One Rockefeller Plaza, New York, NY, 10020
www.aucpress.com

Copyright © 2020 by Mohamed Elshahed

All rights reserved. No part of this publication may be reproduced, stored in a retrieval system, or transmitted in any form or by any means, electronic, mechanical, photocopying, recording, or otherwise, without the prior written permission of the publisher.

Every reasonable attempt has been made to identify copyright owners. Any errors or omissions will be corrected in subsequent editions.

All drawings, graphics, and diagrams are produced by the research team (see the Acknowledgments) except where noted.

All non-archival photographs are by the author except where noted.

Dar el Kutub No. 20785/17
ISBN 978 977 416 869 7

Dar el Kutub Cataloging-in-Publication Data

Elshahed, Mohamed
    Cairo since 1900: An Architectural Guide / Mohamed Elshahed.— Cairo: The American University in Cairo Press, 2020
    p. cm.
    ISBN 978 977 416 869 7
    1. Architecture–Cairo (Egypt)
    720.96216

2 3 4 5   24 23 22 21 20

Designed by Ahmad Hammoud
Printed in China

Contents

Foreword by *Mercedes Volait* 17
Acknowledgments 19
Building Selection 23
Introduction 27
Glossary 43
Maps 53
Historic Cairo **69**
    1. Al-Azhar Administration, 1936 72
    2. Muhammad Abduh Auditorium, 1946 73
    3. Museum of Islamic Art and National Library, 1903 74
    4. Al-Rifai Mosque, 1869–1912 76
    5. Mustafa Kamel Mausoleum, 1947 78
    6. Hassanein Bey Mausoleum, 1946 79
    7. Al-Azhar Park, 2004 80
Downtown **83**
    8. Egyptian Museum, 1902 86
    9. Arab Socialist Union (demolished), 1959 87
    10. Nile Hilton Hotel (Ritz Carlton), 1953–58 88
    11. League of Arab States, 1955 89
    12. Qasr al-Nil Bridge, 1933 90
    13. Omar Makram Mosque, 1948 91
    14. Al-Mugammaa, 1951 92
    15. AUC Science Building (demolished), 1966 94
    16. Aziz Bahari Buildings (Tahrir Square), 1934 95
    17. Cleopatra Palace Hotel, 1962 96
    18. Khoury Building, 1941 97
    19. Baehler Buildings, 1920s, 1934 98
    20. Misr Insurance Company Offices, 1950 100
    21. Misr Insurance Company Offices, 1952 101
    22. Ahmed Kamel Pasha Building, 1936 102
    23. AUC Jameel Building, 1989 103
    24. AUC Library (Greek Campus), 1978 104
    25. Bab al-Louq Station, 1932 106
    26. Chamber of Commerce, 1955 107
    27. Strand Building, 1957 108
    28. Al-Tabbakh Mosque, 1931 109
    29. Awqaf Administration, 1898–1929 110
    30. Alexandria Insurance Company, 1952 112
    31. Immobilia Building, 1940 114
    32. Central Bank, 1930–47 116
    33. Murad Wahba Pasha Building, 1949 117
    34. Ayrout Building, 1937 118
    35. Radio Tower, 1954 119

36. Church and Convent of Saint Joseph, 1909...120
37. Banque Misr, 1927...121
38. Banque Misr Tower, 1985..121
39. Aziz Bahari Buildings (Mustafa Kamel Square), 1938..122
40. Assicurazioni Generali Building, 1939..123
41. Crédit Foncier Égyptien, 1903..124
42. Shaar Hashamayim Synagogue, 1905...125
43. Tiring Department Store, 1912..126
44. Sednaoui Department Store, 1913..127
45. Khedival Buildings, 1911...128
46. George and Helal Shammaa Building, 1952..129
47. Misr Petroleum Company, 1948..130
48. Arabic Music Institute, 1923...131
49. Egyptian Society of Engineers, 1923–46..132
50. Abdel Hamid al-Shawarbi Pasha Building, 1925..133
51. High Court, 1924–34..134
52. La Genevoise, 1937..136
53. Waqf Gamalian Buildings, 1940..137
54. Ouzonian Building, 1949..138
55. Al-Nasr Import–Export Company, 1964...139

Bulaq..141
56. Nefertiti Hotel (proposed), 1962..144
57. Ramses Hilton Hotel, 1976–79..145
58. TV and Radio Administration, 1960..146
59. Ministry of Foreign Affairs, 1994..147
60. Nile Tower (proposed), 2007..148
61. St. Regis Hotel, 2018..149
62. World Trade Center, 1988..150
63. Akhbar al-Yom Building, 1948..151
64. Al-Ahram Building, 1968..152
65. Turguman Regeneration Plan (proposed), 1967...153
66. Maspero Triangle Master Plan (proposed), 2015..154

Sayeda Zeinab & Abdeen...157
67. Cultural Park for Children, 1990..160
68. Waqf of Raafat Bey, 1940...162
69. Al-Sharq Cinema, 1947...162
70. Dar al-Hilal Printing Press, 1945...163
71. Saad Zaghloul Mausoleum, 1931...164
72. Misr Insurance Company, 1947..166
73. Zeinhom Housing Development, 1955–2007..168
74. National Museum of Egyptian Civilization (NMEC), 1984–2017......................169

Garden City..171
75. Al-Chams Building, 1949..174
76. Cairo Center Office Building, 1969...176
77. Embassy of the United States of America, 1989...177
78. Egyptian Company for Real Estate Investment, 1940.....................................178

79. Petroleum Cooperative Society, 1957 ... 180
80. Mobil Building, 1959 ... 181
81. Serageldin Palace, 1908 ... 182
82. Residential Building (2 al-Fasqiya Street), 1938 ... 183
83. Houd al-Laban Building, 1960s ... 184
84. Sabet Sabet Building, 1958 ... 185
85. Arab African International Bank, c.2000 ... 186
86. Ibrahimiya School, 1939 ... 187
87. Residential Building (2 Ittihad al-Muhamiyin Street), 1940s ... 188
88. Doctors' Syndicate (Dar al-Hikma), 1949 ... 189

Manial ... **191**
89. Le Méridien Hotel, 1974 ... 194
90. Qasr al-Aini Medical School, 1923–33 ... 195
91. Manial Palace, 1901–29 ... 196
92. Saraya Ahmed Mustafa Abu Rehab, 1949 ... 198
93. Ibrahim Mosque, 1945 ... 199

Giza ... **201**
94. Cairo University Hall, 1937 ... 204
95. Al-Shafiq Building, 1948 ... 206
96. Halim Dos Bey Building, 1937 ... 208
97. Misr Insurance Company, 1961 ... 210
98. Villa Anis Serageldin (demolished), 1934 ... 211
99. Villa William Habib (demolished), 1933 ... 212
100. Villa Cassab (demolished), 1934 ... 213
101. Villa Dr. Kamal Abdel Razeq (demolished), 1947 ... 214
102. Villa Ibrahim al-Kassas Bey (demolished), 1948 ... 215

Dokki & Agouza ... **217**
103. Aziz Abdel Malek Hanna Building, 1937 ... 220
104. Faisal Bank, 2000 ... 221
105. State Council, c.1990 ... 222
106. Goethe-Institut, 2016 ... 223
107. Mohandes Insurance Headquarters, 1999 ... 224
108. Embassy of the Czech Republic, 1980 ... 225
109. Ahram Beverages Company, 1900 ... 226
110. National Research Center, 1956 ... 227
111. Musaddaq Office Building, 1995 ... 228
112. Mahmoud Othman Building, 1955 ... 229
113. Al-Kateb Hospital, 1946 ... 230
114. Bishara Building, 1937 ... 231
115. Agouza Hospital, 1939 ... 232
116. Shahrazad Hotel, c.1982 ... 233

Mohandiseen ... **235**
117. Madinat al-Awqaf, 1948 ... 238
118. Media City Apartments, 1959 ... 239
119. National Center for Social and Criminological Research, 1959 ... 240
120. Sphinx Cinema, 1965 ... 241

121. Residential Building (26 Gameat al-Diwal al-Arabiya Street), 1986............242
122. City Central Premium Offices, 2017............243
123. Residential Building (16 Lebanon Street), 1980s............244
124. Villa Shawky, 1968............245
125. Villa Badran, 1971............246

Imbaba............249
126. Imbaba Bridge, 1924............252
127. New Amiriya Printing Press, 1973............253
128. Workers' City, 1950............254
129. Tahrir City, 1958............256
130. Giza Park, 2013............257

Zamalek............259
131. Exhibition Grounds, 1936–49............262
132. Opera House, 1988............263
133. Mahmoud Mukhtar Museum, 1962............264
134. 1952 Revolution Museum (unfinished), 1951–2009............265
135. Cairo Tower, 1961............266
136. Nabil Amr Ibrahim Palace, 1923............268
137. All Saints Cathedral, 1988............269
138. Forte Tower (unfinished), 1976............270
139. Islamic Congress Secretariat (proposed), 1957............271
140. Rodrigue Flats, 1945............272
141. Lebon Building, 1950............273
142. Henri and Georges Boinet Building, 1934............274
143. Ali Labib Gabr Building, 1951............275
144. Zamalek Tower (Wahbi Mousa Soliman Building), 1953............276
145. Dar al-Hana (Madame Khayyat Building), 1938............278
146. Villa Umm Kulthoum (demolished), 1936............279
147. Virgin Mary Church (al-Maraashli Church), 1959............280
148. Sedky Pasha Building, 1947............281

Shubra............283
149. Corniche al-Nil Towers, 1992............286
150. Rod al-Farag Market, 1947............287
151. Don Bosco Italian Technical Institute, 1926............288
152. Khazindara Mosque, 1927............290
153. Saint Teresa Church, 1931............291

Daher & Abbasiya............293
154. Church of Collège De La Salle School, 1955............296
155. Al-Halabi Print House, 1937............297
156. Residential Building (35 Sabil al-Khazindar Street), 1931............298
157. École Alliance Israélite Universelle, 1928............299
158. Waqf Inji Zada, 1937............300
159. October Bridge, 1969–99............301
160. Boutros Ghali Memorial Church, 1911............302
161. Saint Mark's Coptic Cathedral, 1968............303
162. 23 July Development, 1962............304

163. Ain Shams University Lecture Halls, 1969..........305
164. Faculty of Engineering, Ain Shams University, 1933..........306
165. Gamal Abdel Nasser Mosque, 1966..........307
Heliopolis..........309
  166. Waqf Asmaa Hanem Halim, 1948..........312
  167. Heliopolis (Ferial) Hospital, 1955..........314
  168. Saint Catherine's Church, 1950..........316
  169. Le Méridien Hotel, 1987..........317
  170. Society for Culture and Development, 1997..........318
  171. Heliopolis War Cemetery, 1941..........318
  172. Baron Empain Palace, 1911..........319
  173. Cathedral of Our Lady of Heliopolis, 1910..........320
  174. Fayza Hanem Owais Building, 1949..........322
  175. Mahallawy Building, 1949..........323
  176. Residential Building (Sesostris/Mamoun Streets), 1911..........324
  177. Cinema Farouk, 1949..........325
  178. Heliopolis Company Buildings, 1908..........326
  179. Elias Bey Rizq Building, 1948..........328
  180. Regine Khoury Building, 1934..........328
  181. Fattouh Bey Guinenah Building, 1941..........329
  182. Merryland Apartments, 1958..........330
  183. Merryland Park, 1963..........332
  184. Madinat Ghernata, 1928..........334
  185. Debbane Bey Building, 1940..........335
  186. Gamal Abdel Nasser Museum, 2017..........336
  187. Villa Kamel Bek Abdel Halim (demolished), 1932..........337
  188. Villa Mrs. Valadji (demolished), 1933..........337
Nasr City..........339
  189. Nasr City Plan, 1953..........342
  190. Al-Azhar University Campus, 1962–65..........344
  191. Cairo International Stadium, 1960..........346
  192. Expo City (proposed), 2009..........347
  193. Unknown Soldier Memorial, 1975..........348
  194. Military Parade Stands, 1960..........349
  195. Government Sector, 1960..........350
  196. Nasr City Company for Housing and Development, 1959..........351
  197. Housing Model 20, 1959..........352
  198. Housing Model 10, 1959..........353
  199. Housing Model 15, 1959..........354
  200. Nasr City Cinema (demolished), 1962..........355
  201. Al-Rahma Mosque, 1982..........356
  202. Housing Model 22, 1959..........357
  203. Housing Model 33, 1959..........358
Maadi..........361
  204. Residential Building (Road 256), 1962..........364
  205. Saint Thérèse Church (proposed), 1950s..........365

206. Maadi Mosque, 1938......366
207. Villa Sayed Karim, 1948......367
208. Maadi Garden Villas, 1949......370
209. Maadi Palace Building, 1996......371
210. Supreme Constitutional Court, 1999......372
211. Maadi Towers, 1987......373

Outskirts......375
212. The American University in Cairo, 2008......378
213. Bank ABC, 2018......380
214. Unity Building, 2015......381
215. Cairo International Airport, 1963......382
216. Abusir House 2, 2003......384
217. Harraniya Arts Center, 1951–72......386
218. Farouk Resthouse, 1946......387
219. Grand Egyptian Museum, projected 2022......388
220. Pyramid House, 2009–19......389
221. National Cancer Institute, projected 2019......390
222. Dar al-Handasa Office Building, 2013......391
223. Designopolis, 2012......392
224. Japanese Garden, 1917......393
225. Studios Misr, 1935......394
226. Skyline, projected 2022......395

Notes......400
Bibliography......402
Index of Architects......406

Foreword

I still remember the excitement of coming across issues of *Al Emara*—as the title of *Majallat al-'imara* was romanized on the magazine's covers—decades ago in Cairo. The architectural journal, established in Egypt in 1939, was the first of its kind to be published in Arabic and offered an exceptional window on the projects and achievements of Egyptian professionals. The discovery followed a conversation in 1984 with a fellow student who was also conducting research in the dusty holdings of Dar al-Kutub, Cairo's National Library, but who had mastered much better the library's card drawers and indexes. While interested in modern Egyptian architecture for some time, I had gathered no indication from the literature that such a journal had ever existed, let alone supported the ideas and concerns of the International style, promoting furthermore their Egyptian and Arab expressions. Faculty at architectural departments in Cairo and Alexandria had never heard of the magazine. Its pages belonged to a world that had fallen into complete oblivion. Egyptian architects had been present in international Modernist circles since the 1930s and 1940s, but no one seemed to be aware any more, as I realized after publishing my first monograph on the topic (*L'architecture moderne en Égypte et la revue al-'Imara (1939–1959)*, Cairo: CEDEJ, 1988). After all, revolutions are meant to be harsh ruptures with the immediate past, and 1952 was no exception.

In the West, another narrative had taken precedence in the wake of decolonization and at the acme of 'architecture without architects.' For anyone trained then in the history of twentieth-century design, the Egyptian experience equated solely with attempts made by Hassan Fathy at reviving mud-brick construction. Recent extensive research in the archives of Hassan Bey has shown that his was a broader universe, one that was deeply rooted in the ethos of the Egyptian 1930s and could not be reduced in any case to vernacular masonry. By then, there was indeed a largely shared belief that Modernism beyond Europe and the United States was primarily, if not exclusively, the working of colonial agency and society. In other words, the input could not come but from the West. To some extent, this ideological prejudice still holds firm today in mainstream knowledge, despite efforts made by architectural historians to uncover "Other Modernisms" (the theme of the Ninth International DOCOMOMO Conference in 2006) across the world and regardless of the fact that, in the Egyptian case, the first eleven years of the whole print run of *Al Emara* (1939–59) have been fully accessible online since 2010, thanks to a joint initiative of Archnet and Harvard University.

With this unique resource, supplemented by many other materials collected over the years, Mohamed Elshahed has set out to reconstruct the lost story of Cairo's architectural Modernism through a selection of buildings. Possessing an intimate knowledge of the giant city, he has chosen to include samples exemplifying typical and canonical trends as well as specimens expressing peculiar formulas. Constructions from the 1950s and 1960s are somewhat closer to his heart than early twentieth-century examples, as readers will immediately notice, but the selection covers what was produced throughout the century. More crucially, Mohamed is not trying to force Cairo into the canon of avant-garde architecture. His aim is not to demonstrate that the Modernist buildings of the Egyptian capital should compete with the conventional Top Ten or Twenty of pioneering architecture. The purpose is to show that the city possesses a genuine modern built landscape that has value *per se*. Many will agree that there is a life for modern architecture besides icons and manifestos! Exposing Cairo Modernism on its own terms does break, however, with standard narratives in twentieth-century architecture and art history, where so little space is provided to Modernism outside the West. But paying attention, if not tribute, to its expressions and exponents, is a prerequisite to enlarging our understanding of the Modern and devising a more inclusive history of its global making. The revision is long due and is gaining momentum. This architectural guide is a most welcome addition to the recent literature on the Modern worldwide, that is, to one that acknowledges the place and role of the Global South.

Mercedes Volait
Centre national de la recherche scientifique
Paris

Acknowledgments

Cairo is a city that inspires and troubles me. This book was written during a difficult time personally as I lost both my parents within the space of a few months. These are also difficult times for Cairo, as it is quickly shedding the layers of architecture and urbanity that my parents' generation built and inhabited. I hope this book will inspire residents and visitors to see Cairo in a new light and to appreciate the modern constructions that have shaped it over the past century. I also hope the book will lead to the protection and preservation of some of the buildings included in it, for the sake of the city and its historical memory.

This book was only possible with the assistance and dedication of architect Hala Ismail Higazy, who managed the teams that surveyed districts, identified buildings, conducted research, and drew plans. Hala collected data and organized it in immaculate lists, spreadsheets, and documents, facilitating the task of writing the book. My gratitude goes to Hala and all the young architects who eagerly worked toward the production of this book.

Thanks to members of the research team who carried out multiple tasks including surveying, research, and drafting. They are Amr Yusuf, Engy Khaled, Islam Aboualdardaa, Maha Hatem, Mennatallah Hamdy, Rasha Emad, Mohamed Abdelaziz, and Islam Ali. Surveying and research were carried out by Shahd Omar, Adham Kalila, Alya El Chiati, Fady Francis, Mostafa El-Baroody, Ahmad Omar, Shahira Yahia, and Mai Eid. Plans were drawn by members of the core team as well as Omar Abou-Taleb, Maryam Kamal, Mona Samir, Mostafa Kamal, Reham Hamad, Hemmat Fouad, Salma Ahmad, Menna Essam, Mahmoud Elsalamouny, and Ahmed Abdelhakim.

This project is supported by Barjeel Art Foundation; many thanks to its founder Sultan Sooud Al Qassemi, whose efforts to document and publish the modern architecture of Sharjah parallel the efforts behind this book. Part of the writing of this book was carried out while I was a fellow at the American Research Center in Egypt in early 2018. The center was fully supportive and provided an institutional base during the months of my fellowship. Thanks to Djodi Deutsch and Mary Sadek for their welcome and continued support.

At the American University in Cairo Press, I am grateful to Nadia Naqib for approaching me to produce this book. I am thankful for the opportunity to write a book that is so fundamental for understanding Cairo today and to have it published in Egypt. Also at the press, Laila Amr Abdel Ghany's resourcefulness is to be credited for securing many of the images in the book. I am also indebted to Neil Hewison for his meticulous editing, patience, and enthusiasm for the project.

Archival material used in this book comes from my own personal collection as well as others. Thanks to Ola Seif and Balsam Saleh, who provided access to collections housed at the Rare Books and Special Collections Library at the American University in Cairo, which were consulted for this book. They include the archives of architects Sayed Karim, Hassan Fathy, Gamal Bakry, and Ramses Wissa Wassef, in addition to the university's postcard collection. Images from the archive of Mahmoud Riad were generously provided by architect Mahmoud Riad Jr., who is safeguarding his grandfather's papers and is continuing the family tradition of practicing architecture.

Architectural photography is not well developed in Egypt, with the few photographers in this field focusing on new real-estate developments for commercial purposes. Photography in Egyptian streets has become dangerous work; the high security alert makes any photographer suspect who points his or her camera at buildings that are not deemed touristic sites. In addition, the difficulty of photographing buildings in many residential districts in the city is compounded by poor lighting, overgrown trees concealing façades, layers of signage and advertising, and highly protective *bawab*s who will immediately chase a photographer and demand the photo be deleted, at best. For all this, thanks to Karim Hayawan, Hesham Mohamed Hassan, Nadia Mounier, Ola Seif, Sabry Khaled, and all other photographers whose images appear in this book. The work of Wafaa Samir as photo editor was crucial for bringing the heterogeneous images utilized in this publication together as seamlessly as possible.

Designing this book was a collaborative process with Ahmad Hammoud, who elegantly melded such diverse material and images into an accessible, well-presented book.

Mercedes Volait pioneered scholarship on modern architecture in Egypt. I am deeply indebted to her friendship and mentorship, and to her work, namely her 1988 publication *L'architecture moderne en Egypte et la revue al-'Imara (1939–1959)* and the 2005 book *Architectes et architectures de l'Égypte moderne (1830–1950): genèse et essor d'une expertise locale*. These publications provide a solid foundation for my own interest and research on twentieth-century architecture in Cairo.

Numerous individuals provided advice and support or shared their lists of important buildings in their districts: all of these contributions affected the current publication in some way. Many thanks to Mariam Korachy, who advised on Maadi; Ahmed Mostafa Mansour, who advised on Heliopolis; and Amr Adel Abotawila, who advised on Imbaba. I am grateful to Khaled Fahmy, Shaimaa Ashour, Shahira Fahmy, Yasmine El Dorghamy, Omniya Abdel Barr, Kareem Ibrahim, Mahy Mourad, and Sabelo Narasimhan for their support and to my friend Ibrahim Ahmed for guiding me through the process. I owe my passion for modern architecture to my friends and teachers Gabrielle Esperdy and Zeynep Çelik.

I am indebted to the family of architect Sayed Karim for their generosity and welcome. The legacies of Sayed Karim and his magazine *Al Emara* were the focus of Egypt's participation at the 2018 London Design Biennale, titled "Modernist Indignation," which I curated and which was awarded the biennale medal for most outstanding overall contribution, a win that would not have been possible without Zein Khalifa and Suzanne Gaballa. This was my humble effort to pay tribute to Karim, a great architect and thinker whose career was cut short by the Nasser regime in 1965.

Finally, work on this book was completed in the companionship of Marco Aziz, who provided advice and feedback and pushed me to continue working during difficult times. This book is dedicated to him.

Building Selection

The burden of selecting 226 structures to represent nearly 120 years of architectural developments in one of the world's largest and most densely urbanized cities should not be taken lightly. The purpose of this guide is not to present an exhaustive survey but rather to highlight representative samples from across the city. The buildings included in this book are not necessarily masterpieces, a category that often shapes the selection of buildings for guides like this. While some are uncontested landmarks, most are architecturally interesting but not avant-garde; others are easily missed or willfully ignored by historians, tour guides, and local experts who arbitrarily assign heritage value to buildings. First and foremost, buildings in this guide are included as material evidence of the evolution of the city; they are partly the result of the aesthetic decisions made by the architects and their patrons, but also the result of economic, political, cultural, and municipal conditions impacting the time and place of their construction.

The present-day architectural quality of the selected buildings is the result of many years of care or neglect, of consecutive alterations or maintenance to the original. Building descriptions are as faithful to the original design as possible, with notes regarding major alterations or changes that have happened over the years. It is important to note that given the unstable status of many of the included buildings, writing a physical description solely based on the present is a futile exercise. A new floor can be added, balconies enclosed, an entrance hall redesigned, or façades painted in new colors. For Cairenes, the sanctity of design is trumped by practical needs and changing tastes. The user of this guide will therefore need to put some effort into peeling away layers of dust and signage and to mentally reconstruct the original appearance of a building, with the aid of archival photos included in the book when possible.

The selection of buildings is also shaped by archival sources and available data. The last comprehensive survey of twentieth-century Egyptian architecture was published by Tawfiq Abdel Gawad, co-editor of *Al Emara*,

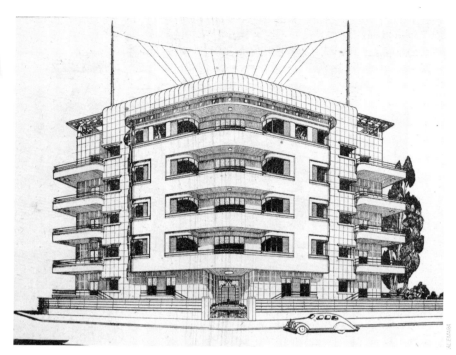

Illustration of Fattouh Bey Guinenah Building in Heliopolis, designed by architect Albert Khoury and published in *Al Emara* in 1941.

in 1989.[1] Architect Sayed Karim wrote the preface to the book, published in Arabic, and it includes many buildings covered in this present volume. Despite Abdel Gawad's central position among the architects of the period, his book includes numerous errors in building names, architect names, and construction dates. The lack of primary sources or a central architectural archive or authority hinders research and writing, and renders many constructions invisible if no drawings or photographs survive as evidence that such buildings ever existed. The majority of the buildings in this book have not been published previously. When possible, references to *Al Emara* and other souces were provided. All responsible efforts were made to ensure correct identification details accompany each building in this book. Any shortcomings or mistakes will be corrected in subsequent editions.

MODERN ARCHITECTURAL HERITAGE AND THE LAW

Since 1900, Cairo has lost many key buildings in an onslaught on nineteenth- and twentieth-century properties, unprotected by the law that arbitrarily requires the passing of one hundred years for a building to be given heritage status. Article 1 of Law 117/1983 states that "artifacts produced by different cultures as a result of arts, sciences, literature, or religion; which are indicative of different historic periods from prehistory to a hundred years ago" may be considered for heritage status. This law has often translated as a deadline for owners to damage or demolish their buildings, since heritage status as it is currently prescribed in Egyptian law does not translate into financial benefits to owners. This has spawned a lucrative clandestine business specialized in inconspicuously damaging otherwise structurally sound heritage-worthy buildings in order to avoid listing and to create the case for issuing a demolition permit. Techniques used range from flooding foundations to injecting acid into the structure, to speed up decay and engender collapse. While demolition permits are provided by local authorities, the heritage listing process is centralized on the national level and requires the involvement of the Ministry of Culture, the National Organization for Urban Harmony, and the prime minister.

This means that the bulk of Cairo's modern buildings worth protecting have already disappeared. Villas went first, due to their manageable size for demolition; however, recent efforts such as the destruction of the former National Democratic Party headquarters (1959, #9) and the flattening of the entire Maspero Triangle both point to a grim future for Cairo's modern buildings. The large scale of a building and its solid structure no longer guarantee its longevity: it too can be demolished.

Part of the urgency of this book is to document buildings past and present, and this includes those that have already been demolished. A new law expanding the definition of heritage buildings to include modern and contemporary constructions is necessary, and an open decentralized process of heritage listing must take place along with the activation of local municipal government for the management and organization of local urban affairs. Finally, the legal system must not restrict the use of heritage-listed buildings; rather it should encourage in a controlled manner their continued use for the economic benefit of the owners and their wider community.

Introduction

Cairo is essentially a twentieth-century city. Its expansion and development during the past century surpassed the pace and scope of its growth over the previous millennium.² According to the census of Egypt, the population of Greater Cairo grew from two and a half million inhabitants in 1947 to more than twelve million in 2009.³ More people meant more buildings, though not necessarily more architecture. Between 1952 and 1965 over fifteen thousand public housing units were built in Cairo, barely absorbing the city's growing population in need of affordable housing.⁴ Architects provided designs for some of Cairo's residents with more visible impact in the 1920s to 1960s, with their work clustered in specific areas and mostly catering to the city's bourgeoisie or state commissions. The majority of the population built without the services of trained architects.⁵ Today, the legacy of the city's homegrown architects who shaped its landscape is entirely absent from public knowledge. If asked, most Cairenes could not name a handful or even one of the city's prolific architects from the past century. Despite this, architecture was big business in twentieth-century Cairo. Real-estate development boomed around the turn of the century until 1907, and again in the 1930s and 1950s.⁶ Mortgages and insurance policies were powerful engines for Cairo's urban development during the first half of the century. Architectural production was extensive, and architects often took on the role of contractor. The profession was driven less by theory and more by real-estate demand. Modernist architectural features were ubiquitous. They were common in districts such as Dokki, Agouza, and Heliopolis, inhabited by the new classes that formed after the 1919 Revolution, who embraced the Modernist house or apartment as the materialization of new notions of class, identity, and modernity.⁷

Cover of *Al Hadika wal Manzil* (House and Garden) magazine, dated 14 August 1939. While architecture was not the subject of this general-reading and lifestyle magazine, it featured on its standardized cover a rendering of a cubic Modernist suburban house with flat white façades, a flat roof, and unembellished window openings. The idealized representation of the modern home is marketed to readers of the magazine as a desirable object, versions of which could be attained in newly developing areas such as Dokki.

27

With modernization comes destruction. Although Cairo escaped damage during the Second World War, there has been significant loss of the city's architectural heritage since then—particularly modern constructions, which are seen as possessing little cultural value—with many buildings erased without documentation or severely mutated. In many ways this is nothing new for Cairo. In 1945 architect Sayed Karim described Cairo's slow incremental deterioration in times of peace as causing the city more damage than that experienced by European cities in the war. He added that catastrophic damage allowed European architects to innovate and to rebuild cities according to modern concepts and designs, something that was not afforded to Egyptian architects.[8] In January 1952 riots against British occupation in downtown Cairo damaged hundreds of properties. The so-called Cairo Fire, however, had little impact on the city's architectural development. Arson targeted stores and shopping emporiums as well as banks and airline offices and most fires were contained.[9] Furthermore, the fires were limited to the downtown area, leaving the rest of the city without damage. The Cairo Fire, in which Karim's own office fell victim to the flames from the stores below, did not amount to the catastrophe that could have generated a new urban order.

Cairo is an unstable city; it constantly changes its skin, transforming its urban and architectural character in a piecemeal fashion and at a speed that far surpasses the pace of scholarship and documentation. The city tests the permanence of buildings, as structures built to last generations often have short shelf lives and are replaced or modified multiple times within the span of a century. Many of Cairo's iconic buildings today replaced earlier structures. The monumental Immobilia Building (1940, #31) replaced the Neo-Islamic palace Hotel Saint-Maurice (1879) that housed the French Consulate; the sprawling October Bridge (1969–99, #159) required the demolition of several buildings along its path such as the Anglican All Saints Cathedral (1938, see #137), a cornerstone of colonial Cairo. The Arab League Building (1955, #11) and the Nile Hilton (1958, #10) were built on land previously occupied by the army barracks built in 1856 that later housed British troops from 1882 until 1947 when it was demolished. The massive Intercontinental Hotel replaced the old Semiramis Hotel (1907). Next door to the Egyptian

Museum (1902, #8), the former headquarters of the National Democratic Party (1959, #9), originally erected to house Cairo's municipality, was demolished in the early days of conceiving this book. Efforts to save the building from demolition, for its architectural or historic value, failed. The building's Modernist design was equated in public discourse with ugliness, a necessary maneuver to facilitate its demolition. Numerous houses, apartment blocks, public buildings, and entire districts built in the span of the twentieth century across Cairo's vast geography have been demolished in the past three decades to satisfy the insatiable real-estate market currently producing buildings that lack any architectural point of view. Other demolitions make room for piecemeal development projects led by state institutions. Modern structures disappear without record; they casually 'melt into air' as if they had never existed.[10]

Two men oversee the demolition of a two-story Modernist house in Heliopolis in November 2018. Hundreds of houses built from the 1930s to the 1960s in planned middle- and upper-class areas have been demolished starting in the 1990s. However, since 2011 the pace of demolitions has intensified as land value appreciates, municipal corruption is unchecked, and the speculative real-estate market expands. Due to their small scale, the houses are demolished quickly and are replaced by high-rises lacking architectural design, which remain largely vacant for years, appreciating in value.

Modernism in Egypt has not been granted national heritage status, as if history stopped at the threshold of the twentieth century. There are no specialist government or private bodies recognizing, archiving, documenting, or protecting Modernist buildings. In Egyptian universities architectural education marginalizes and often omits the history of modern architecture. While there are departments of architecture in nearly all major universities, enrolling hundreds of students every year, they graduate without taking a survey course on the history of modern architecture in Egypt, a major blind spot in architectural education. This situation has led not only to the loss of this important architectural heritage in the city but also the irreversible loss of entire archives of architects whose oeuvre was reduced to rubble after they passed away. The lack of recognition and documentation of Modernist design means that there are no professionals prepared with the tools to conserve a modern building. Renovations of modern buildings are rare, and they

often amount to redesign rather than refurbishment. For example, the Automobile Club in Downtown, built 1923, had a minimalist façade but it received a facelift in 2008 that resulted in the addition of Classical European decorative features seen today as signs of status and prestige. Plaster Corinthian capitals, cornices, and columns are often added to embellish previously Modernist façades that have fallen out of fashion. A fundamental problem with the heritage system in Egypt is that it treats listed buildings as monuments not to be lived in or used, while the twentieth century produced only buildings that continue to be part of everyday life such as apartments, private houses, stores, and office buildings. A listed building in the current system must be fenced, removed from its context, or turned into a museum—something that contradicts the nature of many a heritage-worthy modern building that continues to serve its function.

Egyptian architects sought commissions across the Middle East. Pictured are architectural projects by Sayed Karim. First, a proposed block of duplex apartments designed in 1948 as part of Karim's New Baghdad urban plan. Second, a proposed apartment tower designed in 1948 as part of his New Damascus urban plan. Third, Al Andalus Cinema, one of several cinemas designed by Karim in Kuwait City, completed in 1960.

Cairo, however, continues to be an important city for understanding the history of Modernism in general and in the Middle East in particular. For example, Modernist architecture in the city erected during the 1930s did not conform to the utopianism and socialism associated with many European pioneers. Residential buildings erected in Zamalek and Downtown with Modernist aesthetic values (clean lines, free of decoration, with open spaces, concrete expressionism) were often spacious, luxurious, and inefficient, as they boasted expensive finishes, excessive rooms, service stairs, and servant quarters in each apartment. They fall outside standard narratives of Modernism that assume it was clearly defined by European experiences and was exported to new territories unedited. While Europe was experiencing war, destruction, and reconstruction, Cairo was booming architecturally and survived the war. The 1952 coup d'état, marketed as a revolution, actively realized modern architecture as a signifier of building a better tomorrow. In addition, from the 1930s onward, Cairo's Modernism was not the work of imported architects and experts—as is common in other Middle East settings, particularly the Gulf—but the fruit of local expertise.

Today, while the city is experiencing an unprecedented amount of construction, it is telling that the only Egyptian architect popularly known is Hassan Fathy, one who espoused rural architecture and had little impact on Egypt's urban landscape. Architects in Cairo urgently need to gain access to knowledge about the architects of the past century to provide inspiration, points of departure, or continuity in order to create a contemporary Egyptian architecture that is aware of its predecessors. By the 1960s Cairo was home to eighteen thousand trained architects, most practicing anonymously as part of the developmental state apparatus. Some drew plans for entire cities, government buildings, housing, and private dwellings outside the country in locations from Algeria to Kuwait. Their work remains understudied, undocumented, and even forever lost. The sheer scale of Cairo compared with its neighboring capitals and the city's abundance of architects meant that the amount of construction was unmatched anywhere nearby. In recent years books and exhibitions have uncovered the legacy of Modernism in the Middle East, focusing largely on the work of American and European architects in the region.[11] Cairo is the missing link between the established centers of modern architecture and the new territories built and urbanized from the 1950s onward across the broader Middle East.

BUILDING MODERN CAIRO
Modern Cairo was positioned at the intersection of cultural, political, and artistic networks that produced a dynamic, heterogeneous city that embraces change and the new. Cairo's modern architectural culture has always been porous. The city's architectural landscape fuses

Architectural conferences and symposia took place regularly in Cairo, particularly in the period following the end of the Second World War. A group photograph from 1949 at an architectural gathering shows (from left to right) architect Mustafa Fahmy, English town planner (Greater London Plan of 1944) Sir Leslie Patrick Abercrombie, Ali Labib Gabr and his wife, Ahmed Sedky, and Abdulmoneim Heikal.

elements from a variety of sources in buildings designed by descendants of Syro-Lebanese émigrés, Eastern European Jews, Italians, and French, as well as home-grown architects who traveled to Liverpool, Illinois, Rotterdam, Zurich, and Rome to further their education, actively engaging with architectural cultures in those locales and bringing technical expertise back with them to Cairo, rather than simply acting as agents importing architectural styles. They read French and Italian architectural magazines and followed trends in Brazil, Mexico, and India. The work they produced rarely committed to a singular architectural style, and they seldom used names of specific styles to refer to it. Often the same architect was able to produce buildings deploying vastly different architectural parlance. The mélange is reflective of Egypt's place in the eastern Mediterranean as a crossroads, a sponge that soaks up influence and regurgitates it in new forms. Hybridity and the ease of moving across artistic and stylistic lines to produce architectural form define modern Cairo since the nineteenth century.

Cairo provided a rich ecosystem for a sophisticated architectural culture to develop. A fine-arts school was established in 1908 and museums for ancient Egyptian and Arab art were already in place, with new buildings completed in 1902 and 1903. Architectural experimentations in revivalism and historicism dotted the city, from the Neo-Mamluk Awqaf Administration Building (1898–1929, #29) to the Hindu-inspired Baron Empain Palace (1911, #172). A popular revolution in 1919 awakened a national ethos and opened debates on the search for a national architectural style. A new social class emerged after the revolution that desired new modern lifestyles and new modern homes. Architects were in demand. By the 1920s Cairo University was producing Egyptian architects trained by a cosmopolitan faculty with focus on technique and construction skills. Many traveled abroad to continue their education and returned to establish architectural offices and to teach at the university. A professional engineering society was formally established in 1920, and architects built, published magazines, delivered public lectures, and convened conferences. The first Arab Engineering Conference met in Alexandria in 1945 followed by the much larger second conference held in Cairo in 1946 with participants from Syria, Lebanon, Palestine and beyond. After the war, Cairo emerged as the meeting place for Arab engineers and architects seeking to redefine their professions to play a bigger role in national development and modernization projects across the region.[12]

A major shortcoming of this period of professional development is the limited representation of women. Although women have had a remarkable presence in architectural education since, throughout the twentieth century and until now the profession has been dominated by men. Out of seventeen architects in the 2013 documentary *Arab Women in Architecture*, only one, Shahira Fahmy, is from Egypt. Women, however, played a major role in Cairo's architectural patronage. Doria Lotfi, whose husband was Sayed Karim, was the patron of *Al Emara* during its later years, and many of the buildings in this book were commissioned by women.

By the 1950s, concrete cubic houses and apartment buildings with rational façades and spacious floor plans became commonplace across the city. Throughout this period, as Gwendolyn Wright puts it, "most architects were ardent Modernists, as were their clients, who employed terms like '*hadith* (new or modern), '*asri* (contemporary or modern), and *madani* (civil or refined).'"[13] Parts of this story are familiar, as similar cultural and architectural developments happened from Mexico to Turkey.[14] A multi-focal international Modernism that did not conform to the strict dichotomy of East/West was emerging, and Egypt was part of it.[15]

1900–39

At the start of the twentieth century the city's architecture was eclectic, cosmopolitan, and hybrid. The Egyptian Museum (1902, #8) by French architect Marcel Dourgnon is a Neo-Classical structure with a central hall, skylights, and a façade adorned by Egyptian figures. In

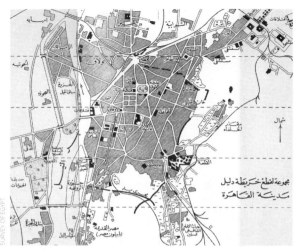

This highly detailed map of Cairo published by Egypt's Survey Authority in 1912 shows a city still clinging to what is referred to today as Historic Cairo, with settlements extending to the west in the Downtown area, Garden City, and Abdeen, and to the north in Bulaq, Daher, Ghamra, and Shubra. Across the river, the village of Dokki is named on the map, Roda Island is empty, and the northern half of Zamalek is just taking shape.

Giza, between the khedival palaces, stood the Ahram Beverages Company (1900, #109), a muscular industrial facility with an austere façade that hints at Tuscan fortresses, with one of the earliest uses of reinforced concrete in Egypt. At the same time Prince Muhammad Ali of the ruling dynasty built himself a palace with lush gardens in Manial (1901–29, #91), combining elements of Islamic architecture from Egypt and as far as Morocco and elsewhere. Eclecticism, or the lack of commitment to a fixed style, and newness, or the attraction toward innovation regardless of its source, were already hallmarks of Cairo's architecture. Between 1903 and 1906 new suburban developments—Garden City, Heliopolis, and Maadi—sprouted around Cairo, creating fresh terrains for architecture to flourish. Constructions in these areas largely consisted of residential buildings, ranging from modest houses to richly decorated palaces. These were built in styles ranging from Art Deco to Neo-Islamic to Modernist, and many examples were hybrids of multiple styles. The Neo-Islamic Heliopolis Company colonnaded buildings on Ibrahim al-Laqqani and Baghdad streets (#178), completed in 1908 and designed by Belgian architect Ernest Jaspar, feature a square minaret in place of the usual dome as a corner articulation for a residential building. By contrast, the Serageldin Palace in Garden City (#81), completed in 1908 and designed by Italian architect Carlo Prampolini, combines elements of Neo-Baroque and Neo-Renaissance with a rusticated façade, a marble double stairway, and thematically decorated rooms.

The outbreak of the First World War impacted the city's architectural culture in a limited way, mostly affecting Cairo-resident architects and patrons of architecture with links to the Austro-Hungarian Empire. British authorities in Egypt closed their businesses—such as the

Tiring Department Store (1912, #43), which was forced into liquidation by 1920, with its building changing hands since—or forced their departure—as with prolific architect Max Herz Pasha, who was responsible for numerous restoration projects of Islamic monuments in the city as well as designing modern constructions. Otherwise the city's architectural culture remained unchanged, lacking direction until the 1919 Revolution marked a significant turning point. A range of architects designed restrained Imperial-style buildings for the state in the 1920s such as the Parliament (1924), Cairo University (1925–37, #94), the High Court (1924–34, #51), and the Egyptian Society for Political Economy, Statistics, and Legislation on Ramses Street (1928). Others continued to rely on a regionally anchored eclectic historicism, as in Antonio Lasciac's Banque Misr building (1927, #37). The work of Egyptian architects such as Mustafa Fahmy and Ahmed Charmi moved in the direction of situated Modernism, deploying an architectural lexicon of elements drawn from the history of Islamic architecture in the city. Examples include the Azhar University campus (1936) by Charmi and the Egyptian Society of Engineers building (1923–46, #49) by Fahmy. Mustafa Fahmy looked beyond Islamic heritage for the construction of a national architecture. His designs for the mausoleum of the nationalist leader of the 1919 Revolution Saad Zaghloul (1931, #71), Giza train station (c.1932), and King Farouk's rest house at the Pyramids (1946, #218) are explicit resurrections of ancient Egyptian architecture for new functions while using modern materials and construction techniques.

An advertisement for construction materials ("Do not hesitate in choosing the best kind of brick") features the Aziz Bahari Building (on Tahrir Square) designed by architect Antoine Selim Nahas and completed in 1934.

From the start of the 1930s a new architectural trend swept the city, namely Modernist designs that relied less on revivalism and more on functionality, restraint, and the expressive use of construction materials such as concrete and brick. Syro-Lebanese architects like Antoine Selim Nahas, Charles Ayrout, and Albert

Zananiri built extensively during this decade. Some catered to new forms of wealth, seeking to capitalize on architecture in the form of luxurious apartment blocks such as Nahas's two pairs of Aziz Bahari Buildings in Tahrir Square (1934, #16) and Mustafa Kamel Square (1938, #39). Others focused on modestly sized houses and apartment buildings with a high-impact design and a small footprint, as in the work of Charles Ayrout in Heliopolis and Downtown. At the end of the 1930s Cairo was a booming city with an architectural practice that defined itself as Arab and Egyptian for the first time since the arrival of Napoleon in 1798.

1939–89

The tumultuous period bracketed by the start of the Second World War and the end of the Cold War witnessed the peak and the decline of Cairo's modern architectural culture. The outbreak of conflict in 1939 put the brakes on the city's rapid urbanization and architectural development, largely because of the war economy and the shortage of materials. Construction companies in Cairo were largely owned by Italians, and when Italy entered the war British authorities placed Italian-owned businesses under sequestration, affecting construction projects. Some construction continued, and architects included bomb shelters in the basements of some buildings as a selling point to potential buyers. The same year, the publication of the first issue of *Al Emara* (al-'Imara, 'Architecture') marked a turning point in Cairo's architectural culture.[16] The magazine was founded and edited by architect Sayed Karim, many of whose buildings are featured in this book, and architects Tawfiq Abdel Gawad and Muhammad Hammad assisted him on the editorial team. Karim's beliefs corresponded with an internationally popular notion that "modern design—design of our time—is not a style. It is a solution to modern problems in modern terms."[17] The purpose of the magazine was to "serve art [*al-fann*] for the sake of art, serve knowledge, and the exchange of architectural culture [*al-thaqafa al-handasiya*]."[18] It was the world's first Arabic-language architectural journal, dedicated

Cover of issue 3–4 (1939) of *Al Emara* magazine, featuring Villa Abdul Latif Bey Mahmoud in Zamalek, designed by architects Anis Serageldin and Sayed Karim, who was also the editor and founder of the magazine. *Al Emara* published sixty-seven issues from 1939 to 1959.

to contemporary design with emphasis on the work of Egyptian architects. Other content included architectural projects abroad, art criticism focusing on Egyptian modern art, and technical commentary on building materials and construction techniques. The magazine energized the profession as it publicized and promoted the work of architects providing their services to satisfy the demand for increased architectural production.

The design of the Immobilia building (1940, #31) was decided by a competition won by architects Max Edrei and Gaston Rossi. It was completed on the eve of the Second World War with financing gathered by prominent Egyptian-Jewish banker Elie Mosseri, who had previously helped build another key monumental building, the King David Hotel in Jerusalem (1931). The scale and Modernist aesthetic of the Immobilia made it a landmark before it was completed. It was the largest construction of its kind, with two enormous blocks rising to unprecedented heights, with an exterior that is unembellished, characterized by sweeping curves, crisp lines, and bold massing. Its interior was understated yet luxurious, with fully serviced apartments with large square-footage, modern amenities, and high-end finishes. Such large-scale buildings were increasingly built in the 1940s and 1950s, often consisting of one or two blocks with stores along the street, followed by one or two floors of offices and the rest apartments, including duplexes or villas with roof gardens at the top. In these large developments a gallery or private street was often cut through the site to give access to the entrance lobbies and to provide additional storefronts. Architects were concerned with how to maximize rentable space while respecting the city's building code, which put caps on heights and required setbacks.

The jury for the architectural competition held for the design of the Immobilia building met on 10 June 1937 to decide the winning design out of thirteen entries. The jury included Ismail Sedky Pasha (executive of the company and head of the jury), architect Mustafa Fahmy (head of the Tanzim Department), Abdel Hamid Soliman Pasha (former minister of public works), Paul Albert (head of engineers at the Suez Canal Company), and Rene Cattaoui Bey (senator and head of Egypt's Jewish community).

Sayed Karim's Ouzonian Building (1949, #54) and Zamalek Tower (1953, #144) are both monolithic concrete blocks, with *brise soleil* (sun breakers) as a prominent façade feature. The Zamalek Tower contains apartments and duplexes topped by penthouses with roof gardens, while the downtown Ouzonian is a multi-use building with offices, apartments, a hotel, and duplexes. Visually these buildings belong to an already global architecture, with similar structures built in Latin America, Africa, and South Asia. In Egypt, Sayed Karim's International Style was partly inspired by a global zeitgeist but also by local politics and culture. Both the Zamalek Tower and the Ouzonian Building are located in districts dominated by the work of foreign architects from an earlier generation. The International Style of Karim's generation of buildings was determined less by fixed stylistic maneuvers and more by the expression of national modernity, without reverting to pastiche. Beyond their aesthetics, however, these were still relatively elite structures for the privileged, so Modernist design in Cairo did not necessarily signify doing away with class hierarchies.

Sayed Karim pictured in his office, standing over a scale model of Nasr City. After the Second World War Karim produced urban plans for several cities including Baghdad (1946), Damascus (1947), and Jeddah (1949). His Greater Cairo plan was completed in 1952 and it incorporated a Modernist expansion that later became Nasr City when it was adopted by Nasser and established by presidential decree in 1959. The city was promoted as a "new capital" and "city of the revolution."

A notable architect in this period is Naoum Shebib, whose work emphasized materiality as the expression of Modernism. The architect/structural engineer was responsible for Nasserist Cairo's most prominent landmark, the Cairo Tower (1961, #135). Shebib also designed Cairo's first and second residential high-rises in Downtown (1954, #35) and Garden City (1958, #84) and the parabolic Saint Catherine's Church (1950, #168) in Heliopolis. His buildings were expressions of concrete's versatility. Another notable figure is Mahmoud Riad, a prolific architect favored by the state and national companies such as Misr Insurance from the late 1940s through the 1950s. His Cairo Municipality—later the Socialist Union and National Democratic Party headquarters (1959, #9)—and the Arab League Building (1955, #11) are both essential buildings for understanding the nationalist remaking of Cairo after 1952.[19] The Arab League building in particular embodies the politics of the times and the aspirations of Cairo as the political heart of the region. It is composed of a tower slab flanked by two shorter

volumes for administration and the assembly hall. The resulting central court is adorned with Moorish patterns reinterpreted with blue mosaic tiles grafted on the building's otherwise unadorned façade.

Egyptian architects also proposed Modernist urban plans for Cairo's expansion. Riad planned Awqaf City in 1947, which was later implemented as Mohandiseen ('Engineers' [City]'). Another large Modernist urban plan was Nasr City ('Victory City'), implemented in 1959. Nasr City included middle-income housing blocks, villas, and new government buildings. Its centerpiece was a landmark stadium; a much-needed structure for hosting political rallies with a capacity of over one hundred thousand spectators. Nasser Stadium—now Cairo International Stadium (1960, #191) was the first structure completed in the new city, along with a military-parade grandstand. Both structures utilized concrete in functional yet visually stunning ways. The various government offices in this aspiring new political capital, akin to Chandigarh or Brasília in its conception, consisted of functional slab blocks with horizontal articulations and strip windows. The idea was to move such offices outside the old heart of Cairo and to house the state bureaucrats in the new housing blocks nearby. A team of architects designed the apartments with Sayed Karim at the helm. Karim's distinctive H-shaped apartment blocks were arranged diagonally in relation to the city's streets so as to create open space in front and at the back of each block, realizing an Egyptian iteration of the Modernist concept of 'towers in the park.' The apartments were efficient yet spacious by international standards for postwar state-built housing, with apartments consisting of three or four bedrooms and others split between two floors.

In addition to popular housing aimed at lower-income Egyptians, the Nasser regime invested heavily in the construction of a wide variety of buildings to appeal to the new middle class, from theaters and cinemas to social clubs and summer resorts, cafeterias, and sports facilities. Pictured are the Cairo Puppet Theater in Ataba and the indoor sports hall at the Police Academy in Abbasiya, both completed in 1964. Such constructions, which always employed International Style or Brutalist aesthetics, were essential for the political stability of the regime.

Functional Modernist designs, which proliferated in the 1950s and 1960s, evolved from two decades of architectural practice prior to 1952. However, the close affinity of such aesthetics with a failing political project put into question the validity of the architecture produced during that era. The Egyptian state had become increasingly authoritarian and ultimately, despite some successes in expanding services, failed to deliver on its promises for lasting social equality. While Egypt experienced national trauma following the 1967 Six-Day War and entered into a national existential crisis recorded in the cinema and literature of that time, internationally Modernism was seen as an expiring architecture.

The 1970s can be characterized as a decade of search for identity. While intellectuals and professionals searched for Egypt's true identity, the majority of the built environment from then on was produced outside the confines of architecture as a profession. Contractors rendered the architectural profession increasingly irrelevant, and informal building activity proliferated. Within the besieged architectural profession, calls for a return to basics and a reevaluation of the vernacular gained momentum as Hassan Fathy entered the canon of international architectural discourse. Architects such as Abdel Wahed El-Wakil built on the Hassan Fathy approach in his designs of private residences for the affluent, seeking modern spaces grounded in a conscious construction of identity that ambiguously claims to be simultaneously down-to-earth, Egyptian, Islamic, and Arab.

Architect Ramses Wissa Wassef's Virgin Mary Church (1959, #147) in Zamalek successfully recuperates vernacular architecture without subscribing to absolutism or fully rejecting modern materials. It exhibits a monolithic ribbed structure for its nave, while introducing elements that recall traditional eastern Christian architecture. His earlier Mahmoud Mukhtar Museum (1962, #133), also in Zamalek, was a building that appeared Modernist from its exterior with its rectilinear colonnade, while the entire design was a meditation on space and light as an architectural homage to the sculptures exhibited in the museum. Wissa Wassef's engagement with vernacular architecture was grounded in a phenomenological reading of space rather than Fathy's material driven approach to vernacular design, fixated on mud brick and a conscious rejection of modern technology.

The AUC Jameel Center under construction. The building combines Brutalist form with the addition of reinterpreted elements from Cairo's Islamic architecture such as ablaq and *mashrabiya* screens.

The period of political and economic stagnation of the Mubarak presidency was largely unremarkable architecturally as architects struggled to reconfigure their role in society. A few landmark buildings were erected, like the Cairo Opera House (1988, #132) as part of a wave of large developmental projects involving international funding that were presented by the Mubarak regime as evidence of its modernization. A series of towers along the Nile, such as the World Trade Center by SOM (1988, #62), signaled Cairo's modest place in the emerging global economy.

1989 TO THE PRESENT
With the end of the Cold War, Cairo entered the era of globalization unspectacularly. Some architects continued to flirt with the notion of situated Modernism—that is, the use of architectural vocabularies that vaguely point to local traditions (arches, domes, etc.). Abdelhalim Ibrahim Abdelhalim's Children's Cultural Park (1990, #67) in Sayeda Zeinab presented an assemblage of such architectural elements in a manner reminiscent of nineteenth-century garden follies, architecture as mere signification, or a collection of fragments. Postmodernism did not find a home in Cairo during that time, as there was not a vibrant local critical assessment of Modernism in Egypt that could produce an architecture that was consciously postmodern. However, fragmentation and façadism grew in popularity as architects and clients relied heavily on pastiche to signify wealth and status, often despite the country's poor economic performance. By the end of the 1990s other appropriations of pseudo-historical motifs emerged in buildings such as the Faisal Islamic Bank

Tower (2000, #104), consisting of offices and twenty luxury apartments. This building features extensive calligraphy on its façade and its entrance portal is topped by a *muqarnas*-inspired decorative element. The dawn of the new millennium also witnessed the revival of ancient Egyptian pastiche, rather than Arab or Islamic, appearing in key public commissions such as the Supreme Court (1999, #210) by architect Ahmed Mito. Pyramidal forms and abstracted ancient Egyptian references also appear in the concrete-and-glass office buildings of the technology business district known as Smart Village, established in 2000.

Twenty-first-century Cairo witnessed several projects that fit within two trends. The first revisits the notion of a situated Modernism, building on the successes and failures of previous attempts. Successful examples of this trend include the Abusir House (2003, #216) by architect Tarek Labib, an eclectic meditation on materiality and form that resurrects vaults found in traditional Coptic architecture in the form of parabolic archways, combined with expressive uses of red brick and Siwa salt bricks. Another example is al-Azhar Park (2004, #7) designed by Maher Stino of Sites International. This large-scale project combines urban regeneration, landscape design, and heritage preservation. The design incorporates geometries drawn from the city's Islamic architecture.

The second trend is the integration of environmentally conscious design. Notable examples include the campus of the American University in Cairo (2008, #212) master-planned by Abdelhalim Abdelhalim and Sasaki Associates, with individual buildings designed by international architects, like Ricardo Legorreta's student housing. The buildings incorporate passive solar design elements that reduce the impact of the desert sun on indoor temperatures. Other examples of environmental design include the headquarters of Crédit Agricole Bank (2015, #214) and ABC Bank (2018, #213), both by Engineering Consultants Group. Both buildings, located in New Cairo, incorporate double-skin façades and other design features that reduce energy consumption. The Crédit Agricole building is the first in Egypt and North Africa to be awarded the Platinum LEED certificate.

Glossary

Architectural Styles

Art Deco
A design style fashionable in the 1920s and 1930s with a range of architectural expressions from streamlining motifs to bold geometric decorative patterns and forms. In Cairo, the style was popular for cinemas as well as residential buildings in Heliopolis, Downtown, Garden City, and Zamalek.

Art Nouveau
A design style from the late nineteenth century to the start of the twentieth century that moved away from imitations of the past. In architecture it was often limited to decoration and detail by architects who rebelled against formalism, classical design, and industrial standardization.

Beaux-Arts
An academic architectural style championed by the École des Beaux-Arts in Paris from the 1830s to the end of the nineteenth century. It relied on classical formulas combined with elements from various European traditions such as Renaissance, Baroque, and Rococo, with the heavy incorporation of sculptural decoration.

Brutalism
The term was coined in England in 1954 to describe recent works by Le Corbusier in Marseille and Chandigarh that are characterized by the use of rough exposed concrete (*béton brut*). It evolved into an international architectural approach to design championed by Alison and Peter Smithson in England, Paul Rudolph in the USA, and Sayed Karim in Egypt.

Functionalism
An international approach to architecture that grew in popularity in the 1930s following the proposition made by Le Corbusier in 1923 that houses should be designed as "machines for living" devoid of superfluous elements that lack function or practical use.

Georgian
A set of architectural styles produced in England in the

eighteenth and early nineteenth centuries and spread in British colonies into the twentieth century.

Imperial
A set of architectural styles used in British and French imperial political projects with a variety of characteristics and decorative features; large scale and the use of Neo-Classical and Baroque elements are common.

International Style
An umbrella term for various approaches such as Functionalism or simply Modernism. In 1932 the Museum of Modern Art in New York hosted its first architectural exhibition accompanied by the publication of *The International Style* by the curators Henry-Russell Hitchcock and Philip Johnson. The exhibition and book solidified the notion that a new architecture had emerged since 1922 that could be described as international, as they included examples from Germany, Holland, and France. The curators identified three principles of the style: volume of space, regularity, and flexibility.

Metabolism
A Japanese architectural movement of the 1960s inspired by megastructures and patterns of organic growth, producing an array of buildings and proposals based on modular design that can be adapted and expanded over time.

Modernism
Twentieth-century architecture focused on Functionalism, the rejection of embellishments and ornaments, and the production of architectural and urban solutions suitable for modern times. Modernist buildings are characterized by asymmetrical compositions and cubic shapes, and use modern building materials and construction techniques. In Egypt, the style was employed by a range of architects who did not adhere to the theorized notions of Modernism produced by European pioneers from the 1920s onward. Instead it was seen as the language of the times that could be combined with elements drawn from other sources.

Neo-Baroque
The highly ornate Baroque style flourished in Europe in the seventeenth and eighteenth centuries. It was an architecture of propaganda and prestige adopted by

royalties and the Catholic Church. In the late nineteenth century the style was revived particularly in France, Britain, and Germany to express state and imperial power. The style spread to other territories through the École des Beaux-Arts in Paris, which placed the style at the core of its curriculum.

Neo-Classical
A movement that began in the 1750s in Europe as a reaction against the excesses of Rococo and Baroque architecture and called for the establishment of principles based on reason and the academic study of the formal and spatial qualities of ancient Greek and Roman architecture. In the nineteenth century Neo-Classicism became richer in decoration and more stately in composition and scale, serving as political propaganda by modernizing nation-states and European imperial projects. Neo-Classicism is a precursor to the historicizing and lavishly decorated Beaux-Arts style.

Neo-Fatimid
The Fatimids ruled North Africa, Egypt, and Palestine from the tenth through the twelfth centuries. Fatimid architecture drew from a variety of sources including Coptic and Byzantine. In Cairo, a city founded by the Fatimids, their architecture flourished and began to produce a set of buildings and elements that became the sources of a few attempts for revival in the twentieth century, not as a complete style but rather as a set of references such as minarets, gateways, and arches drawn from specific monuments.

Neo-Gothic
A nineteenth-century revival of elements and forms of medieval European architecture such as pointed arches and vaulted ceilings as a counterpoint to Neo-Classicism.

Neo-Islamic
A revivalist architectural style that combines elements from a variety of sources associated with the architecture of Muslim societies, with no commitment to a particular era or historical style.

Neo-Mamluk
Mamluk architecture was built between 1250 and 1516 in Greater Syria, Jerusalem, and Egypt, which were ruled by the Mamluk sultans based in Cairo. The revival

of Mamluk architecture in Egypt took place from the second half of the nineteenth century into the beginning of the twentieth century, particularly for official buildings as well as lavish residences for Egyptian and European elites. The study and conservation of Mamluk architecture led to renewed interest in particular surface decoration features of the style (*ablaq* masonry, use of pointed *muqarnas*, monumental calligraphy in Naskhi script, interlaced floral and geometric patterns) that were used for new buildings, often with non-religious functions. Neo-Mamluk architecture served as a national style during this period as a counterpoint to European and Ottoman architectural influences in Egypt.

Neo-Moorish

Moorish architecture developed in the Maghreb, Spain, and Portugal from 711 to 1492, producing a wide variety of elements that inspired a revival movement in Spain and beyond in the nineteenth century. From synagogues in North America to public buildings in Spain and palaces in Egypt, Neo-Moorish buildings drew inspiration from Andalusian architecture as an outcome of European romanticism and the fascination with the orient. Decorative patterns drawn from the Alhambra and horseshoe arches were common features in the style.

Neo-Pharaonic

The appropriation of ancient Egyptian architectural elements and motifs in the construction of new buildings, with new functions. It was first prevalent in Europe and North America from the start of the nineteenth century and appeared in Egypt at the beginning of the twentieth century as a way of establishing a national architectural style but with limited application, such as the mausoleum of nationalist leader Saad Zaghloul.

Neo-Renaissance

Italian Renaissance architecture of the fifteenth century became a source of inspiration for nineteenth-century constructions of varying applications of elements from the original style in different national contexts such as England, France, and elsewhere. Common features in the revival style are grand stairs and clearly ordered façades distinguishing lower, middle, and upper levels, as in the design of Italian palazzos.

Neo-Tuscan
A nineteenth-century style overlapping with Neo-Renaissance, first appearing in England, that produced Italianate buildings with features resembling late medieval and Renaissance architecture from Florence, particularly palazzos and fortresses. The style was popular in the early twentieth century for palaces and upper-class apartment buildings in locations such as Milan and Alexandria (the Montazah Palace).

Ottoman
Architecture of the Ottoman Empire, developed in the fourteenth and fifteenth centuries in Bursa and Edirne, absorbing Iranian, Armenian, Seljuk, Mamluk, and Byzantine influences. It evolved over a period of five hundred years, with its own periodization from early to classical, Baroque, and late Ottoman styles. Features such as large mosque domes and pencil minarets are common in religious buildings, but Ottoman styles were also developed to serve infrastructural works such as bridges and civic and secular buildings. Ottoman architecture was harmonized during the lifetime of Mimar Sinan (1491–1588), a military engineer who is one of the few named architects of the pre-modern Islamic world.

Postmodernism
A reactionary style that emerged particularly in the United States in the late 1960s and flourished in the 1980s as a critique of Brutalism and Modernism in general. Moving away from functionalism toward symbolism, white surfaces to the garish use of color, notions of the building as a whole to one as a collection of fragments, the style deployed humor, contradiction, and historical references to appeal to the masses.

Rococo
The culmination of Baroque architecture in the mid-eighteenth century, particularly in France, just before the rise of Neo-Classicism. It is characterized by richly decorated interiors with delicate, often gilded details.

Streamline Moderne
An international style of architecture, popular in the 1930s around the world from Mumbai to Cairo and Miami, that emphasized curving forms and long horizontal lines, lack of embellishments, and the inclusion of nautical elements such as round windows.

Other Terms

ablaq
A decorative technique of alternating light and dark courses of masonry.

awqaf
see *waqf*.

bawab
The rise of modern apartment buildings in Egypt as new forms of collective habitation beyond family links led to the emergence of the *bawab* as gatekeeper, and they have been a mainstay in middle- and upper-class residential buildings since. They serve multiple functions from security to running errands for residents.

brise soleil
An architectural feature, usually an arrangement of screens or vertical or horizontal fins, designed to shade façades and window openings from the direct sun in hot climates.

clerestory
The upper part of a wall pierced by windows.

Coptic capitals
Capitals crowning pillars in Coptic church architecture are usually of Byzantine inspiration with floral motifs or following Ionic or Corinthian orders. It is common for churches to have no duplicate capitals.

corbel
A bracket jutting from façades to support the weight of another part of the structure such as a balcony. With the use of modern materials such as reinforced concrete the need for corbels was diminished, though due to the popularity of Classical façades plaster corbels were applied to maintain stylistic appearance. Architect Sayed Karim attacked the use of corbels in buildings constructed of concrete in Cairo, calling the practice an architectural lie.

cornice
A horizontal decorative ledge crowning a building or a window or door opening, particularly in Classical and Neo-Classical styles.

dentil
Found in Classical Greek and Roman architecture as

well as Neo-Classical styles, these are small ornamental blocks arranged in a row on the underside of a cornice.

entablature
In Classical architecture, the horizontal upper section of a building resting on columns, composed of the architrave, frieze, and cornice.

Ionic columns
The Ionic order is one of the three orders of Classical architecture, along with Doric and Corinthian. Ionic columns are characterized by twin spiral scrolls crowning a fluted column shaft.

keel arch
A shouldered arch, pointed at the apex, resembling the keel of a ship. It was a feature of Fatimid architecture, for instance in al-Aqmar Mosque in Cairo, built in 1125.

khanqah
A building designed for the gathering of members of a Sufi order.

Kufic
The oldest Arabic calligraphic form, developed in Kufa, Iraq in the seventh century. In Cairo, Square Kufic is used as a decorative surface treatment on the Unknown Soldier Memorial.

kuttab
A school for Arabic and religious studies, usually attached to a mosque or *sabil* as part of a *waqf*; in some cases in Cairo in modern times it was also a place for the general education for children.

machicolations
Originally a protected opening found in defensive architecture in the medieval Middle East; later uses are purely decorative.

majlis
A formal sitting room for receiving guests in palatial and domestic architecture.

malqaf
An architectural element designed to ventilate interior spaces by capturing wind.

mashrabiya
A projecting window bay enclosed with turned-wood screens to allow ventilation while maintaining privacy in dense urban environments.

mihrab
A niche in a mosque indicating the direction of Mecca.

muhandiskhana
An engineering and polytechnic school. One was established in Cairo in 1821 in Bulaq, teaching subjects such as engineering and land surveying.

muqarnas
A decorative architectural element in various traditions of Islamic architecture that is composed of stalactite-like vaulting with small niche-like cells, placed at the culmination of recessed arches and niches such as monumental entrances in Mamluk architecture. In Islamic revival styles it appears in new places such as the tops of windows and as column capitals.

pediment
A wide, low-pitched gable at the top of the façade of a building in Classical and Neo-Classical architecture.

pendentive
An architectural element that transitions from a square room to the circular base of a dome, taking the shape of a triangular segment of a sphere.

piloti
A slender, stilt-like column or pier of steel or reinforced concrete that is a common feature of modern architecture to lift buildings off the ground and give the appearance of lightness.

porte cochere
A covered porch-like structure at the entrance of a building designed for cars or carriages to pass through to pick up or drop off occupants.

pylon
A monumental gateway in ancient Egyptian temples composed of two tapering towers flanking the entrance.

rusticated
A decorative technique in which stone blocks are finished with rough-textured, projecting outer faces. Its origins are in Roman and Renaissance architecture, but the technique was often employed in Neo-Classical public and institutional buildings such as banks.

sabil
A drinking fountain usually established for public charity.

sahn
An open or closed courtyard, usually in a mosque but also in domestic architecture.

shukhshaykha
A wooden screened structure placed over a skylight in the main room of a traditional Cairo house to allow ventilation and indirect light.

trefoil arch
An arch incorporating the shape or outline of three overlapping rings.

waqf (plural *awqaf*)
A charitable endowment often intended for the upkeep of a religious or educational building, or a hospital. *Waqf* was a wealthy, independent economic system that was an important driving force for Cairo's urban and agricultural development until the state intervened in the 1950s and assumed control over it.

wet rooms
Rooms in a building designed to have a water source, most commonly bathrooms and kitchens.

zawya
Literally 'a corner,' a place where a saint or holy person lived or was buried.

Scan QR code to be directed to
cairosince1900.com/go
Enter building number as listed in the book to
be taken to its GPS location on Google Maps.

MAPS

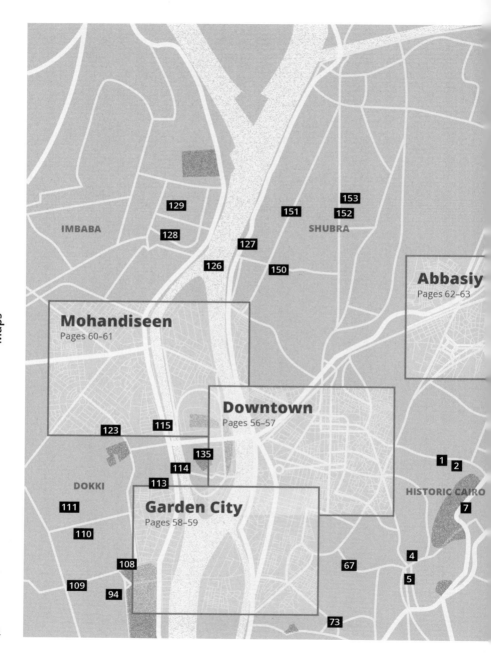

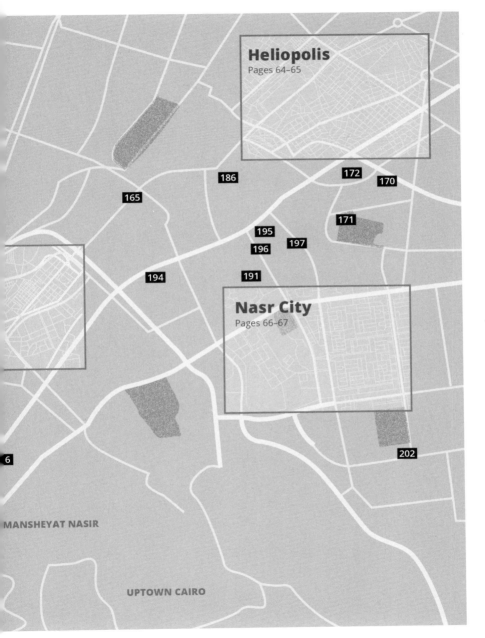

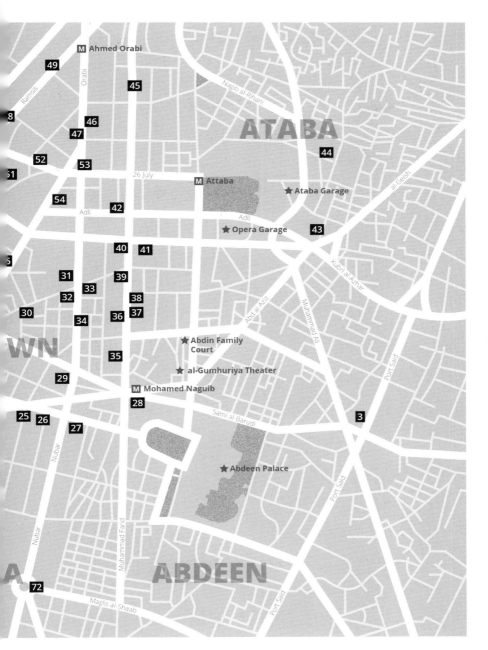

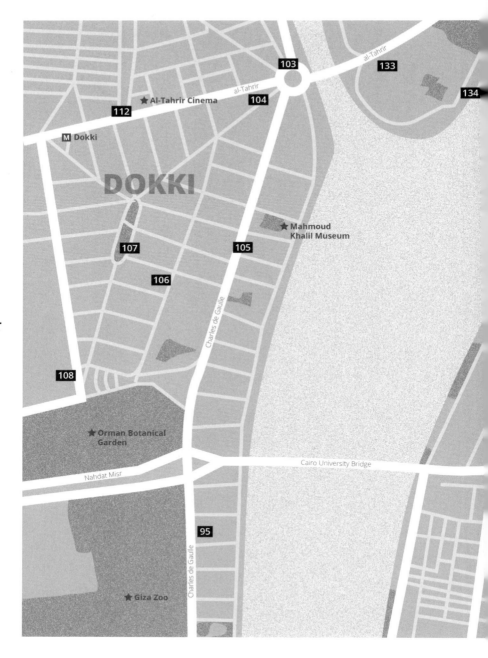

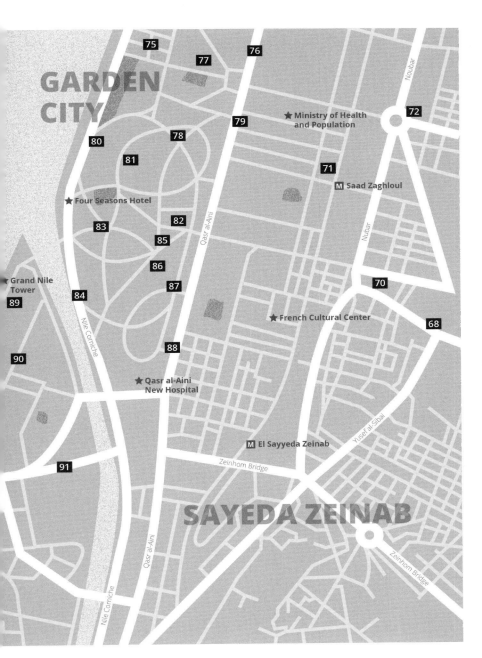

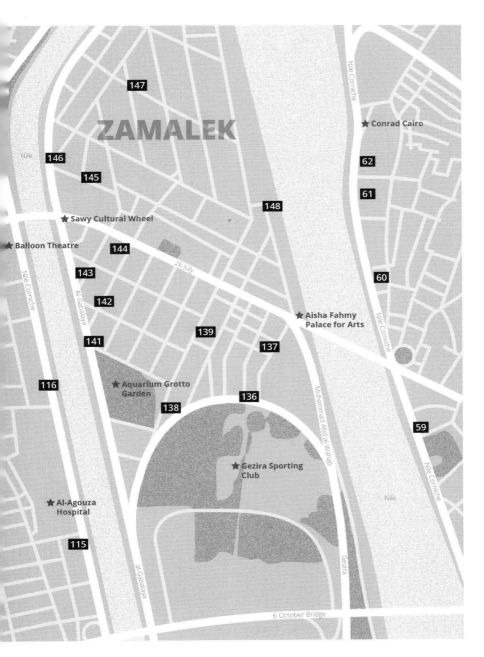

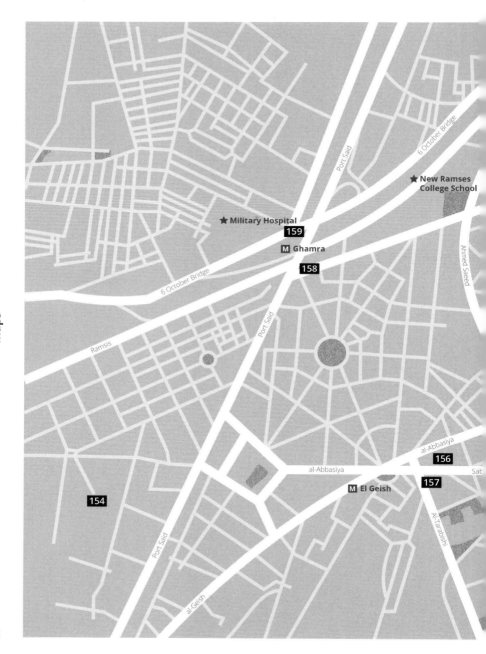

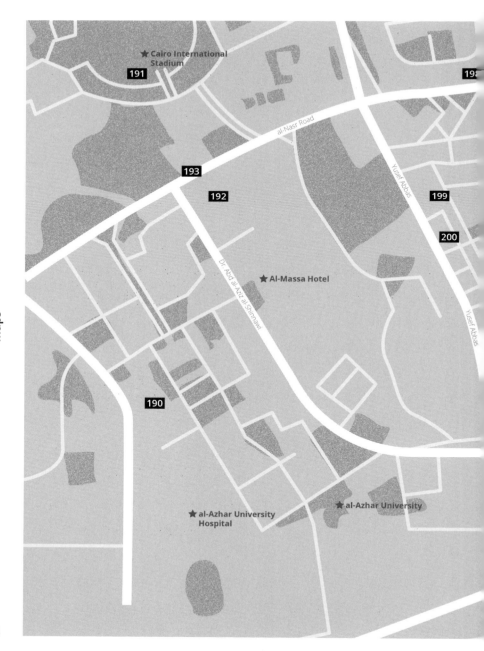

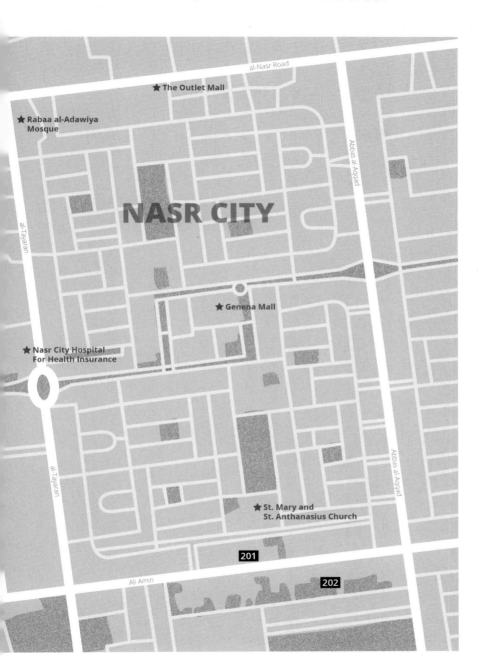

HISTORIC CAIRO

Al-Azhar Mosque (foreground), built 972, and al-Azhar University's Muhammad Abduh Auditorium (background), built 1946, with its clock tower topped by its original bulbous dome.

Historic Cairo

Since it was founded in 969 until well into the nineteenth century, Cairo was limited to the area now known as Islamic or Historic Cairo, which encompasses the districts of al-Muski, al-Gamaliya, al-Darb al-Ahmar, Bab al-Shaariya, and Bab al-Khalq. The area is bordered by Downtown to the west, Abdeen and Sayeda Zeinab to the south, Salah Salem Road to the east, and al-Husayniya to the north. Among the area's ancient buildings are modern constructions that blend in by way of historicism. The study and documentation of historic architecture in the nineteenth century produced an array of architectural elements that were reinterpreted by modern architects to create new buildings in old dress. Other buildings with varying modern styles were inserted along al-Azhar Street connecting the heart of the historic city to al-Ataba, the link between the ancient city and its nineteenth-century extension.

Al-Azhar Street was first constructed in the nineteenth century to provide an east–west thoroughfare. Completed in 2001, the Azhar Tunnel was constructed under the street to provide a high-speed link between Salah Salem Road and Downtown. Despite the area's UNESCO listing in 1979, it has suffered great losses of architectural heritage, particularly domestic architecture, which gave way to newer high-density forms of housing. Increased densification and poor infrastructure have made twentieth-century constructions vulnerable to demolition. Examples that have survived include the 1930s campus of al-Azhar University.

Al-Azhar Administration

Address: 102 al-Azhar Street, al-Gamaliya
GPS: 30.046722, 31.262738
Year: 1936
Architect: Ahmed Charmi

With a location between al-Hussein and al-Azhar mosques in the heart of Historic Cairo, on a triangular site surrounded by three streets, Charmi was confronted by a monumental design challenge for the new offices of Mashyakhat al-Azhar. The stone-and-concrete building is at once grand in appearance yet humble in scale, fitting well within its historic urban context. Charmi pulled from the catalogue of elements (some quoted, others invented) that he favored in his effort to construct a modern national style rooted in Egypt's Islamic heritage. The west and east corners of the three-story building along the main movement of traffic are strongly articulated. The west corner is the two-story portal façade, with the door fronted by a portico marked by a large pointed arch. The raised ground level is reached via seven steps. An inscription, 'al-Azhar Administration,' carved in marble is centered above the arch, followed by *muqarnas* and a crenelated parapet. At the east corner is a two-story semicircular volume with a portico of pointed arches carried on slender columns, supporting a balcony that is shaded by a canopy. A recessed fourth floor was added on the roof during subsequent renovations.

Muhammad Abduh Auditorium

Address: 105 al-Azhar Street, al-Darb al-Ahmar
GPS: 30.046094, 31.264009
Year: 1946
Architects: Ahmed Charmi, Fahmy Momen

The ceremonial lecture hall of al-Azhar University is dedicated to Muhammad Abduh, Islamic jurist, religious scholar and reformer, and a key figure in Islamic Modernism. In plan the hall is a quarter circle bookended by two rectangular volumes with several recessed rectangular volumes housing the building's circulation and offices. While the lecture hall is four stories tall, with a spacious, light-filled, airy design, the bookends are two stories with grand rectangular entry halls leading to the stairs for the balcony level above. The decorative program is rich, always presented as a modern interpretation of elements from Cairo's Islamic architecture. *Muqarnas* capitals, for example, top the columns that adorn the entry hall. Despite the generous use of decorative elements, the overall effect remains muted and modern. Radial concrete beams support the roof of the hall. A soaring clock tower rising from the corner of the building gives the structure a monumental quality and marks the hall as the cornerstone of the al-Azhar University campus, also designed by Charmi. The tower was originally crowned by a spire that mimicked those of the surrounding minarets; however, it was redesigned during subsequent renovations with a colonnaded portico of pointed arches topped by a dome.

Museum of Islamic Art and National Library

Address: Port Said Street, Bab al Khalq
GPS: 30.044583, 31.252686
Year: 1903
Architect: Alfonso Manescalco Bey

The Neo-Mamluk museum, the style of choice for the ruling family, was built to house the growing collection of artifacts and objects gathered from Arab and Islamic monuments, which had been previously displayed at various sites across the city such as al-Hakim Mosque. The identity of the architect is not fully confirmed, but evidence indicates that Alfonso Manescalco Bey, chief architect in the Ministry of Public Works at the time, provided or supervised the building plans, while Max Herz Pasha, chief architect of the Comité de Conservation des Monuments de l'Art Arabe—an organization established in 1881 by Khedive Tawfiq for the preservation of Islamic and Coptic monuments—supervised interior finishing and display arrangements.

The complicated building houses two institutions, a museum and a library, which are accessed from two separate portals on different streets. The museum is entered from Port Said Street through a raised centrally positioned recessed portal reached by a set of steps. The portal is marked by a double-height pointed arch, a shape that repeats throughout the design of the building in different scales for windows and interior archways separating galleries. The middle section of the museum elevation is three stories and protrudes slightly from the two-story symmetrical horizontal structure. The flat parts of the façade are clad in sandstone. The façade is articulated with repeated vertical bays of three large windows on the ground floor and a double-arch window flanked by two niches on the top floor. The bay design is highly detailed, as it is composed of various elements inspired by Mamluk architecture. The crenelated roofline crowns the ensemble of historical elements largely drawn from religious architecture utilized here for a secular institution. Two wings with a total of twenty-five galleries are located to the right and left of the entrance hall. Double-height galleries are designed with large windows to maximize natural light for viewing objects. The floor plan is seamless, articulated by pillars and large, airy arches that separate the various galleries.

The library is entered from Muhammad Ali Street through a deep recess topped by a double-height pointed arch. A flight of steps leads to the portal followed by an entry hall leading to the main staircase. While the museum occupies the ground floor, the library is mostly on the first and second floors of a volume aligned with Muhammad Ali Street. Currently the National Library holds its collection of rare manuscripts, papyri, and rare books in the building, which, after a redesign project by architect Ahmed Mito that started in 1999, now includes several museum displays of manuscripts, including a rare collection of Qur'ans, as well as a reading room. The interior decoration of the National Library section was altered significantly during the renovation, with new finishing materials and the addition of a skeletal metal structure that runs through all the spaces of the library starting at the portal. The structure carries lighting and ventilation systems, and culminates at the roof of the building.

The museum has undergone several renovations since it opened in 1903, with a major rehabilitation in 1983. Most recently some renovation work was completed in 2010 and again in 2017, which entailed the redesign of the steps at the entrance, the color of the galleries and the entire display system. After the 2014 bombing of the building the library section was renovated yet again, and it remains closed at the time of writing.

Al-Rifai Mosque

Address: Salah al-Din Square
GPS: 30.032779, 31.257156
Year: 1869–1912
Architects: Hussein Fahmi Pasha, Max Herz Bey, Carlo Virgilio Silvagni

When it was completed in 1912, the *Egyptian Gazette* declared al-Rifai Mosque "Cairo's most beautiful modern building." Envisioned as a royal mosque, with tombs for members of the royal family, it was commissioned by Khushyar Hanim, the mother of Khedive Ismail Pasha. Al-Rifai replaced a modest but revered Sufi *zawya* with the monumental Neo-Mamluk structure that matches its Mamluk neighbor, the Sultan Hassan Mosque (1363). The mosque's origin lies in the nineteenth century; however, construction was halted in 1880 with the main body of the building partially completed but its façades, roof, dome, and minarets, as well as interior decorations, left unfinished. In 1906 construction was resumed by the orders of Abbas Helmi II, who ruled Egypt from 1892 to 1914. Work was completed by Max Herz Bey assisted by contractor Carlo Virgilio Silvagni, who completed original architect Hussein Fahmi Pasha's design with some modifications, particularly concerning the building's decorative program as well as the minarets and domes.

The building's unconventional symmetrical plan departs from historical precedents, yet its decorative program is entirely based on the revival and reinterpretation of carefully studied elements of Mamluk architecture. Along the north and south walls are a series of smaller rooms that contain Sufi relics and royal tombs. The shrine of Sheikh al-Rifai (1118–81), the Iraqi founder of the Rifai Sufi order, is located toward the back of the mosque in the center, separating the main prayer hall from a long gallery-like ceremonial hall accessed through its own ceremonial entrance at the western façade, reached by a grand stair. Two main portals for everyday use are located along the south wall, reached by steps set within richly decorated deep niches. Two minarets are also located along the south façade, flanking the two entrances.

The *mihrab* is located at the center of the east wall, aligned with the shrine in the back and the ceremonial gate. The spacious prayer hall is supported by four large pillars placed at the junctions of a grid that divides the hall into nine square modules. These four pillars, embellished with marble columns, support the roof with a dome resting on a tall drum at the center of the hall. A second dome is placed at the center of the south wall above the space between the two portals where the shrine of Sheikh Yahya is located. Two protruding wings at the north and south ends of the east façade housed a *kuttab* (school) and *sabil* (charitable fountain) respectively. The offices of the Rifai Sufi order and a library currently occupy these spaces. The decorative program of the building is busy. The exterior is articulated with a series of tall narrow niches with stained-glass windows as well as *muqarnas*, corbeled domes, and inscriptional friezes. The interior is colorful, with painted timber, marble panels cladding the walls, and decorative plaster panels. Fine glass lanterns add to the richness of the space.[20]

The mosque is the final resting place of Mohammad Reza Pahlavi, the exiled last Shah of Iran, who died in Cairo in 1980. King Farouk, Egypt's last monarch, is also buried at the site, after his remains were returned from Italy, where he died in exile in 1965.

Mustafa Kamel Mausoleum

Address: Salah al-Din Square
GPS: 30.029587, 31.257262
Year: 1947
Architect: Ahmed Charmi

One of a series of mausoleums built in the 1940s to commemorate important personalities and national figures, the mausoleum for nationalist leader Mustafa Kamel (1874–1908) was built in 1947 but his remains were not moved to their new location until 1953. It houses a small museum dedicated to the young activist. Other politicians, such as Muhammad Farid, who supported Kamel, were later interred at the mausoleum, making it a key site in Egypt's pantheon of national figures.

The main portal is set in a deep niche topped by a pointed arch. The building consists of a central double-height square space topped by a dome, forming the main body of the concrete structure. The dome rests on a drum with clerestory windows, allowing light into the space. Additional volumes protrude on all sides of the main space to serve as the entrance hall, additional burial space, and a small museum. These cubic volumes are staggered, giving the overall structure a complex massing. Decorative details on the exterior and interior are stripped-down, reinterpreted historical elements such as the *muqarnas* in the transitional zone of the dome on the interior, which is mirrored on the exterior with an abstract cubic reinterpretation of pendentives. Architect Ahmed Charmi developed an architectural language suitable for a national style of architecture that combines modern materials and shapes with reworked elements from Egypt's Islamic heritage.[21]

Hassanein Bey Mausoleum

Address: Salah Salem Road
GPS: 30.044889, 31.271139
Year: 1946
Architects: Hassan Fathy

After the sudden death of renowned geographical explorer, athlete, and statesman Ahmed Hassanein Bey, he was buried in the historic Northern Cemetery. His brother-in-law, architect Hassan Fathy, designed the mausoleum in a Neo-Mamluk style, fitting well in its context. The building departs strongly from Fathy's famous oeuvre of mud-brick rural architecture, as it is classical in composition, monumental in scale, official in its approach, and built of stone masonry. The building was approached through a narrow delicate garden (now gone) leading to the doorway. Decorative elements borrow from high examples of Mamluk architecture from the twelfth to the fifteenth centuries. For example, the dome is decorated with a zigzag pattern recalling the dome of the Khanqah of Sultan Faraj ibn Barquq, nearby.

Vertically, the mausoleum is composed of three parts: a square shaft, a triangular transitional zone, and a circular dome. Moreover, each of the four façades is divided into vertical thirds, with the middle section recessed into a shallow niche topped by *muqarnas*. The tripartite design continues in the transitional zone, as its middle section is punctuated by a symmetrical composition of openings, flanked by two triangular forms that mediate between the square below and the circle above.[22]

Al-Azhar Park

Address: Salah Salem Road
GPS: 30.040003, 31.265628
Year: 2004
Architects: Sites International and Sasaki Associates

The 30-hectare site of the park had been a dumping ground for several centuries, with debris reaching a height of 45 meters. Commissioned by the Aga Khan Trust for Culture, the park was the centerpiece of a large urban-regeneration project that included the restoration of over a kilometer of Cairo's Ayyubid Wall previously buried under rubble, extensive historic restoration across al-Darb al-Ahmar district bordering the park, and economic development in the neighboring community. The design centers on a north–south pedestrian spine, a promenade lined with palm trees and defined by lighting and water features. To the north, the spine reaches a series of stepped terraces leading to a restaurant sitting on the highest point on the site designed by architect Rami El-Dahan. To the south, it points in a straight line to the Salah al Din Citadel (1183) and the Muhammad Ali Mosque (1848) in the distance, before the promenade bends slightly to the west where a pond overlooked by a pavilion is located. In contrast with the rigid geometry of the spine, a series of meandering paths covers the site, providing sweeping views over the historic city in the foreground and the towers along the Nile in the distance. Cairo's heritage of Islamic architecture provides inspiration for details throughout the park.[23]

Historic Cairo

DOWNTOWN

Streamline motifs such as horizontal lines, rounded balconies, and nautical windows were employed in large residential buildings built in the 1930s, such as this one on Tahrir Street overlooking Falaki Square.

Downtown

The area popularly known as Downtown (Wist al-Balad in Arabic) is a triangular zone, its northwestern boundary defined by the diagonal Ramses Street, with Azbakiya Garden to its east and Abdeen Palace on its south side. The area is composed of Tawfiqiya and Ismailiya, two adjoining nineteenth-century urban expansions west of the historic city. The urban street pattern laid out in the 1860s was contemporary with the latest planning standards of the time, with nine squares connected by a grid of streets overlaid with a network of radial and diagonal avenues. The initial structures built in the area were mansions with leafy gardens, but starting at the turn of the twentieth century nearly all of these were demolished to give way to new typologies of buildings, namely Cairo's first large multi-level apartment blocks, a departure from earlier forms of collective living found in the old city. The Said Halim Pasha Palace, designed by Antonio Lasciac and completed in 1899, is the last of the area's grand palaces, whose garden extended to Mahmoud Bassiouny Street, where three large apartment blocks stand today.

With the beginning of the twentieth century the area had transformed into Cairo's entertainment and commercial center, with theaters, department stores, and banking institutions, and—by the 1930s—cinemas. Large-scale architectural projects, some sponsored by the state, others commercial endeavors, were erected after the end of the Second World War. Riots and arson in January 1952 damaged hundreds of buildings, leading to a new wave of construction. Nasserist nationalization policies transferred the majority of Downtown's buildings into state ownership.

Despite its nineteenth-century origin, Downtown's architectural landscape today is entirely a product of the twentieth century, with a few exceptions dotting the area. Documentation and preservation efforts increased following the 1992 earthquake, though this has been done inconsistently. The history of the area is marred with misconceptions, often being described as European and misleadingly compared with Paris. However, Downtown's eclectic architecture defies stylistic categorization, as hybridity defines most of its buildings. Some of the city's most prominent Modernist buildings, carried out by Egyptian architects, are located in the area. Downtown has seen several rehabilitations, such as the creation of pedestrian streets and the painting of façades, but this has fallen short of modernizing the area's infrastructure and finding a financially sustainable system for the proper upkeep of its buildings.

Egyptian Museum

Address: 15 Mariette Pasha Street, Tahrir Square
GPS: 30.047572, 31.233602
Year: 1902
Architect: Marcel Dourgnon

Egypt's first architectural competition, held in 1894, was for a new purpose-built museum near the east bank of the Nile, in the Ismailiya district, to display the growing collection of Egyptian antiquities. Marcel Dourgnon's Neo-Classical T-shaped design for the two-story building includes a grand sunken atrium at the center with skylights, for the display of colossal statues and large stone objects. The museum is entered through a garden leading to the raised ground floor. A domed double-height space near the entrance acts as a distribution point to the galleries to the right and left and to the atrium directly ahead. The second floor is reached by two grand stairs at the ends of the east and west wings. Corridors run around the building on both levels to facilitate circulation. All gallery spaces are double height, with plenty of natural sunlight entering through clerestory windows and skylights.

There are several balustraded circular openings that allow for visual connections between the two floors as well as for natural light to reach the ground floor. To maintain the feeling of openness, pillars lining the atrium give way to large semicircular arches that support the flat concrete roof. The classically designed main elevation is divided into five sections, with a protruding central bay with the main entrance set within a large arch supported by two columns. Two Beaux-Arts relief sculptures of female figures in ancient Egyptian dress flank the semicircular arch. The two side wings were each articulated with three arches shading a portico that has since been enclosed. Two additional protruding bays at the east and west ends of the elevation complete the symmetry. The fate of the building once its collections are moved to the Grand Egyptian Museum (#219) has not been determined.

Arab Socialist Union
(demolished)

Address: Corniche al-Nil
GPS: 30.047670, 31.232174
Year: 1959
Architect: Mahmoud Riad

This building became known first as the headquarters of the Arab Socialist Union (1962–78), then of the National Democratic Party (1978–2011). However, it was initially built to house the short-lived Cairo Municipality, a different form of municipal government from the current governorate system. The building consisted of a fourteen-story rectangular block placed along the east side of the site, with an attached three-story base that protruded from the back and a second four-story volume at the south of the site containing the auditorium. The overall L-shaped composition created an open space at the center of the site to reflect a spirit of openness, as the fenceless space allowed Cairenes to approach the monumental building with ease. The building primarily contained offices and meeting rooms, a library, and archive spaces. Public services were placed on the lower three floors of the tower within the protruding base, while limited-access administration occupied the tower above. The architecture was characterized by its austere Functionalist design, with a regular grid of windows on both the east and west elevations of the block. A cafeteria was placed on the top floor, with views over the Nile. The proportions of the tower were designed so that all offices were aligned with the exterior, maximizing natural light and air, with a hallway in the center of the floor plan on each floor. Circulation shafts were placed at either ends of the narrow block. Having been the headquarters of the ruling National Democratic Party, the building was torched in January 2011 and demolished in 2015.

Nile Hilton Hotel
(Ritz Carlton)

Address: 1113 Corniche El Nil
GPS: 30.045902, 31.231939
Year: 1953–58
Architects: Welton Becket, Mahmoud Riad

Only the second international Hilton Hotel after Istanbul's, this building marked the full arrival of Americanism in Cairo and served as an important cornerstone in the Cold War as a meeting place for international politicians. The land had been vacant after the nineteenth-century military barracks that stood there and had been the headquarters for the British occupying army since 1882 were demolished in 1947. Schemes for a hotel with a similar shape and appearance to be placed at this site circulated as "Nile Hotel" as early as 1953. The arrival of Conrad Hilton to the project brought with him American architect Welton Becket, who mostly handled the interior design of rooms as well as public areas of the hotel such as the reception, lounges, casino, bars, and restaurants. The earlier scheme for the building by Mahmoud Riad was modified only slightly, for instance by the removal of the proposed pedestrian bridge from the hotel to the Nile. In the final design the exterior was a gleaming white slab with a stripped-down, Functionalist façade of equally sized balconies, reflecting the equally sized rooms. Protruding volumes at the base of the block housed restaurants, stores, and the casino. The crisp horizontal lines and exterior stairs zigzagging up its sides added to the building's International Style. The interior of the hotel was minimally decorated with extensive use of Egyptian stone, blue mosaics and teal-painted surfaces adorned with replicas of ancient Egyptian reliefs. An extensive redesign completed in 2015 significantly modified the exterior, now fully enclosed behind a curtain wall that encapsulates the grid of balconies, and entirely reworked Becket's interior, which had been largely lost in previous renovations.[24]

League of Arab States

Address: 92 al-Tahrir Street, Tahrir Square
GPS: 30.044569, 31.233220
Year: 1955
Architect: Mahmoud Riad

Mahmoud Riad's design for the headquarters of the League of Arab States (Arab League) was the first of what became a new face for 1950s Cairo along the Nile. Similar to the Arab Socialist Union building (#9), the Arab League is designed as a nine-story rectangular block with attached three-story volumes arranged in a U-shape, with a semi-open courtyard in the center. The design mediates between internationalism and regionalism by incorporating decorative elements drawn from the Arab world, such as the Moorish patterns adorning the main and ceremonial portals, with the form and functionality of the International Style.

The building includes the large meeting room for representatives of the member states, located in the west wing, and offices for administration in the tower. Additional meeting rooms, lounges, a library and archive room, and a public reception are located along the base of the tower. The tower consists of offices along its two long elevations, with a hallway in the center and circulation shafts at the two narrow ends, which are each adorned with a large clock.

Qasr al-Nil Bridge

GPS: 30.043762, 31.229764
Year: 1933
Architect: Dorman Long & Co. Ltd.

The first bridge crossing the Nile anywhere along its path was completed in Cairo in 1871 at the same spot as the current Qasr al-Nil Bridge. However, by 1930 the old bridge was no longer sufficient given the increased need to urbanize westward and the growing number of automobiles in the city, surpassing thirty thousand vehicles. The new bridge was constructed in thirty months and completed in 1933, at 382 meters long and 20 meters wide. The modular design of steel arched beams resting on piers at even intervals allowed for the pieces to be manufactured in England and shipped for speedy installation. Much of the work done on the site focused on stabilizing foundations and building the piers. The four lion sculptures that adorned the first bridge were reinstalled on new shorter plinths backed by tapering pillars crowned by Art Deco lighting fixtures.

Omar Makram Mosque

Address: Tahrir Square
GPS: 30.043145, 31.233889
Year: 1948
Architect: Mario Rossi

The demolition of the military barracks at Ismailiya Square in 1947 initiated a series of urban and architectural projects that aimed to transform the square into the city's civic center. One of the projects was carried out by the Awqaf Administration to replace a small derelict *zawya* for al-Sheikh al-Abit located on the site. In light of the nationalist fervor in the aftermath of the exit of British troops from Cairo, the new mosque was dedicated to nationalist leader Omar Makram (1750–1822). The eclectic mosque design combines volumes of various forms—a square, a rectangle, and a semicircle—into a single composition. The plan of the raised ground floor is divided into three parts: the prayer hall, the courtyard, and the ablution area. The rectangular prayer hall, facing southeast, is supported by columns and arches carrying the flat decorative ceiling. The *sahn* (open courtyard), with an Andalusian entrance portico from the street, hosts funerals and events. An attached semicircular three-story protrusion at the west side houses an ablution area on the ground floor and an office, the imam's room, and a library on the upper floor. The decorations are drawn from Rossi's three-decade career in Egypt, which mostly focused on producing Neo-Islamic buildings and decorative interiors. The entrance is unconventionally placed in the corner portico facing the square, topped by the soaring Neo-Fatimid minaret.

Al-Mugammaa

Address: Tahrir Square
GPS: 30.042686, 31.234999
Year: 1951
Architects: Muhammad Kamal Ismail, Fahmy Momen

The largest administrative building in the Middle East, the monumental Mugammaa was the centerpiece of the remaking of Ismailiya Square following the demolition of the military barracks nearby. Construction started in 1947 as part of the postwar urban projects undertaken by the state. The project aimed to create a single building for all government departments to be represented in order to help the public complete all their official business at one address. With a traffic circle already taking shape at the south end of the still undefined square, the architects arced the main elevation on the center point of the circle. The streets that surround the building on the other three sides govern the shape of the structure, so it is not symmetrical in plan, its west side larger than the east. The two sides of the building protrude slightly, creating arms that give definition to the plaza at the base. After the first ten floors, the 55-meter-high building recesses twice to accommodate regulations on height limits. The main portal is marked by five double-height, pointed arches in the center of the main elevation. An entry hall leads to a round colonnaded atrium rising the entire height of the fourteen-story structure.

The atrium acts as a distribution point for the many hallways, where the building's 1,309 rooms are arranged around the perimeter of the structure. Welcoming more than twenty thousand visitors daily, the building is served by ten elevators. Four large air shafts penetrate all floors, bringing fresh air and light to all rooms

and hallways along the interior. Fenestration is arranged in vertical columns across the façade at even intervals. While the building is often dismissed as lacking any architectural style, the staggering of recesses on the two side elevations and the rounding of the top corners in the back of the structure are Art Deco features. The addition of stripped-down elements inspired by Islamic architecture, such as the pointed arches, are an effort to graft locality onto the building's international design.

Downtown

AUC Science Building
(demolished)

Address: Tahrir Square
GPS: 30.043440, 31.236473
Year: 1966
Architect: Medhat Hassan Shaheen

In 1963 American University in Cairo (AUC) president Thomas Bartlett expanded the university's science program, which necessitated a new facility. The six-story Science Building housed departments of physics, chemistry, and mathematics on its first three floors and laboratories and computer labs on the top floor. The floor plans of the bar-shaped building consisted of a hallway in the center flanked by rooms. All rooms included large glass windows to maximize light, though on the south façade the windows were protected by a screen of *brise soleil* of small rectangular openings fixed to the exterior.

Two large uninterrupted glass windows on the ground and first floors were for a teachers' room and the head of the department office. Vertical circulation shafts designed to occupy minimal space were placed at both ends of the building. The building was considered a pioneering example of sustainable architecture in Egypt for its passive solar design. After standing empty when AUC moved to its new campus, then sustaining considerable damage during the 2011 Uprising, it was demolished in 2015.

Aziz Bahari Buildings

Address: 3 al-Tahrir Street, Tahrir Square
GPS: 30.043901, 31.236499
Year: 1934
Architect: Antoine Selim Nahas

Designed by the architect as a complex of three residential buildings, the two overlooking the square directly are conjoined into a single ten-story unit, while the third stands independently in the back of the site, rising to eight stories. The buildings occupy a total of 1,552m² out of the 1,811m² plot. An 8-meter-wide passageway, conceived as a covered garden, separates the two conjoined blocks on the ground level and gives access to their two entrances. The entire ground floor is given to store space, with the exception of the entry halls, stairs, elevators, and service stairs for each of the blocks. The first floor of the front unit is dedicated to offices. The plan and main elevation of the unit is perfectly symmetrical. Typical floors from two to eight contain apartments ranging in size from three to four rooms. The reinforced-concrete structure is designed so that the internal walls can be rearranged between apartments to combine or reduce apartment sizes. Stone cladding in the passageway is articulated with a series of pillars, niches, and dentils above the doorways. The same motif is repeated on the exterior, lining the bottoms of the balconies. Interior finishes include white-marble entry halls and stairs, mosaic-cement tiles for public hallways and lobbies, parquet floors for living areas, and wood-plank floors for bedrooms.

This was the site of Astra Café, which counted Naguib Mahfouz among its patrons; the café has been replaced by fast food restaurants. This is the first of two Bahari building complexes designed by Antoine Selim Nahas in Downtown. The second set is located at Mustafa Kamel Square (#39).[25]

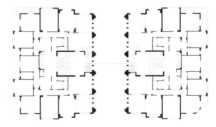

Typical Floor Plan (2nd to 8th Floors)

Cleopatra Palace Hotel

Address: 2 al-Bustan Street
GPS: 30.046289, 31.235257
Year: 1962
Architects: Ahmad Sidki, Ahmad Fuad

Occupying a prominent triangular site overlooking Tahrir Square and the Egyptian Museum, Cleopatra Palace Hotel is a fifteen-story International Style concrete block. The structure is composed of two elements: a triangular three-story base aligned with the streets, delimiting the 716m^2 site, and a rectangular tower with a smaller footprint facing the square. *Brise soleil* screens are placed on the narrow façade facing the museum while the side façades are punctuated with rows of windows for the offices and hotel rooms. The building has two entrances, one on al-Bustan Street servicing the hotel, and a second entrance on Qasr al-Nil Street servicing the offices.

The hotel was originally designed with around seventy rooms for low-budget travelers. The rooftop featured a nightclub and restaurant with a terrace. A circulation tower with elevators and stairs is placed at the back of the tower. After decades of neglect the building was renovated in 2017, which led to the redesign of all interior spaces. The office entrance retains the original design, incorporating marble cladding.

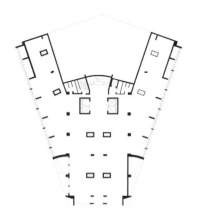

Typical Floor Plan (1st and 2nd Floor Offices)

Khoury Building

Address: 18 Mahmoud Bassiouny Street
GPS: 30.048623, 31.235946
Year: 1941
Architect: Raymond Antonius

Despite its grand appearance, the Khoury Building is a tenement designed for middle-income residents of the area, with apartments ranging in size between 80m^2 and 120m^2. With a footprint of 550m^2, the ground floor contains five stores, an entrance lobby, two garages, and two small apartments. The following six identical floors each contain four apartments, each with a living room and three to four additional rooms for living, dining, and sleeping. The building's exterior is typical of the period, with an unarticulated ground and first floor followed by interplay of flat surfaces and recessed balconies. For shading, external blinds are installed on all windows, and shutters on balcony doors.[26]

Baehler Buildings

Address: Talaat Harb Square
GPS: 30.047962, 31.238923
Year: 1920s, 1934
Architect: Unknown (original), Leon Nafilyan (additions)

In 1898 the four-story Hotel Savoy was built on a triangular site overlooking today's Talaat Harb Square. Within two decades the location appreciated quickly, which led Charles Baehler, chief shareholder of Egyptian Hotels Ltd., to replace the short-lived hotel with a larger, taller structure of palatial apartments and grand shops. Today the Baehler Buildings are composed of three structures built in two phases. First, the iconic seven-story block built with Haussmanian inspiration, completed with an overdesigned parapet crowning the structure mimicking turn-of-the-century Parisian rooflines. The identity of the architect of this structure is not confirmed. Two additional blocks were completed in 1934, designed by French-Ottoman architect Leon Nafilyan.

Those structures, situated along Qasr al-Nil, are separated from the first block by a private street lined by two shopping arcades. In total the three blocks contain 130 luxurious apartments, ranging in size from two to four bedrooms, with living spaces placed along the streets and service spaces arranged around the large internal court or light wells in the centers of the blocks. Six separate entrances service the blocks, which are internally divided into six sections. Along the street seventy-two shops line the bases of the buildings. The exterior of the first block is characterized by a clear order of balconies, windows, and protruding window bays. The two blocks by Nafilyan exhibit characteristics of Art Deco.[27]

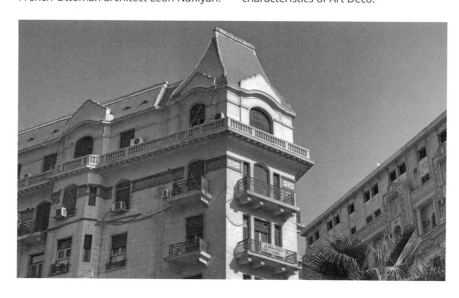

Downtown

Misr Insurance Company Offices

Address: 7 Talaat Harb Street
GPS: 30.045496, 31.237317
Year: 1950
Architect: Mahmoud Riad

The design of this office building architecturally exploits the corner of the site. The entrance is located at the corner, within a recessed portico on the slightly raised ground floor. Above that, the first floor is treated with a protruding horizontal ribbon that curves in a quarter circle, giving way to a cylindrical element at the corner of the main body of the building composed of six floors. Flanking the cylinder are small semicircular balconies on floors three to six. The main body of the structure matches the height of the company's neighboring buildings, and two additional floors were recessed to maintain harmony with the urban context. The L-shaped floor plan of the upper floors arranged along the corner allows for light and air to enter offices from the back and front of the building.

Misr Insurance Company Offices

Address: 9 Talaat Harb Street
GPS: 30.045832, 31.237575
Year: 1952
Architect: Sayed Karim

The larger of the two Misr Insurance buildings at this corner, Sayed Karim's design is in conversation with Riad's building for the same company across the street. It consists of three stacked sections: a base of stores and mezzanine level, eight identical floors of apartments currently used as offices, and four gradually recessing floors with duplex apartments. The U-shaped floor plan allows for light and air to enter the building from the front and back. The most remarkable aspect of the building is the treatment of the exterior. Ribbons wrap around the corner of the building, emphasizing horizontality and creating shaded balconies to reduce the effect of the sun on indoor temperatures. On the Talaat Harb Street elevation are balconies that are currently enclosed, with a grid of alternating breeze-block screens.

Ahmed Kamel Pasha Building

Address: 174 al-Tahrir Street
GPS: 30.044820, 31.238471
Year: 1936
Architect: Ali Labib Gabr

This building was commissioned by the head of the Alexandria Municipality as a private investment, with a duplex and roof garden for the owner on the top floors. Situated on a narrow triangular site, the building soars with its rounded corner of deep balconies. The structure is stripped of any ornamentation; instead, its aesthetic qualities come from the interplay of solid lines and deep recesses for balconies, which create shadows. The tall ground floor contains six stores, the entrance lobby, and a small apartment. The spacious entrance is clad with black-and-white marble leading to the stairs and elevator. Six typical floors each contain a five-room and a four-room apartment, complete with service spaces and service stairs to kitchens. The owner's duplex extends into the seventh floor at the corner, extenuating the building's height.[28]

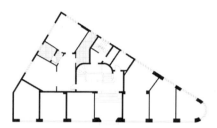

Ground Floor Plan

AUC Jameel Building

Address: 171 al-Tahrir Street, Greek Campus
GPS: 30.044095, 31.239103
Year: 1989
Architect: Dar al-Handasa

Built diagonally across from the AUC Library, the nine-story Jameel Building is a tower block of exposed concrete. Mamluk-inspired trilobed arches, rising above the recessed ground floor and creating a colonnade at campus level, mark the three-story base. The overall composition of the structure is that of an inverted ziggurat, with the top three floors extending slightly over the three below, which are in turn slightly larger than the three stories of the base.

The building can be described as a rare example of Neo-Islamic Brutalism, as it combines the materiality and heaviness of Brutalist concrete architecture with the introduction of Cairene historical motifs such as the arches, realized with alternating yellow and red sections, referencing *ablaq* masonry. Other Neo-Islamic motifs include wooden screens, referencing *mashrabiya*s, which function as sun breakers on the façade. Strong horizontal ribbons that shade the recessed windows define the upper floors.

AUC Library

Address: 28 al-Falaki Street, Greek Campus
GPS: 30.043597, 31.238457
Year: 1978
Architect: Hugh Jacobsen

The former Library of the American University in Cairo is a Brutalist concrete V-shaped structure that turns its back on its urban context with bunker-like concrete exterior walls. Instead, the library is oriented inward toward the university campus, where glass walls along the inner corner of the V-shaped opening allow diffused light to enter reading rooms and sightlines toward other university buildings. A triangular awning of *brise soleil* extends above the V-shaped opening toward the campus to control direct sunlight. It is composed of a diamond-shaped latticework of concrete beams. The ground floor can be accessed from within the campus or from a gate at the corner of the site. The main library entrance, however, is located on the first floor, reached by a stepped platform from the campus side, creating outdoor seating for communal gatherings, leading to a footbridge into the first floor. Three identical floors with open-floor plans allow for flexibility in arranging bookshelves in the darker parts of the space, while desks and reading tables are arranged toward the glass walls overlooking the campus.

Each elevation of the stark exterior is articulated by twelve large rectangular openings that funnel back across the thickness of the walls to become slit windows with an indirect view of the street. The corner of the building is carved away to create a shaded deep niche with an entryway to the campus. The structure is constructed with untreated exposed reinforced concrete with steel fittings such as stairs and railings. Since the AUC moved to its suburban campus, the building has been rented as office space.

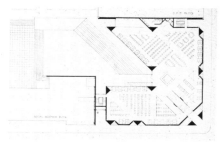

Main Library Floor

Downtown

Bab al-Louq Station
(demolished)

Address: Bab al-Louq Square
GPS: 30.044474, 31.240240
Year: 1932
Architect: Muhammad Raafat

In the 1930s the train link between Helwan and Bab al-Louq was modernized, with new diesel trains replacing steam engines and with new rail crossings at intersections. The old station was demolished to clear the street connection between Abdeen and Tahrir (then Ismailiya) squares. The new terminus was built on Mansour Street with a single platform in the center between the two tracks. The entrance was reached via five steps leading to a double-height station hall flanked by three rooms on each side, a total of six. Three rooms served as passenger waiting areas, one as a ticket office, one as left luggage, and another for the station director. Two additional exits to the left and right were located immediately before the platform. The station's reinforced-concrete structure was enveloped with a brick skin. The main façade was articulated with five narrow vertical windows, illuminating the main hall. The canopy over the platform consisted of a thin concrete roof rounded at the end and supported over a single file of pilotis at the center. The station was demolished in the 1960s and the Helwan railway was later incorporated into the Cairo Metro system and pushed below ground in this part of the city.[29]

Chamber of Commerce

Address: 6 al-Tahrir Street
GPS: 30.044585, 31.240966
Year: 1955
Architect: Sayed Karim

The nine-story Chamber of Commerce is situated on a 1,000m² corner plot in Bab al-Louq. It is composed of a podium covering the entire plot topped by an L-shaped block with a chamfered corner. The raised ground floor is reached by two sets of steps at the corner of the plot leading to the lobby. Behind the lobby is a large multipurpose hall used for trade exhibitions and other events. The rectangular lobby leads via another set of steps to a double stair to the first floor. Two elevators are placed to the right and left of the stairs. A 1,500-seat auditorium in the back corner of the site occupies the first and second floors, while offices for executive management are placed along the outer wall of the protruding rounded podium of the building. From the third to the seventh floors are identical floor plans of offices along the two side wings of the L-shaped structure. The social club for members of the chamber occupies the top two floors. The club was designed with a restaurant, a library, sitting rooms, and a terrace.

A grid of pilotis supports the lower part of the building, punctuating several spaces such as the lobby. Pilotis are also visible on the exterior along the outer wall as they support the protruding podium above. Along the left and right walls flanking the entrance are large stylized relief sculptures depicting trade across the globe. These panels are the work of artist Fathy Mahmoud, who collaborated with Sayed Karim on several buildings during this period, such as the Zamalek Tower (#144).

Ground Floor Plan

Strand Building

Address: 183 al-Tahrir Street
GPS: 30.044290, 31.242130
Year: 1957
Architects: Mustafa Shawky, Salah Zeitoun

The Strand Building was named after the cinema it replaced. Its design follows a model popular in the real-estate boom after the Second World War, consisting of a large consolidated land plot built up with a large mass structure divided into two blocks, with two entrances accessed through a covered passageway cutting through the site. The structure steps back in the upper floors (following setback laws of the time).The creation of the passageway increases store frontages. The two building entrances facing each other in the passageway are designed as fluid open lobbies with no gates. Above, there is a mezzanine level for offices. The main circulation is composed of connected scissor stairs that stitch the two blocks together internally in the center of the building's section, just above the passageway. Flexible floor plans are adjusted per floor for apartments ranging in size from one to three bedrooms, with four 'villas' with roof gardens at the top. Notable interior details include industrial metal-framed windows in the hallways and the stairs, and parquet flooring in apartments, as well as custom-designed apartment doors featuring minimalist brass details. Two Neo-Classical double arches were added at either end of the ground-floor passageway during a facelift completed in 2018.

Al-Tabbakh Mosque

Address: 18 Ali Zu al-Faqar Street
GPS: 30.045133, 31.244414
Year: 1931
Architect: Mario Rossi

The original mosque on the site was a Mamluk building erected around 1243, which quickly deteriorated and was rebuilt in 1542. It fell into poor condition again until it was reconstructed between 1929 and 1931 at the orders of King Fuad. The Awqaf Administration handled the redesign and rebuilding, led by head architect Mario Rossi. The current structure occupies a small rectangular plot of land, with the front elevation aligned with the street. The main prayer hall is rotated slightly to the southeast, with a *mihrab* marking the direction of prayer. Reinforced-concrete columns and beams compose the structure, which is embellished with Neo-Islamic decorative motifs. The four central columns support an octagonal shallow dome with clerestory windows. The building is surrounded on three sides by other structures, leaving only one narrow façade visible to the street, unconventionally designed symmetrically in three thirds. The middle section doubles as the base of the minaret, flanked by two keel-arched niches with a window set in the right one and a doorway in the left. A variety of decorative elements such as stone columns, ceramic tiles, and inscriptions adorn the brick façade. The minaret, with a spiral stair in its center, is elaborately designed with arched openings, *muqarnas*, and brick patterns.[30]

Awqaf Administration

Address: Muhammad Sabri Abu Alam Street
GPS: 30.045608, 31.241571
Year: 1898–1929
Architects: Saber Sabri, Mahmoud Fahmy, Mario Rossi

Diwan al-Awqaf was established in 1835 to manage religious endowments. Construction started on its premises in 1898; however, the building in its present shape was not completed until the eve of the First World War, with additions carried out in 1929. The structure is composed of a basement with windows at street level, followed by a raised ground floor and an additional level above. Offices are arranged around the perimeter as well as two narrow rectangular air shafts, and a planted square courtyard at the center of the building. The trapezoid building occupies a city block, with the main elevation along Sabri Abu Alam Street set back to allow for a lush front garden. The three other façades are built along the street edge, with a secondary portal at the center of each elevation, marked by a tall double-height arch and a tall parapet. At the turn of the century Neo-Mamluk historicism was prevalent, particularly for public buildings, such as the Museum of Islamic Art and National Library (#3) in Bab al-Khalq. The elevations of the building are divided into vertical bays of windows, each articulated with columns, pointed arches, *muqarnas*, geometric patterns, and *ablaq* masonry. The main portal of the building is the most elaborate section of the elevations. It consists of a protruding tall central bay with a wide, double-height pointed arch marked with black *ablaq*, the only instance in the building. Steps to the raised ground floor reach the main portal. Above the entrance is a balcony on the second floor, extending from the office of the head of the authority.

Downtown

Alexandria Insurance Company

Address: 23 Qasr al-Nil Street
GPS: 30.048035, 31.240355
Year: 1952
Architect: Sayed Karim

Located on a corner site, surrounded by three streets, at the heart of Cairo's commercial center, is this luxury residential block commissioned by the Alexandria Insurance Company. Rather than treat the three sides of the building as separate elevations, the architect created a continuous façade of concrete ribbons with a prominent round corner overlooking Qasr al-Nil Street. The ribbons alternate with windows and balconies along the façade. A double-height passageway flanked by robust pilotis cuts through the site perpendicular to the main street. The passageway increases storefronts and gives way to the building entrance tucked beneath the structure in the center. The double-height entrance is designed with elevators and a double stair leading to the first floor, occupied by offices. Sculptural reliefs by the artist Fathy Mahmoud of the Alexandria lighthouse and a personification of insurance, protecting life and a vulnerable family, adorn the passageway at the top and the vestibule's mirrored wall above the elevators.

The second floor contains four apartments and functions as a transitional level for the building's circulation, as the main stair shifts here to the area directly above the passageway. Floors three through eight are identical, with four apartments per floor, each with six rooms; all apartments are equipped with fireplaces in the main hall. Other amenities include hot water and air conditioning. Two service stairs provide direct access to the kitchens, which are placed along the interior of the block and ventilated by air shafts. The top four floors are staggered at a 60-degree angle to accommodate caps on building heights. Four 'villas' are located on the tenth and eleventh floors, with access to sweeping balconies. Additional service rooms are situated on the twelfth floor and a large water tank is built at the pinnacle of the building, completing its pyramidal shape. Along the façade on Qasr al-Nil, four concrete ribs are grafted vertically on the façade, originating from the passageway and extending up the entire height of the building.

This is one of the finest examples of Karim's architecture, not only in terms of its space-solving approach and its architectonic characteristics but also for the particular selection of building finishes. Materials include glass block; brass fittings; mosaic tiles; white, brown, and green marbles; cement tiles; and innovative lighting solutions.[31]

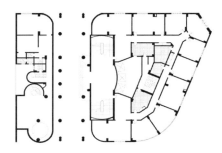

Ground Floor

Downtown

31

Immobilia Building

Address: 26–28 Sherif Street
GPS: 30.048975, 31.242253
Year: 1940
Architects: Max Edrei, Gaston Rossi

This building resulted from a competition held by the Immobilia Company for Real Estate in 1937. Celebrated upon its completion as Egypt's—and the Middle East's—largest modern construction, the Immobilia Building occupies a 5,444m² plot and houses 218 apartments. At 70 meters, it was the tallest building in Cairo. From the sweeping curved balconies on one of Downtown's most prominent intersections, residents could see as far as the Citadel and the Pyramids.The reinforced-concrete structure consists of two separate (north and south) blocks atop a 100-vehicle garage placed below street level. The colossal scale of the building is matched with generously designed entryways to each of the blocks. At the time of its completion this building housed the biggest cluster of elevators anywhere in the region. Other technical services included intercom, heating, radio antennas, and advanced plumbing and electrical systems. Service shafts penetrate the floors of the blocks, allowing for light and ventilation as well as service access to kitchens and laundry rooms.

While large retail spaces front Qasr al-Nil and Sherif streets, smaller commercial spaces are located in the colonnaded passageway leading to the buildings' entrances. The first floor is dedicated to offices and is distinguished from the remaining floors by the use of large industrial glass windows to maximize sunlight. Each of the residential floors consists of twenty-three apartments, ranging in size from two to six rooms.

The hallways and interiors were simply designed and finished with 'Ceramocrete' cement floor tiles, furnished by Vita Mory and Frère Company, established in Bulaq in 1919. Strong horizontal lines formed by the deep balconies characterize the unembellished exterior of the building.³²

Typical Floor Plan

Downtown

Central Bank

Address: 39 Qasr al-Nil Street
GPS: 30.048544, 31.242037
Year: 1903–47
Architects: Dimitri Fabricius (original);
J.P. Serjeant, Max Zollikofer (redesign)

The current building is the outcome of a 1947 remodeling of the structure that already stood on the site. Dimitri Fabricius designed the original bank in a rusticated Neo-Baroque style. Its stone exterior was covered in architectural ornaments such as a broken round pediment above the main portal, cornices, balustrades, columns, and an elaborate parapet. The bank was a cornerstone of the British colonial presence in Egypt. When British troops evacuated Egyptian cities in 1947, the state refurbished the bank by adding a third floor and stripping it of its overworked façade. The new, understated façade was not only contemporary for the period but also symbolized the turning of a new page for the bank. The current design consists of a double-height ground floor forming the base, followed by two floors of offices, and is crowned by a horizontal parapet line extending over the structure. The corner of the building, where the main portal is located, is articulated as a half-hexagon. Streets surround the building on all four sides, thus the plans were devised with offices around the perimeter for maximum light and air, with air shafts in the center of the block.

Murad Wahba Pasha Building

Address: 33 Qasr al-Nil Street
GPS: 30.048823, 31.242583
Year: 1949
Architects: Mustafa Shawky, Salah Zeitoun, Abdel Salam Qinawi, Kamal Sabry

The building's design is the result of an architectural competition held in 1948. Given the site's central location and the high price of real estate, the architects sought to maximize the building's square footage while respecting regulations regarding building heights that were strongly enforced after the Second World War. Setbacks based on the width of the two streets intersecting at the site determined the mass of the sixteen-story structure. The lower part of the building reaches the height limit of 30 meters along the street edge. The central part of the block rises higher, with an 8-meter setback from Sherif Pasha Street. The taller central block is aligned with Qasr al-Nil Street, resulting in the building's overall dynamic massing. An 8-meter-wide gallery cuts across the site on the ground floor, connecting Qasr al-Nil and Banque Misr streets. The building lobby with two main stairs and elevators is accessed through the gallery. Thirty stores line the entire perimeter of the building, facing both the surrounding streets and the gallery in the center. Offices occupy floors two through four, with a total of seventy-five rooms. Floors five through nine are each divided into ten apartments. Floors ten through fourteen are divided into four apartments and two duplexes. Six 'villas' containing six living rooms and a total of twenty-four rooms occupy the top two floors of the building. A 160-car garage occupies the basement. The architects calculated the total monthly rental income from the building, based on their design maximizing floor area, to reach LE7,300, a considerable sum at the time.

Ayrout Building

Address: 13 Sherif Street
GPS: 30.046683, 31.242398
Year: 1937
Architect: Charles Ayrout

The striking 47-meter-high Ayrout Building stands out for its towering corner clad in brick, a signature material in Ayrout's designs. In its ten floors the building offers apartments in varying sizes from two to four bedrooms, in addition to a duplex on the top floors. The base of the structure consists of 5-meter-high stores, with the main entrance to the building on the side street leading immediately to a set of stairs to the elevator lobby above the stores. The apartments begin at the following level, clearly distinguished on the exterior from the base. The two elevations on the corner site are a single continuum of horizontal strips, balcony recesses, and window openings. The horizontality is interrupted only by a soaring vertical element at the corner that extenuates the height of the structure. The vertical corner culminates in an elaborately designed crowning element, a futuristic interpretation of a Tuscan tower. The building is constructed of a reinforced-concrete frame with masonry infill walls.

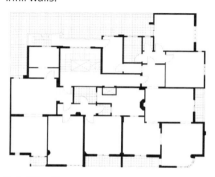

Typical Floor Plan

Radio Tower

Address: 3 Rushdi Street
GPS: 30.046664, 31.243611
Year: 1954
Architect: Naoum Shebib

Radically transforming domestic architecture in Cairo, the twenty-two-story Radio Tower was the city's first tall residential building. The site is narrow, with limited frontage on the main street while the rest of the land goes deep into the city block surrounded by buildings on three sides. To maximize façades, thus creating more apartments with direct sunlight, the architect designed a slender tall tower occupying only half the site. The deep setback allows for the building's height without breaking regulations. There are two apartments per floor, each afforded views to the north and south.

The Rushdi Street façade is a grid of concrete lines defining the equally sized balconies shading the north-facing side of the building. The east and west walls are protected with concrete screens, with alternating panels across the height of the structure. The double-wall design protects the exposed building from the sun, thus reducing indoor temperatures.

Church and Convent of Saint Joseph

Address: Banque Misr Street (intersection with Muhammad Farid Street)
GPS: 30.048022, 31.243829
Year: 1909
Architects: Aristide and Pio Leonori

Historicism in Cairo comes in varieties as diverse as the multiethnic communities that rose to prominence throughout the city's modern history. The monumental Neo-Tuscan cross-shaped church commissioned by Cairo's Italian community is aligned parallel to Muhammad Farid Street, with the main entrance from the side street. Unconventionally, the church extends along a north–south axis, rather than the traditional east–west, due to the restriction of the rectangular site. A double stair leads to the raised ground floor and the Neo-Gothic marble portal. A large central nave flanked by two cross-vaulted side aisles leads to the transept and the apse. Frescoes depicting scenes from the life of Christ, with emphasis on the journey to Egypt, decorate the otherwise sparse interior. Clerestory windows flood the nave with light. The exterior is painted in horizontal stripes recalling late-medieval Italian churches. The center of the cruciform plan is marked not by a dome but by an octagonal drum with a gabled roof. A square campanile tower rises at the southeast corner of the building, adding to the church's monumental presence.

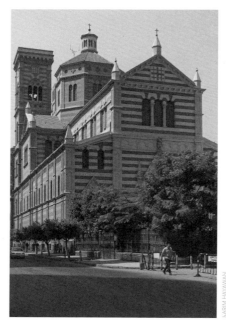

37
Banque Misr

Address: 151 Muhammad Farid Street
GPS: 30.048139, 31.244178
Year: 1927
Architect: Antonio Lasciac

Established in 1920 as the first bank owned and managed by Egyptians, Banque Misr's headquarters were built between 1924 and 1927 in an eclectic 'Arab style.' The six-story structure is an exercise in the decorative arts, with every two floors defined on the main elevation by a distinctive ornamental program. The exterior is treated with stone, decorative balconies, pointed arches carried on double columns, brick facing for upper floors, and two towering elements with clocks articulating the corners. At the base of the building is a double-height grand banking hall lit from its glass ceilings and overlooked by a mezzanine level. The lavishly decorated hall incorporates finely painted wooden ceilings, intricately designed marble floors, and highly detailed wall treatments and metalwork. The upper four floors are built around two courts that ventilate the offices and allow light to enter through the glass roof to the base.[33]

38
Banque Misr Tower

Address: 153 Muhammad Farid Street
GPS: 30.048480, 31.244410
Year: 1985
Architect: Ove Arup

With the liberalization policies of the Sadat presidency, Banque Misr expanded its role in the Egyptian economy as the country's main state-owned bank, with established investments in a wide range of industries. The Brutalist tower, initiated in 1979, sits on a muscular solid base. The concrete structure is clad in Egyptian granite, extracted from quarries owned by the bank. The tower has three distinctive elements: a base, housing banking facilities and services; a tower shaft for offices and administration; and a monolithic crown at the top. While the corners of the tower are solid, the four elevations are designed with strips of windows alternating with rectangular panels arranged in rows, concealing the floor plates and doubling as shading devices to reduce direct sunlight.

Downtown

Aziz Bahari Buildings

Address: Mustafa Kamel Square
GPS: 30.049206, 31.243928
Year: 1938
Architect: Antoine Selim Nahas

The large 3,127m² plot is divided into two corresponding ten-story buildings separated by a colonnaded passageway (later built in with a store). With a combined footprint of 2,442m², the structures were typical of the new typology of large-scale real-estate development in central Cairo popular in the 1930s. Stores with ceilings higher than 5 meters occupy the ground floor. Two additional floors are designed for offices, accessed through separate entrances and stairs. The remaining eight floors are for apartments ranging in size from two to four rooms.

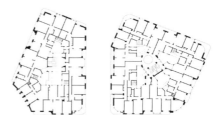

Typical Floor Plan (2nd to 8th Floor)

The structure is built with reinforced concrete and limestone masonry, with extensive use of marble for cladding the storefronts, entrance halls, and stairwells, as well as all bathrooms. The dark marble cladding on the two lower floors contrasts with the light color of the remainder of the structure, making the building appear to float. The marble is installed on pillars, creating the illusion that pilotis support the heavy structure. A grid of concrete sun breakers on the slightly curved corner overlooking Mustafa Kamel Square contrasts with the rounded corners of the long balconies along the building's façades.[34]

Assicurazioni Generali Building

Address: 33 Abdel Khaleq Tharwat Street
GPS: 30.050045, 31.243874
Year: 1939
Architect: Arnold Zarb

Occupying a 2,400m² corner plot, this monumental building, named after the Austrian insurance company that commissioned it, was a landmark in luxury living in Cairo. The 62-meter-high building is equipped with four elevators for residents—including two high-speed models—in addition to seven service elevators and two large elevators for furniture. The entry hall and the two main stairs are lined with black and beige marble. Seven additional service stairs with direct access to kitchens are located in the ventilation shafts. When it was completed in 1939 it offered its residents modern amenities including air conditioning through floor pipes and vents, central hot water supplied from three furnaces, water pumps to ensure regular water pressure in all apartments, seven refuse chutes near the kitchens leading to on-site trash furnaces, and all apartments connected with telephone lines.

The structure is composed of a central core with four corner volumes. The top four stories step back, making the floor area of the top floor about half that of the ground floor. The ground floor is 6 meters high to allow for double-height stores. The first floor was designed with a communal area including a games room, billiards room, and a three-hundred-seat multipurpose room. The second to ninth floors each include thirteen apartments, ranging from two to five rooms. Apartments ranging in size from three to six rooms occupy the tenth to the thirteenth floors.

The building was featured on the cover of the first issue of *Al Emara*, the world's first Arabic-language journal concerned with contemporary architecture and design. The editor, Sayed Karim, called it "a work of modern art."[35]

Crédit Foncier Égyptien

Address: 37 Abdel Khaleq Tharwat Street
GPS: 30.050157, 31.244663
Year: 1903
Architects: Max Herz Bey, Eduard Matasek

Crédit Foncier Égyptien, founded in Alexandria in 1880, was a formidable economic institution that held half the mortgage debts of Egypt well into the 1920s. The building, the first purpose-built bank in Cairo, combines elements of Neo-Classicism and Neo-Renaissance as well as decorative elements of Neo-Baroque and turn-of-the-century modern design that utilizes concrete. Designed by Max Herz Bey, the building is a testament to Herz's versatility, as he also worked on buildings in Neo-Islamic styles, such as al-Rifai Mosque (1912, #4). The Crédit Foncier's symmetrical front elevation is divided into five sections, with protruding bays in the center and two corners and two slightly recessed bays (with four windows each) flanking the entrance. The façade is rusticated on the ground floor, contrasting with the smooth masonry of the second floor. The first floor houses an open space for teller counters and other banking activities. The original, more elaborate design included a drum topped by a dome articulating the corner of the building; however, this was not implemented. The second floor houses management and administration offices.

Shaar Hashamayim Synagogue

Address: 17 Adli Street
GPS: 30.051442, 31.243694
Year: 1905
Architects: Eduard Matasek, Maurice Youssef Cattaui

Originally commissioned by Cairo's Sephardic community, the synagogue is the largest in the city. The present building is the result of the original design in addition to various alterations and renovations carried out in 1922, 1940, and 1980. The square building consists of a large central dome above the main space supported by four triangular pendentives resting on four corner pillars. Beyond the pillars on three sides of the square are side galleries, and along the east wall is the *bimah* (reading platform) and the Holy Ark, reached by a set of marble steps. A second-floor gallery for women overlooks the central space from the north, south, and west sides. The prayer space is lit through clerestory windows on the outer walls. The interior decoration today is the accumulation of a variety of motifs completed at different times, drawn from various styles such as Neo-Baroque, Art Nouveau, Art Deco and Neo-Pharaonic. The synagogue is entered through two raised square porticos on either end of the main elevation, one leading to the main space for men, the other to the second floor for women. Two sets of steps lead to the porticos and the large wooden doors adorned with Stars of David. The structure's cubic form is articulated with four towering corners. A stylized motif of palms appears throughout the building and on the main elevation.[36]

Tiring Department Store

Address: 2 al-Esili Street, Ataba Square
GPS: 30.050798, 31.251055
Year: 1912
Architect: Oscar Horowitz

Victor Tiring, an Austrian merchant born in Istanbul who specialized in Turkish tailoring, founded this store in 1910. Oscar Horowitz, a Czech architect who studied in Vienna and who designed similar shopping destinations within the Austro-Hungarian sphere, designed the building. The Tiring Store in Cairo was completed in 1912, and when it opened it was the city's premier shopping destination for imported luxury goods. The six-story building with a footprint of 1,235m² was designed with open floors and an airy feel fit for modern shopping. Large glass windows maximized natural light in the spaces of the store. A cupola topped by four kneeling figures with Egyptian headdress holding a globe articulates the corner of the building. The department store was only in operation for a few short years, as the outbreak of the First World War led British authorities in Egypt to expel Austro-Hungarians and to liquidate their businesses. Other occupants have used the building informally for decades.

44
Sednaoui Department Store

Address: Khazindar Square
GPS: 30.053401, 31.251310
Year: 1913
Architect: Georges Parcq

Sednaoui was established in 1907 as a family-owned retail business; the Khazindar building was commissioned to be its flagship department store. It consists of a double-height ground floor, followed by three additional stories organized in an open floor plan with specially designed display cases that did not obstruct views. The focal point of the building is its light-filled, glass-roofed large atrium, allowing shoppers to see up and down to other levels with additional merchandise. The feeling of openness is achieved with the use of a steel structure, most visibly in the columns supporting the floors along the atrium. The exterior is designed with a central bay, where the grand entrance is located under a steel-and-glass canopy with name of the store in Arabic and English at the top of the central bay, articulated with two small domes.

Khedival Buildings

Address: 15 Emad al-Din Street
GPS: 30.055608, 31.244349
Year: 1911
Architects: Antonio Lasciac, Gustave Brocher, Georges Parcq

Khedive Abbas Helmi II established the Société Belge-Égyptienne de l'Ezbékieh to carry out real-estate and construction projects. The company's landmark complex of four imposing residential buildings with palatial apartments was the largest construction of its kind in Cairo at the time. Arranged as two pairs flanking Emad al-Din Street, the meeting of the four blocks is marked by four domes. Stylistically the buildings are eclectic, combining elements of French Neo-Baroque with Italian Neo-Renaissance. Each building consists of three stacked sections: large stores and a mezzanine level at the base separated with a balustrade from the following three floors of apartments. The top floor is articulated with a protruding colonnaded balcony with a wooden roof. Each block is entered from Emad al-Din through a passageway leading to a large courtyard with the main staircase and elevator as well as service-stair access.

George and Helal Shammaa Building

Address: 9–11 Orabi Street
GPS: 30.054326, 31.242706
Year: 1952
Architect: Ali Labib Gabr

The Shammaa building belongs to the era of large-scale private real-estate development projects that resumed after the end of the Second World War. These buildings were typically built on large consolidated land plots in the flourishing commercial center. The scale of this building responds to the monumental Misr Petroleum Company building across the street, and is designed to maximize rentable area while respecting the city's building codes at the time. The code led to the recessed upper floors, respecting the height cap of 30 meters along the street edge. A double-height commercial gallery cuts into the volume of the building at the center of the main elevation, thus increasing storefronts and giving access to the building entrance away from the bustling street. A large light well tops the gallery, with glass blocks embedded in the roof to allow diffused light into the space.

The base of the building consists of the storefronts topped by an office level; the shaft consists of six identical floors of apartments. The four recessed floors at the top create staggered terraces for the upper apartments that crown the structure. In order to break the monotony of the large volume, the architect created a dynamic exterior with deep balconies articulating the corners with horizontal lines, contrasting with the vertical arrangements of fenestration and a grid of slightly rounded balconies, three bays wide, at the center of the elevations. In the original design, green granite clad the base of the structure and flower boxes were integrated into the windows and balconies of the fourth floor to add visual texture and soften the built edges.

Misr Petroleum Company

Address: 6 Orabi Street
GPS: 30.053924, 31.242340
Year: 1948
Architect: Mahmoud Riad

One of the largest postwar constructions in Cairo, this building commissioned by Misr Insurance occupies a triangular city block surrounded by three streets. The main entrance on Tawfiqiya Street is in a double-height deep recess in the façade supported by two pilotis. The mass of the structure is staggered with several recesses, so that the top three floors occupy nearly half the footprint of the ground floor. Shell Petroleum Company (later nationalized as Misr Petroleum Company) rented the building while it was still in the design stage. Plans for the office building, with a total of ten stories, focused on providing all offices with sufficient natural light. This led to the creation of a large court in the center of the block for light and air to reach the interior. In essence the building is arranged as three bars along the perimeter streets, each with a hallway in the center flanked by offices along the exterior facing the streets and the interior facing the court. Circulation cores are placed near the corners of the triangular building, each with a grand staircase and two high-speed elevators. Protruding volumes at the corners of the lower floors provide terraces for the smaller upper floors.

A large auditorium on the ground floor, used for screenings and lectures, occupies the center of the block; the court in the center of the building starts at the third floor, above the roof of the auditorium. Large commercial spaces and garages occupy the remainder of the ground floor. Asbestos was used in the first four floors to reduce noise from the bustling streets below. The top two floors were designed for laboratories, and special considerations were given to the archive rooms and the library. The exterior of the building has a massive quality, with sharp lines and symmetry. Several grid systems govern the placement of the large windows that allow maximum natural light in to the office spaces. Clocks were installed throughout the building, in addition to two large 2.25-meter-diameter timepieces on the exterior, at the tops of two towering elements that face the large squares near the site.

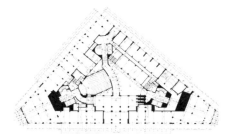

Ground Floor Plan

Arabic Music Institute

Address: 22 Ramses Street
GPS: 30.054573, 31.239477
Year: 1923
Architect: Ernesto Verrucci

Founded in 1914 for the preservation and development of classical Arabic music, the institute was originally designed to host a theater, music library, and rehearsal rooms. The two-story structure is rectangular in plan, with the theater in the center. Other functions of the building are placed along the perimeter with windows. The main entrance, placed at the building's inverted corner, is topped by a slender *mashrabiya* and is set within a wide, pointed arch placed diagonally between the two side elevations.

The side elevations are articulated with vertical bays, each composed of tripartite windows at the ground and upper floors, with the addition of wooden awnings above the second-floor windows in the center of each elevation. The parapet is most elaborate at the corners. Some decorative elements are reinterpreted from Mamluk architecture, while others are entirely invented. The heart of the building, the theater, is richly decorated.

Two royal boxes flank the stage, designed for musical performances. Additional boxes are placed on the second floor to the sides and back of the theater auditorium. The structure is crowned by an ornamented dome near the corner. The building hosted the Cairo Congress of Arab Music in 1932.

Egyptian Society of Engineers

Address: 28 Ramses Street
GPS: 30.0562422, 31.2413567
Year: 1923–46
Architect: Mustafa Fahmy

The Egyptian Society of Engineers was founded in 1920, and their headquarters was built in two phases: first a single-story structure was completed in 1923, and as the society grew a second story was added in 1932. This small rectangular structure belongs to Mustafa Fahmy's oeuvre of public buildings and professional syndicates designed in a modernized Islamic style. The building is composed of a basement with clerestory windows at the sidewalk level, followed by a raised ground floor reached by a set of steps, and a second story with a library. The symmetrical façade is composed of three sections, with a protruding, taller middle section marking the portal. Three tall windows set within pointed arches punctuate each of the side wings on the ground floor. Rectangular windows topped by *muqarnas* on the upper story are paired with the windows below. When the building's height was extended the original design was maintained, and the elaborate parapet of the original structure was reassembled after the work. In the 1960s a Brutalist concrete extension was added to the back of the building, hosting a large auditorium and offices.

Abdel Hamid al-Shawarbi Pasha Building

Address: 75 Ramses Street
GPS: 30.053606, 31.239162
Year: 1925
Architect: Habib Ayrout

This corner building is composed of three semi-independent structures unified by an uninterrupted façade or envelope. When it was completed it was the largest building in the surrounding area, before the Mixed Court building was realized. The elevation of the six-story building comprises three horizontal sections: the base with stores and a first floor for offices, the middle section of the building with four undifferentiated levels, and a crowning top floor distinguished from the rest by a loggia articulated by double columns placed at an interval around the entire structure. The corner is further accentuated with a cupola decorated with winged sphinxes. The elevations are organized with a regular grid of balconies interrupted by vertical bays of windows that culminate at the roofline with semi-circular arches. A rich decorative program of Art Deco and Beaux-Arts details, Ionic column capitals, floral motifs, and Egyptian sphinxes adorn the building's exterior.

Completed three years after the discovery of King Tutankhamun's tomb, the Shawarbi is an example of the incorporation of European-style Egyptomania in a residential building in Cairo. In the middle of the elevation on 26 July Street is a double-height archway that leads to a private passageway, one of two that separate the three blocks composing the building. These passageways not only divide the large site into manageable smaller parts but also create additional stores and allow light and air to reach living spaces arranged along the internal façades of the blocks. Entrances to the three blocks are accessed from the passageways. The blocks, housing spaciously designed apartments ranging in size from two to four bedrooms, each have additional air shafts for ventilation for wet rooms (kitchens and bathrooms). The first floor of the buildings is composed of office spaces. The office of architect Sayed Karim—for his practice and for the magazine *Al Emara*, which he founded and edited—was located in the building, which was damaged in the Cairo Fire of 1952.

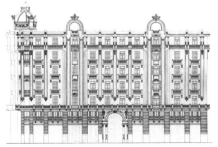

High Court

Address: 26 July Street
GPS: 30.052585, 31.239480
Year: 1924–34
Architects: Léon Azema, Max Edrei, Jacques Hardy, Victor Erlanger

This monumental building, originally designed for the city's Mixed Tribunals, was the result of an international competition, with winners announced in 1924. While construction started in 1925, the building process was slow and faced delays, pushing its inauguration back to 1934. In 1949 the Mixed Tribunals were canceled and the building was renamed the High Court, the centerpiece of a unified legal system administered in Arabic before Egyptian judges.

The stone-clad court design does not directly quote particular historical sources. It is eclectic and restrained, with an austere exterior and a grand hall at its center. Together with Azbakiya Park, the court gave definition to Downtown's commercial spine, Fuad I Street (now 26 July Street). The main elevation facing the street is composed of a grand entrance portico, reached by a flight of steps leading to eight colossal ribbed columns with no capitals or bases. Reinvented versions of decorative elements such as dentils are added sparsely for definition. The rectangular entablature carries the Arabic letters of the name of the court, which are flanked by two disks engraved with the scales of justice. Behind the columns, in the center of the elevation, are three tall glass windows with the portals at their base.

In plan the three-story court is complicated, and its general shape is irregular, following the pattern of the streets that already defined the site. In essence there are two main components: a T-shaped middle section, starting with the front elevation, leading to the ceremonial grand hall with vaulted coffered ceilings; surrounding the hall are bar buildings tracing the perimeter of the site. The spaces between the T and the other parts of the structure are voids, left as air shafts. The perimeter buildings form a complicated network of hallways, courtrooms, and offices. Interior details and finishes include geometric metalwork, decorative cement tiles, and marble. The court's secondary entrance is toward Ramses (then Queen Nazli) Street, where a civic spine of various institutions was already established.

Ground Floor Plan

Downtown

52

La Genevoise

Address: 21-26 July Street
GPS: 30.053014, 31.240858
Year: 1937
Architect: Max Zollikofer

A Geneva-based Swiss insurance company commissioned the building, which is prominently located on Fuad I (now 26 July) Street, facing the High Court. The company agreed with the owners of the adjacent properties to create 10-meter-wide streets between the buildings, thus increasing the number of façades to four from only two. This boosted the value of all the properties and allowed for more rentable store spaces. The streets were carved out of the 1,320m² plot and the expenses were shared among all beneficiaries. This left a buildable area for La Genevoise of 1,090m². Two rectangular vertical volumes on the principal and side façades mark the building's exterior, each punctuated by four columns of windows. This verticality is complemented by bold, deep balconies, most prominently on the corner, giving the building a dynamic façade of solids and voids, and vertical and horizontal lines.

Originally the building was intended to rise to twelve stories, making it the tallest structure in the city at the time, but those plans were altered when the owner decided to reduce the height to nine stories. Before the final construction drawings were drafted the company aimed to provide long-term lease agreements to potential occupiers of different floors such as apartments, offices, and hotels. Based on these agreements the final shape of the floor plans was determined, making it an unusual building for its time, as it was tailor-designed to suite its diverse users. The building entrance on the main street leads to private residences and offices, while a second entrance on the side street is dedicated to the Carlton Hotel, occupying the sixth and seventh floors. Office space on the second and third floors was designed with flexible partitions that can be adjusted, based on the required office area. Eight apartments per floor, ranging in size from one to two bedrooms, are located on the third, fourth, and fifth floors. Two 'villas,' or duplex residences, including one for the head of the insurance company, are located on the eighth and ninth floors.[37]

Waqf Gamalian Buildings

Address: 15, 15A, 17 26 July Street
GPS: 30.052947, 31.242486
Year: 1940
Architect: Muhammad Kamal Ismail

With its distinctive streamlined modern lines, circular balconies cantilevered at the corners, and its immense scale, the Gamalian is an unmatched landmark in Cairo. The Waqf Administration initiated this project on land it manages for a family endowment dating to 1682. The architect created three independent structures separated by three 9-meter-wide passageways intersecting at a marble fountain in the center of the site. The three entrances, one for each block, are located in this semi-private space, relatively quiet and secure from the bustling city streets surrounding the building. By dividing the large plot, the design allows direct sunlight and fresh air to all rooms of the three structures without relying on internal air shafts for ventilation. Only bathrooms and kitchens are ventilated via air shafts, placed in the core of each of the three blocks.

The north and east blocks are each composed of a base (ground floor and second floor of offices) topped by seven identical floors of apartments, in addition to a recessed top floor. The apartments are designed with clear separation between reception areas (sitting and dining rooms, service areas, and guest bathrooms) and private quarters (bedrooms). The spacious rooms were designed with additional ceiling height. The south block, on the busiest corner of the site, is designed to house a 120-room hotel, with a separate entrance facing the street. A double-height glass atrium at the top of the hotel corner leads to a roof terrace with a restaurant.

The building was serviced with high-speed elevators and it included amenities such as hot water, heating, radio, and telephone connections in all apartments. Interior finishes were restrained, except for the use of a variety of marbles in the entrances and hallways. Due to a shortage of materials during the Second World War, non-essential building finishes such as marble cladding were completed later.[38]

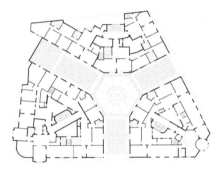

Ground Floor Plan

Ouzonian Building

Address: 37 Talaat Harb Street
GPS: 30.051870, 31.241581
Year: 1949
Architect: Sayed Karim

This building was designed to accommodate varied uses, including stores, offices, apartments, and a hotel. It occupies 800m^2 out of the 980m^2 plot. A spacious entrance on Talaat Harb Street leads to three elevators and a sculptural staircase leading to the offices above. Separate service elevators and stairs are located to the side. The first nine floors equate in their total height to the six floors of the neighboring Classical building. From the ninth floor upward the floor area shrinks as the building sets back incrementally until it reaches a floor area of 270m^2 on the seventeenth floor. The seventeenth and eighteenth floors compose the 'villa' originally intended for the owner of the building.

The initial design, altered slightly during implementation, included eight stores (now five), office spaces (ranging in size from one to seven rooms, each with service spaces including an 'archive room') as well as an eighty-room hotel, serviced apartments of one or two bedrooms with bath and kitchenette, and a terrace with a restaurant and bar.

The building's main façade is designed with concrete *brise soleil* to reduce direct sunlight, to create visual rhythm, and to distinguish the lower floors occupied by offices and hotel from the upper floors with the serviced apartments and the villa. The villa occupies a cubic volume with extruded vertical lines contrasting with the horizontality of the several floors below.[39]

Al-Nasr Import–Export Company

Address: 30 Talaat Harb Street
GPS: 30.049853, 31.239764
Year: 1964
Architect: Muhammad Ramzy Omar

Established in 1958 and nationalized in 1961, al-Nasr Import–Export Company was one of the largest international trade companies in the region, with twenty-five international offices in Africa, Europe, and the Arab world. The office building, completed in 1964, is located on a corner site measuring 1,600m^2 along Talaat Harb and Abdel Hamid streets. The building program includes storefronts along the commercial artery of Talaat Harb, a branch of the National Bank, a multi-function auditorium, and two hundred offices of varying sizes distributed along the façades of the eight typical and two recessed floors. The placement of offices along the façade maximizes indirect natural sunlight. The basement of the building houses mechanical rooms and a garage.

Architect Muhammad Ramzy Omar divided the overall volume of the building into several smaller parts to satisfy building regulations regarding height. The façade along Talaat Harb is kept at eight floors, with an additional two stories recessed. Along the narrower side street the entire building steps away from the street's edge, allowing for the maximum height of ten floors, with only single-story commercial space extruding from the main mass to maintain the building's edge and footprint. Also along the side street is a six-floor volume with a glazed façade, marking the auditorium. Additional office spaces are stacked and recessed above this volume. With the exception of the curtain wall along Abdel Hamid Street, the building's façade is entirely of cast concrete, with strong horizontal extrusions doubling as sun breakers. The Functionalist façade unifies the office spaces with the use of standardized windows.

BULAQ

Façade of the Nile City Towers, designed by Atelier d'Art Urbain Architects, a complex of three mixed-use towers, the first completed in 2001.

Bulaq

Bulaq is a large triangular area defined by the Ramses train station in the east, the Imbaba Bridge in the north, and the October Bridge in the south; it has the Nile as its west edge. The few remaining structures from old Bulaq include the Sinan Mosque, built in 1571. Historically the district developed as a Nile port near Cairo, connected to it when a tree-line road, Bulaq (now 26 July) Street, from Azbakiya was constructed in the nineteenth century, transforming the area into an important industrial zone. Bulaq was home to the city's muhandiskhana (polytechnic and engineering school) from 1821 to 1854. The construction of Bulaq Bridge in 1912, connecting the area to Zamalek and onward to Imbaba, further stimulated Bulaq economically.

In addition to being the location of the Middle East's first printing press, constructed in 1827, Bulaq grew to include the headquarters of

Egypt's leading newspapers al-Ahram (#64) and Akhbar al-Yom (#63). The area developed as a working-class neighborhood behind the industrial zone. Bulaq's central location has made it the site of several proposed plans to demolish its industrial infrastructure and poor housing. An early plan by Mahmoud Sabry Mahboub from 1930 proposed extending Downtown's urban pattern into Bulaq, redesigning the entire area and removing all industrial infrastructure and housing. Throughout the twentieth century industrial facilities and several slums in Bulaq, such as Turguman, were demolished to make way for Cairo's central bus station and landmarks such as the TV and Radio Administration building (#58) and the Ministry of Foreign Affairs (#59). The Maspero triangle, Bulaq's southern residential district, was demolished in 2018 to prepare the ground for a large-scale mixed-use commercial development.

Nefertiti Hotel
(proposed)

GPS: 30.050514, 31.231779
Year: 1962
Architect: Sayed Karim

In a ceremony on the tenth anniversary of the 1952 Revolution, Gamal Abdel Nasser laid the foundation stone for a large development project at the south corner of Bulaq, overlooking the Nile. Envisioned as a tourist center, the scheme consisted of several buildings connected by shared podiums occupying a triangular plot bordered by the Nile to the west, the recently completed TV and Radio Administration building to the north, and Galaa Street to the south. The largest of the proposed buildings was a 100-meter-tall thousand-room hotel, the Nefertiti. Other facilities included a conference center, restaurants, roof gardens, swimming pools, offices, and a transport hub. The complex was designed in the International Style, with crisp horizontal lines, cantilevered structures, and a variety of shading techniques and *brise soleil* variations. The complex was meant to replace an industrial facility on the site, but was never completed. The colossal Ramses Hilton Hotel later occupied part of the plot.

Ramses Hilton Hotel

Address: 1115 Corniche al-Nil
GPS: 30.050514, 31.231779
Year: 1976–79
Architects: Warner, Burns, Toan, and Lunde; Ali Nour al-Din Nassar

At 118 meters tall, this is Cairo's most visible example of Brutalism. The thirty-six-story triangular tower rises from a four-story podium housing the main lobby, service areas, event rooms, restaurants, and a roof terrace with a swimming pool. The complex occupies a 10,500m² plot that was previously occupied by the city's tramway company and a tram depot. It has an entrance from the Nile side leading directly to the atrium and casino, one from Galaa Street for hotel guests, and a third along the side street designed for the arrival of large groups and tour buses. The hotel was a landmark for the new wave of mass tourism that commenced in the 1970s, as the iconic Nile Hilton, completed in 1958, was no longer sufficient to accommodate the numbers of visitors. The Ramses Hilton's triangular floor plan gives rooms on two sides Nile views, with one side facing the city. Each floor contains twenty-four rooms and six suites arranged along the perimeter of the structure, while the core is reserved for service facilities, elevators, and stairs. The façades are designed as regular grids of deep recesses for windows. To break the monotony of this design, the tower shaft is divided vertically into four stacked sections, each articulated at the corners with protruding volumes containing the suites.⁴⁰

58

TV and Radio Administration

Address: Corniche al-Nil
GPS: 30.053052, 31.230585
Year: 1960
Architects: Galal Momen

Hailed at the time of its completion as Egypt's fourth pyramid, the mammoth TV and Radio Administration building has a footprint of 10,000m². While the original design was made in 1956, ground was not broken until 1959. Construction was completed at such an astonishing pace that the first television broadcast was made from the partially completed building on 23 July 1960, the eighth anniversary of the 1952 Revolution. In plan the building consists of two parts, a large rectangle covering the east side of the plot and an attached half-circle on the Nile side. In section too, the building is composed of two parts, a twelve-story podium and a square tower rising sixteen additional stories in the center of the block. While the rounded part of the podium is articulated with sweeping horizontal lines and strip windows, *brise soleil* define the façades of the remainder of the structure. An antenna tower placed atop the structure extenuates its height. The building is accessed through three entrances, a primary one on the Nile façade and two side entrances for employees and for celebrities, each leading to its tailored reception and waiting area. Twenty-three elevators, including two large ones for moving studio sets, service the complex. The building program is immense. It includes a large auditorium, workshops for set-making, dozens of sound and television studios, and offices for all aspects of production from writing to editing. The building was equipped with the latest US broadcasting technology, after an agreement with the Radio Corporation of America.

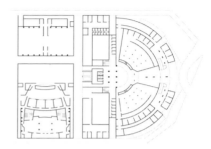

Ground Floor

Ministry of Foreign Affairs

Address: Corniche al-Nil
GPS: 30.055344, 31.229455
Year: 1994
Architect: Arab Contractors/ ACE Consulting Engineers

With a distinctive base, shaft, and crown, the design of this 143-meter, thirty-nine-story tower relies on the classic elements of a skyscraper. The seven-story podium, with a footprint of 3,600m², contains reception and public areas, service facilities, and meeting rooms. Fourteen slender pilotis line each side of the square podium. A second row of identical columns located directly behind is filled in with glass. The double layer protects the street-level part of the building from public view and shades it from the sun. The skyscraper's shaft steps back from the edge of the base, with a total floor area of around 2,500m². It comprises thirty identical floors housing offices. Its façade is composed of a grid of thermal windows. The crown of the tower, housing a restaurant and event space, is slightly set back and features an extended roofline forming a canopy mimicking the base of the building.

Bulaq

Nile Tower
(proposed)

GPS: 30.060235, 31.227994
Year: 2007
Architect: Zaha Hadid

This proposed seventy-story tower would have been the tallest building in Egypt's history. Rising above a narrow triangular plot sandwiched between the corniche and the Nile to the west and the bustling market and former industrial area of Bulaq to the east, it was commissioned by a private owner to make a bold statement. With 60,000m² of residential space in addition to a 35,000m² hotel, the landmark tower would have been entirely glazed with a draped, continuous, subtly undulating surface. The Nile-facing façade bulges at the top and again at the base of the tower. Diagonal creases define the north and south façades and create visual tension, as the overall form of the tower appears to slightly rotate. A glazed plaza housing all the shared and semi-public programmatic elements is located at the base. The building would have significantly surpassed the country's cap on building heights, set at 144 meters according to fire-safety regulations.

61

St. Regis Hotel

Address: 1189 Corniche al-Nil
GPS: 30.063032, 31.227479
Year: 2018
Architect: Michael Graves Architecture & Design

This 197,000m² development along the Nile comprises an L-shaped south tower and a second north tower, sharing a seven-story podium. To avoid the appearance of large monolithic volumes, the massing of each of the two towers is deconstructed with a series of recesses. For example, the north tower is composed of a shorter, circular frontage attached to a taller, rectilinear mass. The fenestrations and façade treatments, alternating between curtain wall and stone cladding, further break down the overwhelming scale of the building. The ceiling of the lavish *porte cochere* is adorned with gold mosaic tiles reflected on custom-designed paving. Vehicles enter the covered entrance through a semi-ellipsoid opening, a shape repeated elsewhere in the interior of the building. The development includes 292 hotel rooms, including sixty-three suites, as well as ninety-nine serviced guest apartments and 117 St. Regis Tower residences. All the services and common spaces are located in the podium, including restaurants, library, lounges, water garden, spa, and wellness center, and the hotel lobby is located on the fifth floor. Materials such as custom clear-glass blocks, bronze, mother-of-pearl inlaid wood panels, and Swarovski crystals are used throughout the interior. Ornate arabesque patterns, carved wood, and *mashrabiya*-like details add a layer of pastiche to the design.

Bulaq

World Trade Center

Address: 1191 Corniche al-Nil
GPS: 30.064081, 31.227477
Year: 1988
Architects: Ali Nour al-Din Nassar; Bruce Graham; Skidmore, Owings, & Merrill

This complex of buildings consists of two 100-meter-high thirty-story concrete towers for apartments and a hotel located along the back of the site and a 65-meter-high twenty-story concrete office tower toward the front. A five-story podium at the base of the towers houses service facilities and a shopping mall. The architecture is typical of the Americanism exported at the time to business and commercial centers around the world. Grids that govern the placement of windows and balconies define the sand-colored exterior of the boxy structures.

The World Trade Center is an example of a typology that emerged in the 1980s that aimed to transform consolidated plots of land into large-scale high-rise developments entirely cut off socially and architecturally from their urban surroundings.

Akhbar al-Yom Building

Address: 6 al-Sahafa Street
GPS: 30.055578, 31.237842
Year: 1948
Architect: Sayed Karim

Rather than resort to a standard block with a light well in the center of the 1,200m² plot and one frontage on the main street, Sayed Karim designed a U-shaped structure for this newspaper headquarters maximizing natural sunlight and views to the outside. Light enters the building from the front and back, and the circular front façade makes the building formalistically stand out in its otherwise rectilinear urban context. A sunken basement gives way to a triple-height base occupying 1,000m² of the site. This large space houses the printing press and machinery and is overlooked by stations for supervisors and managers. Loading docks and ramps were carefully designed to facilitate movement of trucks in and out of the confined garage. Once inside, trucks are rotated on a plate that directs them toward the loading dock or toward the exit, reducing the space needed to make U-turns.

A 6-meter-wide stair with aluminum railings leads to the glazed entryway of the circular marble-clad lobby. The airy entry hall is supported by four pilotis on the periphery of the circular space. From the lobby, visitors can access administration through a stairway and two elevators, ride directly to the eleventh floor via two high-speed elevators, or climb a ceremonial stair leading to the second level, where a large event space is located. A large glass sphere and a globe—with indications of the locations of international *Akhbar al-Yom* offices and correspondents—are suspended above the ceremonial stair. There are two additional entrances to the building, one for administrators and another for workers in the press. Six identical floors occupy the U-shaped structure sitting above the base of the building, for journalists and administration. The circulation shafts and the wet areas are placed at the two ends of the U. By designing the structure toward the outer skin of the building, the office spaces enjoy an open floor plan, with no visual interruptions. A system of movable lightweight partitions was designed to allow staff to create their own spaces. Glass block was used when possible to allow sunlight while maintaining privacy.[41]

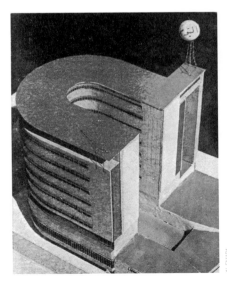

Al-Ahram Building

Address: 34 al-Galaa Street
GPS: 30.055784, 31.238971
Year: 1968
Architect: Naoum Shabib

Following the success and wide appeal of the Cairo Tower, Muhammad Hassanein Heikal, editor-in-chief of *al-Ahram*, commissioned Naoum Shebib in 1962 to build a new headquarters for the newspaper. The new structure adjoined an existing single-story, factory-like printing press. Four distinctive volumes house the newspaper's programmatic elements: administration, press office, distribution, and printing facilities. Meeting rooms and common spaces dot the twelve-story structure, in addition to a bar, a canteen, and an auditorium. The building is entered through a glazed spacious hall with a sculptural spiral stair leading to a mezzanine. The heart of the building is the newsroom, an open-plan office space for journalists, writers, and editors. The building was furnished with tubular chairs and metal office furniture made by the Egyptian industrial furniture company Ideal. Interior spaces as well as part of the façade are clad with a variety of Egyptian stone. Works by Egyptian modernists from *al-Ahram*'s art collection adorn the hallways. The building was home to Egypt's first computer.

65

Turguman Regeneration Plan
(proposed)

Address: 3 Wabour al-Tugroman
GPS: 30.058820, 31.237744
Year: 1967
Architect: Salah Zaki Said

By 1950 Turguman was widely publicized as a slum in central Cairo. Plans for regenerating the area were numerous, but the outstanding example was a proposal by architect Salah Zaki Said from al-Azhar University. He posed the question: "Is it possible to combine the rich social life of popular areas with the measures of healthy modern living?" Designed as a social-housing project that replaces the slum, the plan critically responds to the state's public housing schemes, which lack social space. Instead, the architect proposed an urban fabric of low-rise and medium-rise buildings, mixed-density integrated commercial and residential areas, and services and public spaces. The proposed model is firstly concerned with creating affordable spaces for living, complete with an infrastructure that improves social life.

For Said the following components had to be integrated in the design: a market place, stores, cafés, places of worship, public spaces, varying sizes of streets, and internal courtyards for housing clusters. The modular design starts with a 'cell' composed of housing for fifteen families, who share a small open space. These clusters of low-rise attached housing units are situated among taller apartment blocks, all arranged at right angles to one another, with a mosque, community center, public space, and market in the center.[42]

Maspero Triangle Master Plan
(proposed)

GPS: 30.053338, 31.233478
Year: 2015
Architect: Foster + Partners

The area known as the Maspero Triangle was a tightly-knit popular neighborhood with a rich stock of urban vernacular domestic architecture, most of which developed around the beginning of the twentieth century. Foster's plan is the result of an international competition organized by the Ministry of State for Urban Renewal and Informal Settlements, which sought to demolish the neighborhood and to rehouse residents on a fraction of the land, making the rest of the centrally located area open for investment and development. Foster proposed high-rises for offices, retail, and luxury developments along the waterfront backed by a dense urban network of low-rise housing to accommodate the area's fourteen thousand residents. Key features include a pedestrian footbridge to Zamalek and a series of 'green pocket' public spaces to foster a sense of community in the residential areas.

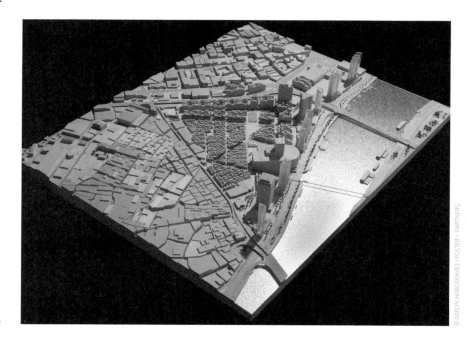

Bulaq

SAYEDA ZEINAB & ABDEEN

Al-Sudan Building on Port Said Street, designed by Mustafa Shawky and Salah Zeitoun and completed in 1957, utilizes a modular shutter design that reimagines both the traditional *mashrabiya* and Modernist *brise soleil*.

Sayeda Zeinab & Abdeen

The administrative limits of Abdeen extend from Bab al-Shaaria Square in the north, down Port Said Street (formally al-Khalig al-Masri Street) to the area surrounding Abdeen Palace, then west to Qasr al-Aini Street, with Talaat Harb Street delineating its western boundary. However, the historic district of the same name is confined to the area surrounding the palace. Sayeda Zeinab abuts Abdeen to the south, with Qadri Pasha Street and Ibn Tulun Mosque at its eastern boundary, Magra al-Eyoun to the south, and Qasr al-Aini Street to the west. Al-Khalig al-Masri was a canal that extended from the Nile in a northeasterly direction, overlooked by traditional houses. Between 1897 and 1899 the canal was filled in to create a diagonal avenue (al-Khalig al-Masri Street) across Cairo from Sayeda Zeinab Square, then called Qanater al-Sebaa, to Ghamra in the north. In June 1900 the city's first electric tram carried passengers on al-Khalig al-Masri Street in Sayeda Zeinab, heading north. After the 1956 Suez Crisis and bombardment of Port Said, al-Khalig al-Masri Street was renamed after the Suez Canal city.

Both Sayeda Zeinab and Abdeen are each centered on a major building: the Sayeda Zeinab Mosque and shrine of the patron saint of Cairo, its current iteration built in 1940, with an expansion in 1969; and Abdeen Palace, built between 1863 and 1872 as the seat of power. Sayeda Zeinab and Abdeen squares, the civic centers of each district, attracted the building of modern structures throughout the twentieth century. Beyond these squares, the districts developed as socially stable popular working-class areas, making them sites for experiments in affordable housing such as the railway-worker accommodation proposed in 1928 or the Zeinhom low-income housing built in 1960 (#73). The areas are also dotted with important sites such as the Mausoleum of Saad Zaghloul (#71) and the Dar al-Hilal Printing Press (#70).

Cultural Park for Children

Address: 20 Qadri Street
GPS: 30.031490, 31.246836
Year: 1990
Architect: Abdelhalim Ibrahim Abdelhalim

The site of this postmodern park had been a green area since Mamluk times. With community participation, this project sought to redevelop the plot with a new park and buildings with cultural facilities for children, such as a library, theater, and museum, in addition to a playground and green spaces. The intention of the new park is to respond to three pressing problems: the need to provide children-oriented spaces in the city, the lack of green space, and the dilapidation of Cairo's historic fabric. The project initiated the upgrading of historic buildings along Abu al-Dahab Street.

The design of the park is driven by four principles: rhythms of symbolic forms, geometry to create order, a promenade of palm trees as an organizational axis, and the social aspect of a space for rituals and ceremonies. A set of architectural elements was established and used throughout the site, including arches and arched windows, vaults, domes, and wooden screens. All construction on the site is in reinforced concrete for horizontal structures and load-bearing masonry for walls. The design was the result of a competition, and it received the Aga Khan Award for Architecture in 1992.

Sayeda Zeinab & Abdeen

Waqf of Raafat Bey

Address: Sayeda Zeinab Square
GPS: 30.032629, 31.241457
Year: 1940
Architect: Ali Labib Gabr

Due to the area's lower economic status, the architect aimed to maximize the profit generated from the building while reducing construction costs and providing affordable high-standard apartments. The building consists of a ground floor with stores and a small apartment followed by eight identical floors, each with three apartments. Cost reductions were made by using cement-tile floors instead of wood, omitting wall insulation, utilizing limestone when possible in place of reinforced concrete, and keeping rooms small and ceilings low. Apartments range in size between 80m^2 and 100m^2, small by the standards of the time set by architects working mostly in wealthier districts.[43]

Al-Sharq Cinema

Address: 172 Port Said Street
GPS: 30.032771, 31.241237
Year: 1947
Architect: Unknown

Built during a wave of cinema construction that took place after the Second World War, the currently defunct al-Sharq was the largest movie theater in Sayeda Zeinab. The design combines Modernist and Art Deco features, most prominent in its entrance, marked by a towering cylindrical section, and in the foyer leading to the thousand-seat auditorium. The current marquee was a later addition. The building is composed of a five-story rectangular block along the street, and the cinema hall extending toward the back of the site. The lower two floors of the block housed offices and facilities for running the cinema, while the upper floors housed apartments accessed by a separate entrance.

Dar al-Hilal Printing Press

Address: 16 Muhammad Ezz al Arab (Mubtadayan) Street
GPS: 30.034146, 31.239683
Year: 1945
Architect: Albert Zananiri

Established in 1892, Dar al-Hilal published some of Egypt's most widely read magazines, such as *al-Musawwar*. New facilities were needed as the publishing house continued to grow. The headquarters stretch along Mubtadayan Street for 106 meters, giving it a monumental presence. At the center of the elevation is the double-height grand entrance with a set of steps leading to the partial first floor. The grand stair is flanked by two elevators and two service stairs, forming the circulation core. The building is composed of a ground floor with a double-height space to the east housing the printing machinery. The west half of the first floor contains spaces for photography, editing, and zinc-press composition, while the east half includes a suspended hallway leading to storage areas. The hallway overlooks the double-height printing-press room below. The following two identical U-shaped floors house meeting rooms and offices for administration, journalists, writers, editors, and publishers. The understated exterior of the building is flat, with four rows of industrial-style windows illuminating the high-ceilinged spaces within. The building is constructed of reinforced-concrete floor plates supported by a grid of columns with masonry infill walls.[44]

Saad Zaghloul Mausoleum

Address: al-Falaki Street
GPS: 30.037479, 31.237973
Year: 1931
Architect: Mustafa Fahmy

The death of nationalist leader Saad Zaghloul in 1927 was followed by a government decision to commemorate him with a grand mausoleum. Mustafa Fahmy adopted Egyptian Revivalism, which had been popular in Europe and the United States since the nineteenth century, in his efforts to produce a modern national style. When it was completed in 1931 the country's new government considered transforming the site into a pantheon of national leaders, but Zaghloul's wife opposed this and the building remained unused until the government changed again. Zaghloul's remains were interred in the mausoleum in 1936.

The symmetrical mausoleum is centered on the tomb positioned in a square hall, with side galleries to the north and south. Twelve papyriform columns placed directly in front of walls or pillars carry a decorative entablature, which gives way to a crowning element, a recessed smaller cubic volume accentuating the building's height. The interior space is lit from twelve large clerestory windows, three on each side of the building's crown. There are three additional tall rectangular windows on the north and south walls. The soaring space is entered through two portals set within elevated porticos reached by steps at the east and west elevations. Two monumental red-granite palmiform columns mark each portico. All elevations are tapered, leaning slightly toward the center of the building and surmounted by cornices in a fashion reminiscent of ancient Egyptian pylons. Local stone crafted with precision is used throughout the structure. The building's rich decorative program includes cobras, winged sun, lotus flowers, and scarabs.

Sayeda Zeinab & Abdeen

Misr Insurance Company

Address: Lazughli Square
GPS: 30.039095, 31.240687
Year: 1947
Architect: Mahmoud Riad

This is the first of three buildings designed by Mahmoud Riad for the Misr Insurance Company. The nine-story Lazughli building was one of the city's first mixed-use developments, intended from the start to house the separate functions of offices and apartments, with each given equal weight. This division is reflected in the design, as the structure is composed of two adjoining parts, with offices overlooking the busy square in the slightly curved section that matches the curve of the traffic circle, while the apartments are arranged in the U-shaped section overlooking Nubar Street. By creating a U-shape, the architect managed to pull most apartments away from direct contact with the noisy street, which had a busy tramline at the time. The open space in front of the entrance to the residential section creates a welcoming oasis for residents and a playground for children.

The office section is entered from Lazughli Square, with three large portals leading to a spacious hall and elevator lobby. It was designed with an open floor plan that allows occupants to rent only the space they need, with flexible partition walls that can be rebuilt according to need. Circulation spaces, including elevators, stairs, and hallways, were designed for easy movement of large numbers of people in the busy office space. In the residential section there are two entrances, each served by a circulation core made up of an elevator and stairs. With a total of four apartments on each level, dividing the circulation into two separate cores means that each serves only two apartments per floor. Amenities include radio antennas, trash chutes and furnaces, hot water, storage space, and garages. Retail spaces are located only along the curved façade of the office section. Marble provided by the Bank Misr Company for Quarries clads all stairs and public halls in the building.[45]

Sayeda Zeinab & Abdeen

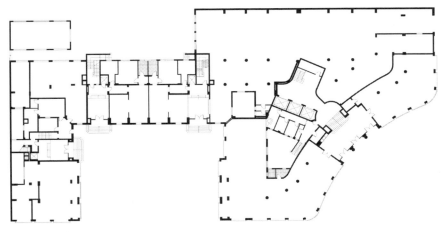

Ground Floor Plan

73

Zeinhom Housing Development

Address: Beyram al-Tunsi Street
GPS: 30.022999, 31.245393
Year: 1955–2007
Architect: Housing Authority

The hills of Zeinhom were leveled to make room for public housing, part of a national program launched in the 1950s. Around sixty freestanding residential blocks were constructed by the early 1960s, following the 'towers in the park' model. Each four-story block, housing eight apartments per floor, is divided between connected sections, each with a stair accessing four apartments per floor. Apartments were compact, with two bedrooms and a sitting area. The spaces between the blocks were meant for communal activities, services, and greenery.

In 1999 a new slum-clearance and housing project commenced on the nearby empty land, expanding the residential units by 181 buildings, constructed over three phases and completed in 2007. In total 2,456 new apartments were added. These later units included two bedrooms and a living space, with a total area of 67m^2.

The typology of the new buildings differs from the slender bar blocks of the 1960s; instead, their apartments are in a pinwheel arrangement around the central core of the square plan. Buildings occupy 40 percent of the land, leaving the rest for green areas. Zeinhom is a model housing project, as it allowed residents of the area to remain in their homes while improving their living conditions. The community participated in the planning process, making it a rare example of a successful low-income housing initiative.

74

National Museum of Egyptian Civilization (NMEC)

Address: Ain al-Sira, al-Fustat
GPS: 30.007442, 31.248475
Year: 1984–2017
Architect: El Ghazali Kosseiba

The International Campaign to Save the Monuments of Nubia (1960–80) led to the establishment of two museum projects supported by UNESCO: the Nubia Museum, completed in 1997, and the National Museum of Egyptian Civilization. The intention was to create a comprehensive national museum displaying objects from prehistory to modern Egypt. The design was the result of an international competition held in 1984. The initial project site was in Zamalek on an empty plot behind today's Opera House.

As the project was delayed its site was moved to the archaeological area of al-Fustat, overlooking the Ain al-Sira lake, but the design was left unchanged. Construction started in 2004, but due to several setbacks the museum only finally partially opened in 2017. It is set to exhibit important collections gathered from Egypt's other museums, including the royal mummies currently displayed at the Egyptian Museum. Japanese architect Arata Isozaki is designing the galleries and display systems. The design is based on a grid system established across the entire site to inform the project's landscaping and architecture. The museum is composed of two parts: first, the entrance building, hosting lobby, administration, and visitor services; second, the galleries building. While the entrance building is aligned with the grid, the galleries building is angled at 30 degrees. A tunnel bridge connects the two structures.

The galleries building is square in plan with an L-shaped courtyard along the north and east sides of the square. Two double-height floors host galleries, which are built as dark boxes relying entirely on artificial light. Circulation is designed around the inner walls, with occasional openings allowing views into the courtyard.

The interior finishes are not part of the original design. The pinnacle of the building is a pyramid lifted off the building's roof by four pillars. The motif is repeated across the site through lighting features with inverted pyramids. The exterior of the museum's concrete structure is clad in sandstone.

Sayeda Zeinab & Abdeen

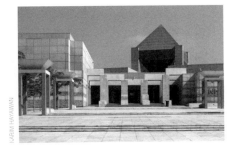

GARDEN CITY

Grand Art Deco apartment buildings lined Qasr al-Aini Street in the 1920s, creating a high-density edge along the eastern side of Garden City.

Garden City

Garden City is a clearly defined residential area delineated by Qasr al-Aini Street to the east, Tahrir Square to the north, the Nile to the west, and Qasr al-Aini hospital to the south. At the turn of the twentieth century the site of Garden City was occupied by agricultural fields and palaces. In 1905 the Nile Land and Agricultural Company acquired the area for real-estate development, and engineer José Lamba provided the sinuous street plan to parcel the site into plots for sale.

Art Nouveau lines influenced the conception of the area's circular street pattern. Despite its name, the project was far removed from Ebenezer Howard's garden city movement initiated in 1898. Howard's plan was to improve the quality of life for workers in increasingly crowded industrial cities. Cairo's Garden City, however, was intended as a wealthy enclave with lush tree-lined streets and an urban pattern that separates it from its surroundings without the erection of physical barriers. The area's initial structures were mansions and palaces, such as the massive palace of Prime Minister Adli Yakan Pasha, designed by Antonio Lasciac and demolished in 2001 to make room for the towering Four Seasons Hotel. Demolitions have hit Garden City for decades, due to its appealing location and high real-estate value. Key residents in the area include the British and American embassies and the Collège de la Mère de Dieu boarding school, in its current building since 1921. In the 1920s large Art Deco apartments were built on the edge of the district, lining Qasr al-Aini Street and along the Nile, and the rest of the area had already been filled with villas and large private residences. Starting in the 1930s, large apartment buildings crept toward the center of Garden City, slightly transforming its initial character. This continued in the 1940s and 1950s with Modernist apartment blocks built for elite residents, including Cairo's tallest structure at the time, the Sabet Sabet Building (#84). Nationalization policies in the 1960s strongly impacted the ownership of the area, leading to several government offices and banking institutions inhabiting Garden City's residential properties or demolishing them to build suitable office buildings in their place.

Al-Chams Building

Address: 1103 Corniche al-Nil
GPS: 30.041584, 31.231702
Year: 1949
Architect: Sayed Karim

The Egyptian Company for Modern Construction (Chams) was established by a royal decree in 1946 to undertake real-estate development projects, one of which was this building overlooking the Nile and occupying a 1,350m² plot surrounded by small side streets on three sides. The building has two equally large entrances, with stairs leading to the entrance hall; the Nile-side entrance is composed of a circular fountain flanked by two pillars and two semicircular stairs; the second entrance, also with two pillars and a stair running through the center, is located on the south side of the building. The raised ground floor, reached by the entrance stairs, is nearly 3 meters higher than street level. It sits above a partially sunken basement level with service rooms and a garage. Besides the spacious entrance hall, the ground floor houses a concierge room and five apartments with from one to three bedrooms. Seven identical floors each contain five apartments, two facing the Nile and three at the rear. The apartments are each divided into four areas based on function: a reception area, including two sitting rooms and a dining area; the master-bedroom suite, including a private sitting area, dressing room, and bathroom; a separate wing for the additional bedrooms; and a service area, including kitchen, storage, and laundry. A penthouse is located on the tenth floor, facing the Nile.

The main architectural feature in the building's interior is its elaborate entry sequence, and particularly the main stair. This is composed of two connected stairs that meet between floors at a landing. These spacious stairs divide the floor plans into two halves, the Nile-facing half and the rear half of the building. By combining the two stairs into one stairwell, additional area was afforded to the air shafts, which allow for increased natural light and ventilation in the stairs and the service areas of the apartments. Servant quarters and service facilities are located at the top of the building.[46]

Garden City

Cairo Center Office Building

Address: 106 Qasr al-Aini Street
GPS: 30.041384, 31.235478
Year: 1969
Architect: Muhammad Ramzy Omar

This building boasts possibly the earliest application in Cairo of the curtain-wall office-building model. Located on a 2,000m² corner plot along Qasr al-Aini, it stands out for its use of unconventional materials. The tower block includes double-glazed façades with dark reflective glass and aluminum detailing, Carrara marble cladding on parts of the façade, and black Azzurro granite cladding the pillars along the street. The design of the building included fire-fighting systems, a fully realized HVAC system for air-conditioning, drop-ceilings, and a grid of equally distributed ceiling lights over the large open-plan office spaces. The floor plans were kept flexible, with no permanent or heavy structures, allowing each level to be designed independently by the occupant using lightweight partitions. Stairs, four passenger elevators, one service elevator, and restrooms are kept in a service zone along the back of the floor plan to maximize usable area and to standardize the building's floors. Respecting building heights at the time, the office block consists of ten typical floors followed by four recessed ones.

The building includes other services in the design, such as a garage in the basement, fire-escape stairs, a telephone exchange, standby generators, and electrical carriages to enable the cleaning of the curtain walls. The main entrance floor is covered with granite, walls are clad with Carrara marble and brass ornaments, and the floors and walls of the elevator lobbies on every floor are also faced with Carrara marble.

Embassy of the United States of America

Address: 5 Tawfiq Diab Street
GPS: 30.040886, 31.233799
Year: 1989
Architects: Metcalf and Associates

After the Camp David Peace Accords, the US presence in Egypt was cemented and a new embassy building was needed. In it, building functions are separated into publicly accessible spaces (placed at the perimeter of the site) and those accessible only to embassy staff (the tower). A single-story belt of buildings with an outward sloping roof is placed along the perimeter of the site, containing functions such as the auditorium. The reinforced-concrete office tower sits on three-story piers forming a dramatic colonnade below the tower and securing it from intrusion. With its monolithic design and heavy appearance, the embassy is perhaps Cairo's most visible example of architectural Brutalism. The fourteen-story building has a square footprint and has a grid of diagonal recesses for windows that defines its elevations. The Architects Collaborative later designed the ambassador's residence, which was completed in 1995.[47]

Egyptian Company for Real Estate Investment

Address: Ahmed Ragheb Street
GPS: 30.038669, 31.232950
Year: 1940
Architect: Raymond Antonius

This is an example of the encroachment of large buildings on Garden City. The four-story structure, with a footprint covering an entire block surrounded by three streets, houses twenty luxury apartments ranging in size from four to seven rooms. The building is divided into two almost symmetrical wings, with two separate entrances accessed from a small garden placed in the center of the north-facing side of the plot.

All the standard luxury amenities of the time are included, such as hot water, central heating, and radio antennas, as well as fireplaces in all apartments and a forty-car garage in the basement. Erected at the beginning of the Second World War, the building includes a bomb shelter for one hundred people. The building also includes a small, octagonal, double-height synagogue with a separate entrance at the south corner. First-floor apartments are given large terraces at the three corners of the triangular block. Ample balcony space is provided to all apartments. The top floors are divided into duplexes, with internal wooden stairs leading to the roof garden above.

The structure utilizes a reinforced-concrete frame filled with red brick for walls. Architectural details include rounded corners and balconies, and Art Deco metalwork such as railings, gates, and elevator doors.[48]

Ground Floor Plan

Garden City

Petroleum Cooperative Society

Address: 94 Qasr al-Aini Street
GPS: 30.039414, 31.234865
Year: 1957
Architect: Muhammad Ramzy Omar

Twenty years after it was established in 1934 as the first nationally managed company for petroleum products in Egypt, the Petroleum Cooperative Society commissioned a new building for its headquarters to be located in Garden City. The program included a gas service station for automobiles, which was placed at the corner of the 1,800m² site. Due to municipal regulations forbidding the construction of habitable space above gas stations, the building is set back, resulting in its prominent curved façade.

The structure is composed of two joined volumes. The first is a ten-story curved block with eight identical floors and two recessed levels at the top, fronting Qasr al-Aini Street. A second, smaller volume fronts the narrower side street and consists of five floors: four identical ones and one recessed one at the top. The original design of the gas station included a thin concrete canopy supported by two V-shaped columns However, this was removed during later renovations. The building's glazed entrance on Qasr al-Aini is recessed and is marked by four pilotis, allowing pedestrians to pass under the structure.

Brise soleil is the main architectural feature of the south-facing and curved façades. The façade above the entrance facing the main street features horizontal lines with recessed balconies, creating a strong solid–void composition.

Mobil Building

Address: Corniche al-Nil
GPS: 30.038514, 31.230166
Year: 1959
Architect: Abu Bakr Khairat

The T-shaped footprint of this office building is concealed behind its large round façade, which traces the perimeter of the plot on which it sits. The ten-story structure is entered at the center of its curved façade, where the lobby is located at the intersection of the T. The remainder of the ground floor is allocated to the parking garage. Four elevators and a staircase bring employees to the upper floors. From the first floor upward, a second staircase is added to the open circulation core. Offices are arranged along the building's exterior, with natural sunlight and operable windows. *Brise soleil* is extensively used in order to reduce the impact of direct sun on the large expanse of the main elevation.

Garden City

Serageldin Palace

Address: Kamel al-Shinnawi Street
GPS: 30.037939, 31.231322
Year: 1908
Architect: Carlo Prampolini

This palace has a complicated social history, being commissioned by the founder of Crédit Foncier Bank, then briefly occupied by the German Embassy, before becoming a short-lived elite girls' school, until 1930 when it was purchased by Fuad Serageldin Pasha, the Wafdist politician and the last minister of interior under the monarchy. The building is square in plan and designed around a central hall with a grand marble staircase that flanks the entrance of the house, connecting the ground floor, with its reception and public areas, to the second floor with private areas and bedrooms.

The subtly protruding entrance bay includes a portico with three arched openings above the portal. The slightly raised ground floor is reached by a set of marble steps leading to the doorway, with its rounded arch and elaborate metalwork, placed between two rusticated columns. The voluminous rooms are airy and open onto one another with wide archways and double-leaf doors set within Neo-Classical doorframes. The Beaux-Arts plan of the house translates into symmetry and an axial arrangement of spaces. The rich decorative program incorporates Classical elements such as robust stone columns and capitals, as well as Neo-Baroque details. An atrium in the main central hall, topped by a skylight, creates a sectional relationship between the two levels of the house. Rooms were decorated thematically, with richly patterned wallpaper, textiles, marble, and parquet floors, and with wooden shutters on all exterior doors and windows. The exterior is eclectic, with a Neo-Renaissance design and added Classical elements such as Ionic column capitals and pediments above the windows on the second floor. A portico with three arched openings tops the entrance of the house. The privately owned building is listed, though it has remained unused and unmaintained.

Residential Building

Address: 2 al-Fasqiya Street
GPS: 30.036125, 31.232904
Year: 1938
Architect: Youssef Mazza

This luxurious, monumental, heavy and robust structure is divided into three attached sections with three separate entrances. In plan the building is rectangular, with chamfered corners at the east and west ends of the southern façade where the portals and elevator lobbies are located. The spacious marble-clad entrances include stairs to the first floor for the first set of apartments and for access to the main stairs and elevators. The garage occupies the ground floor. Rounded vertical external ribs give the façade its muscular quality as well as regularity and order, dictating the placement of windows and balconies. The protruding bay at the center of the southern façade is composed of a grid of balconies. At the center of the northern façade is a concave semicircular bay carved into the mass of the building with rooms arranged along it. Four air shafts provide light and air to service and wet rooms and accommodate service stairs with direct access to kitchens. All living and sleeping spaces are arranged along the exterior of the building.

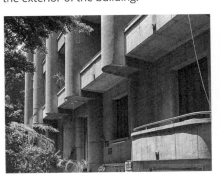

Garden City

Houd al-Laban Building

Address: Houd al-Laban Street
GPS: 30.035808, 31.230533
Year: 1960s
Architect: Unknown

This striking six-story residential structure occupies a triangular site behind the mammoth Four Seasons Hotel. The A-shaped building leans outward at the pointed corner, appearing like the prow of a ship. The hammered-concrete exterior is formed of horizontal shapes and recesses for shaded balconies and the building's recessed windows. The seemingly heavy structure is lifted on two pilotis at the corner, creating a low cutout at the most critical moment in the design, allowing pedestrians to walk under the tip of the structure. A garage occupies the ground floor, while the lobby is raised above street level, reached by marble steps from both sides of the building that lead to the crescent-shaped entrance hall. The circulation core is placed at the back of the plot, with a generously designed triangular stairwell and two elevators. Apartment spaces are arranged along the outer walls of the building to provide direct access to light and air, while air shafts in the core of the structure ventilate service spaces and wet rooms.

Sabet Sabet Building

Address: Corniche al-Nil
GPS: 30.034047, 31.229727
Year: 1958
Architect: Naoum Shebib

At the time of its completion Naoum Shebib's Sabet Sabet Building stood out on Cairo's skyline, as no other building matched its height or its monolithic design. A large glass wall leads into the marble-clad minimalist lobby, with two passenger elevators and one service elevator. Every apartment in the thirty-one-story tower is afforded unprecedented views on both sides of the building, toward the Pyramids to the west and toward the Citadel to the east. Each floor is divided into two equally-sized two-bedroom apartments. A service stair doubling as a fire escape is accessed through the kitchens. The apartment layouts are geared toward the views, with four balconies in each apartment, two on each side of the building, most of which have been enclosed with glass by residents over the years.

The building is an exercise in structural engineering, stretching the limits of concrete construction in Egypt at the time. The foundations are 25 meters deep, reaching the bedrock. Due to the softness of the soil on the banks of the Nile and the high water levels, Shebib engineered a concrete mix capable of supporting the building's height in these conditions.

Arab African International Bank

Address: 10 Aisha al-Taymuriya Street
GPS: 30.035492, 31.232368
Year: c.2000
Architect: Unknown

This building is designed with two interlocking L-shaped sections. The first consists of six typical floors with offices arranged along the street and the second, smaller L is the main circulation core at the back. The most remarkable feature of the building is its modular glass-and-metal exterior, designed with alternating protruding three-sided window frames and window 'brows' functioning as *brise soleil* to reduce the impact of the sun on indoor temperatures.

Ibrahimiya School

Address: 1 Ittihad al-Muhamiyin al-Arab Street
GPS: 30.034717, 31.232234
Year: 1939
Architect: Charles Ayrout

This L-shaped, three-story school was erected in only seventy days. The longer side of the L contains four lecture rooms, laboratories, and teacher rooms on the ground floor, followed by two further floors, each with seven classrooms and a teacher's lounge. A canteen occupies the entire space of the short side of the L on the ground floor, and an art room and a geography classroom on the first floor.

The school's modular reinforced-concrete post-and-beam structure was designed for speedy implementation. The rectilinear building is faced with brick on the ground and first floors and stucco on the top floor. Fenestration is arranged in two equal rows of larger windows on the lower two floors and narrower windows on the top floor, separated by brick arranged in a three-dimensional pattern.[49]

Residential Building

Address: 2 Ittihad al-Muhamiyin Street
GPS: 30.034165, 31.232758
Year: 1940s
Architect: Unknown

Garden City's planning, with intersecting curving streets, resulted in many triangular corner plots. This narrow triangular building erected in the 1940s is an example of how the urban plan directly impacted the architectural development of the area. The six-story building is composed of three parts: a recessed, raised ground floor; four stories of apartments, with a prominent rounded corner presently glazed with large industrial windows; and, finally, a recessed top floor with a roof terrace.

The marble-clad entrance is along al-Fasqiya Street, leading to the circulation core being placed at the back of the site at the widest part of the building. Living spaces are arranged around the exterior, with balconies and shuttered windows.

Doctors' Syndicate
(Dar al-Hikma)

Address: Qasr al-Aini Street
GPS: 30.032359, 31.232619
Year: 1949
Architects: Mustafa Fahmy, Ahmed Charmi

Established in 1940, the Doctors' Syndicate built its headquarters on land granted by the state. Known as Dar al-Hikma, the building was part of Mustafa Fahmy's oeuvre of public commissions combining modern architectural form and material with Art Deco sensibility and his invented Neo-Islamic elements drawn from Cairo's rich architectural heritage. The symmetrical structure is entered through a protruding central bay topped by an arch resting on two *muqarnas* forms. Two urns flank the entrance niche, and marble steps reach the portal leading to the main hall, with rooms distributed on two floors in two wings, to the right and left, and a large meeting hall in the center.

The general arrangement of the building and its elevation are reminiscent of Fahmy's design for the Society of Engineers headquarters (#49) on Ramses Street. The front elevation of Dar al-Hikma is divided into three vertical bays, each with a rectangular window on the first floor, topped by a three-sided balcony set within a subtle recess and marked by a triangular shape along the parapet. The motifs of triangular forms and three-sided balconies are repeated on the building's three secondary elevations.

MANIAL

For his private residential commissions, such as palaces, villas, and mansions, architect Muhammad Sherif Nouman refrained from the prevalent Modernist aesthetic and opted for a romantic Mediterraneanism, with an eclectic mix of pseudo-historical elements. In the Saraya Ahmed Mustafa Abu Rehab, completed 1949, he combines a concrete trellis with twisted columns crowned by *muqarnas* capitals, semi-circular balconies, horseshoe arches, and Neo-Classical corbels.

Manial

Manial occupies the northern part of Roda Island in the Nile. Several palaces and houses had already been built here in the nineteenth century, mostly timber constructions, such as the Manastirli Palace completed in 1851. In 1908 the Ghizeh and Rodah Company was established for real-estate development of the island. That same year two bridges were completed, Abbas Bridge and al-Malek al-Saleh Bridge, which carried the tramline from Ataba to Giza across the island. Two east–west crossings, at al-Saraya Street in the north and Roda Street in the south, are connected by the north–south spine of the island, Manial Street. Land was consolidated and leveled, and a street plan was drawn. The bridges and transport link facilitated urbanization, first with a new wave of mansions and villas for prominent members of society, followed by those for the upper-middle class.

The island's most prominent institution is Cairo University's Medical School, completed in 1933 and occupying most of the northern tip. The densification of the Roda increased rapidly in the second half of the twentieth century, as villas and houses with gardens were replaced by apartment buildings of greater heights and larger footprints. Today the island has stabilized into a middle-class residential district with a wide array of residential buildings from the second half of the twentieth century.

Le Méridien Hotel

Address: 51 al-Uruba Street
GPS: 30.035098, 31.227671
Year: 1974
Architect: Maher Abdel Hamid, Abdel Fattah Bayoumi

The northern tip of Roda Island offers expansive Nile views, and so this 966-room hotel arcs across the site to take advantage of the location. It sits on a podium lifted on pilotis on the Nile side. The glazed lower floors consist of the reception and dining areas and shared and service spaces. The rooms are distributed on eleven floors, all facing the Nile, with the horizontal circulation running along the back of the building. The vertical circulation core is designed as a separate mass attached to the rear of the block. The structure's modular façade is composed of a concrete grid with square protruding balconies for all rooms. The hotel is crowned with a rectangular glazed restaurant and a zigzagging concrete parapet. The building has been disused since 2001 and risks demolition.

Qasr al-Aini Medical School

Address: Cairo University Hospitals Street
GPS: 30.031541, 31.227125
Year: 1923–33
Architects: Charles Nicholas, John Edward Dixon

Founded in 1827, Qasr al-Aini is the oldest medical school in Africa and the Middle East; its current facilities were built around its centennial. The vast campus includes a teaching hospital, a specialized university hospital, laboratories, classrooms, offices, lecture halls, anatomy theaters, libraries, and a museum. It is designed with a north–south spine nearly 600 meters in length, with independent structures—originally identical U-shaped buildings—attached to the spine. Eleven of these original buildings are extant, while others have been altered or rebuilt. They host the various branches of medicine taught at the university. The central administration building is rectangular in plan, with two courtyards and a tower at the center of the main elevation. In contrast to the understated design of the remainder of the campus, the three-story administration building displays characteristics of Georgian architecture. At the center is a protruding entrance portico with steps to the raised ground floor, flanked by double columns supporting the pediment above. The clock tower is composed of five stacked sections, most notably the drum section encircled by columns. The pinnacle of the tower is a crescent emerging from the dome topping the structure. The front elevations of the building's two wings are recessed behind double-height columns, shading the interior. Most of the stone and concrete structures were originally designed with three floors, though there have been numerous additions since their inauguration.

Manial Palace

Address: 1 al-Saraya Street
GPS: 30.028625, 31.229571
Year: 1901–29
Architect: Prince Muhammad Ali Tawfiq, Muhammad Afifi

The 7-hectare palace and gardens, with their complex of buildings and pavilions, are an example of eclectic historicism. Prince Muhammad Ali Tawfiq was an avid traveler and collector with an appreciation for the fine arts, which led him to design the palace himself. Most of the structures on the site are built around the perimeter, while the rest of the plot is dedicated to a botanical garden. The complex includes Mamluk and Fatimid inspiration, Ottoman-style structures, a Moroccan-style clock tower, Persian decorative interiors, and elements of Art Nouveau and Rococo. The rusticated stone wall around the site has two gateways, in the north and west walls. Two slender tower forms of Fatimid inspiration flank the main portal with its horseshoe arch.

The entrance pavilion includes a reception hall on its second floor, topped by a ribbed onion dome. Immediately to the west of the gateway inside the wall is a square stone tower with a Moorish design, which functions as a clock tower and a minaret for the small mosque next to it. The rectangular mosque is entered through a protruding entrance niche, strikingly modern in form despite its rich decorations that include a recessed pointed arch and a *muqarnas* and half-dome ceiling. The exterior of the stone-masonry, single-story mosque is decorated with a ribbon of inscription along the top and an elaborate parapet of cobra heads. The *mihrab* protrudes from the east wall and is marked on the exterior with *muqarnas* and ceramic tiles.

The residence, oriented at a 45-degree angle to the rectangular site, is situated at the southeast corner of the plot. The two-story house is designed with a muted stone exterior with timber details, *mashrabiya*s, and awnings. The entrance is designed as a slightly raised square corner portico with two rounded arches and a single column at the corner. A square tower at the side closest to the Nile supports a square, slightly cantilevered room with glass walls topped with a dome. The carefully designed sitting room is one of fourteen halls that dot the complex, each richly decorated thematically and creating vastly different immersive environments. At the wall of the complex is the Versailles-style *majlis*, a formal sitting area; this is a long, narrow room with windows overlooking the garden to one side, furnished with gilded furniture, red velvet upholstery, and a large elliptical golden-sunburst piece on the ceiling. Other rooms range between Syrian, Persian, and high European styles. The Golden Room in the pavilion along the western wall was built for receptions and public events. Its decoration is partly Ottoman in inspiration, partly entirely invented, such as the gilded columns with lotus-flower motifs. A champion of the arts and crafts, the prince placed a plaque near the entrance to the complex, which lists the names of craftsmen and artisans who worked on the palace over the years.

Saraya Ahmed Mustafa Abu Rehab

Address: Yusif Sherif Street
GPS: 30.0197540, 31.2246220
Year: 1949
Architect: Muhammad Sherif Nouman

This vast private mansion is an example of a building typology that has been lost across Manial. A car ramp and steps lead to the entrance on the raised ground floor. A square vestibule is flanked by an office and a small sitting area. Next is a long, rectangular grand hall running the width of the mansion, with the grand stair at the east end. The grand hall overlooks the square courtyard in the center of the house, around which all the residence's functions are arranged. Trefoil arches lead to the courtyard, which is overlooked by semicircular balconies and terraces from the second floor, with green titles lining the roof around it. The east wing of the ground floor includes a summer bedroom, a daily dining area, and a small sitting area, while the west wing includes the formal dining room, bathroom and kitchen with an attached service stair, and a master bedroom. To the south are a winter sitting room and terrace overlooking the garden in the back. Additional rooms are located on the second and partial third floors, designed with gabled rooflines. Terraces, porticos, and balconies are abundant, giving nearly every room in the house access to an outdoor space. The exterior of the building does not adhere to a particular style; it includes inventive elements such as the bulbous columns carrying the circular arches of the porticos and the custom-designed metalwork on doors and windows. The interior is richly decorated with patterned wallpaper and a wide array of stone, marble, and cement tiles.

Main Elevation

Ibrahim Mosque

Address: al-Khalifa al-Mutawakkel Street
GPS: 30.012111, 31.226276
Year: 1945
Architect: Unknown

It is common to find small prayer spaces repurposing ground floors of residential buildings across Cairo, but this building was designed to combine sacred and profane spaces in one small corner plot. The building's dual functions are rendered architecturally, with the mosque occupying the ground floor while the two floors of apartments are stacked above. The portal of the mosque on the south façade is set in a shallow niche, crowned with *muqarnas* and flanked by slightly recessed windows. The entrance to the apartments on the far end of the west façade, away from the building's corner, leads into a hallway to the stairs. The exterior of the upper floors is punctuated by alternating windows and balconies. A cylindrical minaret is set within the inverted corner of the upper two floors, and the imam's balcony matches the level of the roof. The building was erected as a self-sustaining *waqf* (religious endowment), with rents from the apartments going toward the upkeep and maintenance of the mosque.

GIZA

One of two monumental gates, built 1936, replacing earlier entrances to the Giza Zoo, opened 1891. The Art Deco gates incorporate painted murals, metalwork, and relief sculptures representing animals.

Giza

Land on the west bank of the Nile was agricultural and owned by the state or members of the khedival family, or managed by the Awqaf Administration. From the middle of the nineteenth century to the outbreak of the First World War, Giza witnessed the establishment of several entities such as Cairo's zoo and botanical gardens, an agricultural school (with associated fields), the Royal School of Architecture, and a correctional facility. These structures dotted the agricultural landscape, with several roads already in place. Giza Street with its tramline, today's Charles de Gaulle Street, delineated a narrow strip of land, previously part of Khedive Ismail's estate, sandwiched between the botanical garden and the Nile, which became prime real estate. The Ghizeh and Rodah Company sought to develop the area and proceeded to draw up a street plan and parcel lands. Through the 1920s only a handful of mansions were built. In the 1930s, with the construction of Cairo University, apartment blocks appeared and the residential district of Giza began to take shape.

Suburban Modernist houses flanked Pyramids Road by the 1940s, and Giza Square came into its current shape as a major hub by the late 1950s. In 1958 the Academy of Arts was established in Giza with a campus of Modernist buildings—for the higher institutes of music, ballet, cinema and theater—designed by architect and musician Abu Bakr Khairat. Recent renovations of the campus eliminated its Modernist character with the addition of decorative pastiche on previously whitewashed austere exteriors. Informal enchroachment on agricultural land increased in Giza from the 1970s creating some of Cairo's most densely populated urban settlements.

94

Cairo University Hall

Address: Cairo University
GPS: 30.027404, 31.209265
Year: 1937
Architect: Eric Newnum, Ahmed Charmi

The iconic dome of the ceremonial hall of Cairo University is the centerpiece of the campus built between 1925 and 1937. The hall hosted lectures, speeches and concerts by the likes of Nasser, Jean-Paul Sartre, Umm Kulthoum and Obama, among others.

The main buildings of the campus, including the library, Faculty of Law, Faculty of Humanities, administration building, and the ceremonial hall, are all designed in a stripped-down Imperial Style. The ceremonial hall is located directly behind the administration building and has three entrances: the royal entrance to the north, the dignitaries' entrance to the south, and general admission to the east through the administration building.

With seating arranged on the ground level and two additional tiers on three sides, the total capacity of the hall is 4,100 persons. A double dome tops the hall: the internal dome is 30 meters high, while the height of the external dome, topped by a cupola, reaches 52 meters. At 38 meters in diameter, the dome is supported by radial steel beams and seemingly hovers above clerestory windows that allow sunlight to penetrate the space; it rests on four reinforced-concrete pillars that carry the entire structure, allowing for large expanses of open space. The overall design of the hall is restrained in decoration and Neo-Classical in form. All exteriors are clad in sandstone, while floors in public areas are of white marble.[50]

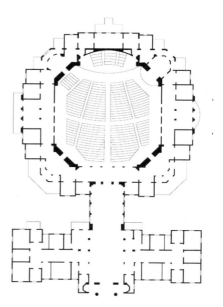

Ground Floor Plan

Al-Shafiq Building

Address: 49 Charles de Gaulle Street
GPS: 30.0268040, 31.2168120
Year: 1948
Architects: Hassan and Mustafa Shafie

Typical of postwar residential projects in Cairo's wealthier districts, al-Shafiq is a massive, sixteen-story structure with high-end apartments, six per floor. The centrally placed, double-height, spacious lobby is glazed along the street. Four round pilotis and a centrally positioned mosaic water fountain, flanked on each side by three tall industrial glass windows along the back wall, emphasize symmetry, concealing the fact that the north wing is slightly larger than the south wing. The elegant lobby is largely unadorned save for the marble floor and wall cladding, in which a diamond shape is repeated. Due to the size of the plot the building is divided into two connected halves, with two different circulation cores, each consisting of a grand staircase, two passenger elevators, and a furniture elevator. There are three service stairs with direct kitchen access. The garage and service rooms occupy the ground floor.

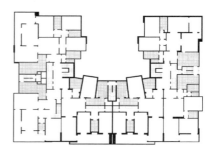

Typical Floor Plan

The mezzanine level was designed for office spaces, while apartments begin at the second floor. In the south wing, each vertical circulation core serves three two-bedroom apartments per floor. The north wing, on the other hand, includes a two- and a three-bedroom apartment on each floor and a duplex apartment on every other floor. The top floor of the building is recessed and includes roof terraces with views over the Giza Zoo. The exterior is typical of the period, with plain elevations defined by a series of horizontal and corner recesses for balconies.

Giza

Halim Dos Bey Building

Address: 11 Murad Street
GPS: 30.017422, 31.214357
Year: 1937
Architect: Charles Ayrout

Creating an eye-catching corner was the main design intention for this five-story apartment building. The chamfered corner creates a third façade, dominated by a stack of bold balconies. The building possesses three distinct parts: an unembellished ground floor; followed by four typical levels of apartments, with robust articulations on the exterior; and a final setback floor with a rounded loggia and roofline that contrasts with the angular roof profile at the fourth apartment-floor level. The result is a dynamic massing that gives the building a large appearance despite its small size. Each floor houses three apartments, ranging in size from three to five rooms. The exterior finishes are typical of Ayrout's architecture, combining concrete with brick.[51]

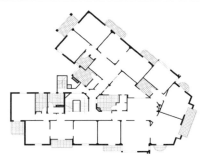

Typical Floor Plan

Giza

Misr Insurance Company

Address: 515 Giza Square
GPS: 330.0149507, 31.2120972
Year: 1961
Architect: Ali Labib Gabr

This building was erected to provide a branch location of Banque Misr in Giza, as well as middle-income apartments. The bank and stores occupy the ground floor, followed by three floors of office space and seven floors of apartments. The architect makes no distinction between the office floors and the residential ones, so that uses of the various floors could be changed. The main challenge in designing this building was to keep costs at a minimum and to maximize rent incomes, while providing affordable apartments. This was achieved with careful calculations of construction costs, reducing ceiling heights, and using cost-effective finishes such as cement tiles. Due to the large footprint of the building, the center of the block is given over to the circulation core and hallways surrounded by four air shafts. These were created to ventilate service rooms, which are placed toward the center, while living and office spaces are distributed along the unembellished exterior.

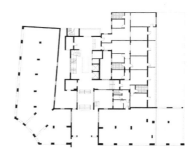

Ground Floor Plan

Villa Anis Serageldin

(demolished)

Address: Haram Street
Year: 1934
Architect: Anis Serageldin

This house was built on a large garden in the suburb of Haram, surrounded by other villas and gardens that flourished in the area in the 1930s. The architect designed a cubic volume with multiple recesses and extrusions. The plan was organized to maximize light and air movement in all rooms. The villa was designed inside out, thus the fenestration and volumetric play of the exterior merely correspond with carefully designed interiors. A notable feature of the house is the external service stair climbing from the second floor to the roof. Flower boxes were placed at nearly all windows, and extruded concrete shades protected the interior from direct sunlight and heat.

The interior of the house was colorful: yellow office, beige dining and sitting rooms, green bedroom for the architect, pink bedroom for his wife, and pink ceilings throughout. In addition, marbles from nearby quarries in Giza were used extensively. The walls and floors of the dining room were clad entirely in Giza marble, while the floors of most of the rest of the house were covered with white marble, and the steps of the main stair have black marble for the risers and white for the treads.[52]

99

Villa William Habib
(demolished)

Address: Haram Street
Year: 1933
Architect: Albert Zananiri

This Rationalist villa is designed around a grid of pilotis that support the entire structure, some of which are exposed on the north and south elevations. The ground floor is used for storage, garage, and a covered garden room toward the back. All the main living spaces are located on the first floor, reached by a set of stairs at the main entrance. The house is oriented east–west, so all rooms face north or south or both. Bedrooms are on the north side for better breezes. Shade is created along the south side with sun breakers and deep recesses. In terms of volume there are two joined parts, a two-story cubic volume containing all the living spaces and a games room, and a long narrow bar containing two bedrooms and culminating in an office at the end of the hallway.[53]

100

Villa Cassab

(demolished)

Address: Haram Street
Year: 1934
Architect: Raymond Antonius

This large, three-story villa was an example of Raymond Antonius's experimentation with building materials, in this case red brick. The design is driven by section, with rooms on multiple levels connected internally. The house can be entered from the ground floor or the main entrance on the first floor, reached by a stair, or via the back door from the garden. The footprint of the ground floor is the smallest, as parts of the upper stories were lifted on pilotis in order to maximize the garden. The ground floor contains a garage, service rooms, a games room, and a sitting room connected by stairs to the first floor, where the main living spaces are located. The first floor is divided into two wings, an area with salon, living, and dining rooms to one side, and an office and 'Arab Room,' with a collection of antiques, located to the other side. The kitchen and service areas separate these two wings. The grand staircase leads to a large hall separating two sleeping wings with a total of five bedrooms. A studio with a rounded front with strip window is located on the third floor, accessed only by the service stair. All rooms have access to ample balconies, loggias, and terraces. A variety of concrete shading devices were built above windows to reduce direct sunlight.

While reinforced concrete was the main building material, the design of the villa showcased brick. Bricks of two different dimensions were arranged on the façade—horizontally in some areas, vertically in others, and with geometric three-dimensional patterns in yet others. Other parts of the façade were plastered with stucco. The result was a house of dynamic massing, interplay of volumes, and a complex skin treatment using a ubiquitous material, brick.[54]

Villa Dr. Kamal Abdel Razeq

(demolished)

Address: Ghaleb Pasha Street
Year: 1947
Architect: Ali Nour al-Din Nassar

This cubist house was designed for a doctor who was a single father. The programmatic requirements were simple and included an office space, reception and living areas, and private sleeping areas, including a master bedroom. The plan of the house is organized as a fan, with the staircase in the center. Upon entering the house, to the left is the service area with the kitchen and bathroom; to the right is the office, with a large glass window overlooking the street. The remainder of the living space was organized in an open plan. On the second floor, the landing from the main stair functions as a distribution point to four bedrooms, with a master bedroom to one side with access to a large terrace and a spiral stair for access to the shaded roof terrace. Various cubic volumes and solid surfaces and protrusions give a fortress-like impression. The chimney forms a strong vertical element that intersects with the horizontal slab shading the roof garden.[55]

Villa Ibrahim al-Kassas Bey

(demolished)

Address: Haram Street
Year: 1948
Architect: Sayed Karim

One of the best examples in Cairo implementing Le Corbusier's "five points of architecture," this villa was part of a group of three belonging to members of the Kassas family. The main living spaces of the house, built on a 700m² plot, are lifted on pilotis. Parts of the ground floor form part of the garden, while the rest consist of a large garden room with a semicircular glass wall, the main kitchen, and the housemaid's room, bathroom, and a large garage. The main entrance of the house is located on the first floor, reached from the outside by a sculptural spiral stair that arrives at a partially enclosed entrance terrace concealed behind a strip opening, which continues across the main elevation to form a strip window along the main living spaces. The entrance stair is one of three in the house; the main stair connects the garden room to the main living space and the top floor, and a third, semicircular service stair is located in the back of the house, connecting all the floors and leading to a roof garden and additional service rooms on the roof.

Within the open plan of the main living space are several sitting areas, including a fireplace area, a dining room, and a living room, which could be closed off by movable partitions. Toward the back of the first floor is the private wing with the bathrooms, office, and a guest bedroom. The office is also directly accessible by another door from the entrance terrace. The top floor is organized in two wings, each with two bedrooms and a bathroom. A living room with a large glass wall separates the two wings and leads to a shared balcony that wraps around the front of the house and is accessible from two of the bedrooms.

While Corbusian in style, the villa incorporates locally available materials in its construction. A reinforced-concrete frame is filled with hollow sandstone bricks for better sound and climate insulation. Other construction details include insulating materials on the roof to reduce heat gain, aluminum window frames throughout, and toughened glass used for the railing of the balcony.[56]

DOKKI & AGOUZA

Atrium of the Goethe-Institut, designed by Worschech Architekten and completed in 2016.

Dokki & Agouza

Until the 1920s today's Dokki and Agouza were part of Cairo's agricultural hinterland, with a few villages. Dokki takes its name from the no-longer-extant village nearby. A handful of villas were sparsely built among the villages and the bucolic landscape. The area was divided among a few landowners who controlled large agricultural properties, including the villages within them that supplied labor. From the 1930s urban encroachment increased along the Nile edge, and *waqf* reforms and land sales in the 1940s opened the terrain for urban development driven by private land companies that divided their properties into plots for sale, each company with its own urban-planning logic. The result is an urban patchwork of parallel and radial streets concentrated around three traffic circles, Naguib Mahfouz Square in Agouza, Soliman Gohar and Fini squares in

Dokki, and the elliptical Mesaha Square in Dokki. The architectural landscape of these newly developed areas was dominated by proto-Modernist single-family houses with small gardens, often built in large numbers by real-estate companies implementing standardized designs. Only a handful of these original houses remain, however. The planning of Awqaf City and subsequent growth of Mohandiseen, starting in the 1960s, led to the replacement of original Dokki and Agouza properties with larger, taller buildings. One of the earliest high-rises in the area is the 1937 Aziz Abdel Malek Hanna Building (#103) overlooking al-Galaa Square. From the 1970s the original districts became increasingly denser, and Dokki's administrative borders expanded westward to encompass the area north of the Botanical Garden and Cairo University, reaching Sudan Street and delimited by the Upper Egypt train tracks.

Aziz Abdel Malek Hanna Building

Address: 98 Corniche al-Nil
GPS: 30.040576, 31.219674
Year: 1937
Architect: Antoine Selim Nahas

The challenge of the site is its small size, just 220m², but its location in front of the Nile and an open traffic circle allows for its height. The slender tower of seven stories houses a one-bedroom and a two-bedroom apartment on each floor; both apartments have Nile views. The slightly recessed eighth and ninth floors house a villa with a roof garden for the owner. Despite the limited space, the building includes a luxurious stair clad with white and black marble, with an elevator and a separate service stair leading to the kitchens. The exterior is purely functional, devoid of any accents or embellishments. The mass of the narrow building is articulated on the three sides toward the square with ribbon-like recessed balconies. However, protruding bay windows from the main living space interrupt the spatial continuities of the balconies, dividing them into two discrete spaces accessed from two different rooms.[57]

Faisal Bank

Address: 149 al-Tahrir Street
GPS: 30.039514, 31.218646
Year: 2000
Architect: Islam Hafez

This building occupies a triangular plot bordered by two major streets overlooking the Nile and Zamalek. There are two entrances leading to the building's two functions, one for the offices in the lower half of the tower, another for the apartments occupying the top ten stories. The office entrance portal, topped by a *muqarnas*-inspired decorative element, is set below a carved niche culminating in a semicircular arch rising the height of the office section. The niche creates a shaded area within the building volume, overlooked by office windows protected from direct sunlight. Twenty luxury apartments, two per floor, are each composed of reception areas and four bedrooms. Triangular balconies partially covered by screens provide shade and articulate the apartments on all three sides.

Extensive Arabic calligraphy functions as *brise soleil* screens arranged vertically on the façade. One of the screens partially covers the exterior triangular emergency stair, which climbs the entire height of the building at the rear.

State Council

Address: Charles de Gaulle Street
GPS: 30.035261, 31.218273
Year: c.1990
Architect: Development and Popular Housing Company

This building for Egypt's administrative court consists of two connected components. The first is a six-story volume along the street, housing twelve courtrooms of different sizes, debating rooms, a library, meeting rooms, and reception and waiting areas. The second is a fifteen-story tower of offices for judges and administration. Brutalism and bold forms characterize the design.

The court building is lifted on a granite-clad podium, with the entrance reached via a flight of stairs leading to the raised first floor. Some courtrooms are legible from the outside as slightly protruding solid forms. These opaque spaces contrast with the strip windows of spaces housing other functions. The parapets of both the low and the high building are exaggerated and extended, appearing like heavy masses resting on the structures below. In the initial design the tower was imagined as a curtain-walled twenty-story block, but it was implemented shorter, with a regular grid of windows.

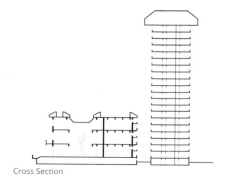
Cross Section

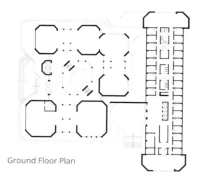
Ground Floor Plan

Goethe-Institut

Address: 17 Hussein Wasef Street
GPS: 30.034161, 31.215162
Year: 2016
Architect: Worschech Architekten

The design of this building creates a series of volumes connected by open-air bridges and walkways. The newly built cubic volume, where most of the public functions are located, is linked with the restored 1920s villa on the site, reused to house a cafeteria and offices. The newly built area is kept to the back of the site, maintaining the center of the plot clear of any construction and thus preserving the garden with its palm trees. The main events hall can be extended into the garden by opening a set of glass doors and metal shutters, allowing for uninterrupted integration of inside and outside. The central atrium, measuring the entire height of the four-story building, includes stairs and an elevator leading to classrooms, offices, and a library. The back edge of the site is defined by open-air walkways overlooking the garden, providing horizontal circulation. Screens are placed along the walkways to protect the privacy of the neighboring residential apartments.

The building is kept minimal and unadorned, with expansive plain white walls throughout. The only recurrent decorative features are the metal screens perforated with the logo of the Goethe-Institut. The screens create an external skin along the garden-facing elevations and allow users to manipulate the amount of sunlight and visual connectivity they want with the surroundings.

Mohandes Insurance Headquarters

Address: Mesaha Square
GPS: 30.034719, 31.214351
Year: 1999
Architect: Ezzat Said

This rectangular, eleven-story office building situated on a corner site overlooking Mesaha Square is composed of identical floors. Its most remarkable feature is its grid exterior, comprising modular window units covering the entire area of its two façades. The grid functions as an organizing system governing the design of the exterior, such as the slight recess, that is four windows wide, and rising to the sixth floor to mark the entrance below. Two double-height voids, functioning as outdoor terraces near the corner on the seventh floor, break the monotony of the grid.

A column rising to the fourth floor further highlights the corner. The deconstructed corner of the building up to the fourth floor creates a niche, as if exposing the structure carrying it, which would usually be concealed behind the façade. The column is designed with a cylindrical shaft, a square transitional element, and a tapered rectangular capital.

Embassy of the Czech Republic

Address: 4 al-Dokki Street
GPS: 30.030840, 31.211634
Year: 1980
Architects: Karel Filsak, Vladimir Toms

The largest Czech embassy in Africa is an entire campus of facilities, including the ambassador's residence, a school, an employees' club, a garden, a swimming pool, and a tennis court. It was the last major construction by Czech Brutalist architect Karel Filsak. The most prominent structure on the site is the thirteen-story block of mostly residential units for embassy staff. The massing of the tower consists of a large rectangular block with two protruding square volumes at the center of the north and south elevations. A large atrium open to the sky at the center of the block allows light and air to penetrate. The tower is encased in a double façade to reduce indoor temperatures. Strip windows and balconies punctuate the inner façade.

The outer layer consists of nine concrete ribbons that function as sun breakers. The ribbons occasionally dip slightly to break the building's regularity and appearance of heaviness. Monumentality is achieved with the overdesigned parapet at the top of the building, appearing like a heavy sculptural piece. A notable interior feature is the concrete waffle ceilings throughout the complex. Embassy offices are spread out at the base of the tower in smaller two- to three-story buildings.

Ahram Beverages Company

Address: Sudan Street at Tharwat Bridge
GPS: 30.028431, 31.201709
Year: 1900
Architect: Unknown

Built in the midst of agricultural land and khedival palaces, the brewery was commissioned by the Belgian–Egyptian Société Anonyme Brasserie des Pyramides. The original symmetrical structure is composed of three main sections running east to west. The central part of the building is of three stories, flanked by four-story towers that appear to be vertical circulation shafts. Two-story volumes with articulated three-story corners flank the central volume.

The stone and brick façade is articulated at the top with machicolations, giving the building a fortress-like appearance. Narrow windows set within shallow arched niches punctuate the façade. The overall composition is heavy, muscular, and austere. Elements of the building's interior suggest it may be one of the earliest in Egypt to be constructed using reinforced concrete—the François Hennebique system, patented in 1892.[58]

National Research Center

Address: 88 Tahrir Street
GPS: 30.036590, 31.204835
Year: 1956
Architect: Ali Labib Gabr

Established in 1956, the National Research Center is today Egypt's umbrella institution for all research fields, including medicine, engineering, chemical industries, agriculture, the environment, the food industry, genetics, and pharmaceuticals. In plan, the symmetrical building is composed of three connected sections: a central upside-down T-shaped section flanked by east and west sections, and two perpendicular south wings. In the central block, three identical floors sit above the ground floor, which includes a large auditorium.

The two side wings are shorter, with two floors above the ground level. Two large circular stairs are placed at the junctions of the east and west wings with their south wings. While the central section is occupied by the administration, the wings are fully dedicated to laboratories and offices for researchers. Offices are laid out facing the front along a hallway running the entire length of the structure. The two rear wings include central hallways flanked by offices overlooking the garden. A series of buildings was subsequently added to the site.

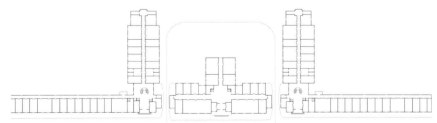

Ground Floor Plan

111

Musaddaq Office Building

Address: 29 Mohi al-Din Abu al-Ezz
GPS: 30.038454, 31.201183
Year: 1995
Architect: Gamal Bakry

By eliminating a sharp corner, Gamal Bakry creates a continuous façade with a uniform grid of windows organized in rows matching this structure's ten floors. The modular façade design reflects the identical open-office plan of all the levels, which include a circulation and a wet core to the rear. The rose-colored façade is articulated with blue window shades, reducing direct sunlight and building temperature. The shading devices can be rolled up, exposing the window behind entirely, or they can be extended out in a closed position, allowing fresh air while controlling light. The result is a dynamic façade that is constantly changing with use by employees at the building.

Mahmoud Othman Building

Address: 2 Abd al-Rahim Sabry Street
GPS: 30.039085, 31.214057
Year: 1955
Architect: Sayed Karim

This is another manifestation of Sayed Karim's interest in creating vertical collections of 'villas,' or duplexes. Three streets surround the building, which contains sixteen units on eight floors. Odd-numbered floors are for the living spaces of the duplexes and even-numbered floors are for bedrooms. The ground floor is occupied by stores, a lobby, and service rooms. Two elevators, a stair, a hallway, and two air shafts form the core of the building.

Apartment entrances are on the odd-numbered levels, connected directly by the stairs, which skip over the even-numbered floors. The duplexes range in size from two to three bedrooms. The units along the front elevation have access to two balconies overlooking Tahrir Street. The balconies on the odd-numbered floors are triangular, as they mediate between the diagonal of Tahrir Street and the building's rectangular footprint aligned with the two parallel side streets.

The result is an architectonically complex front elevation. Within each of the eight double-heights (four on each side), triangular recesses on floors two through nine contain two large windows and two balconies. The living-room balcony on the lower floor of each duplex is large and triangular, overlooked by the smaller rectilinear balcony of one of the bedrooms above. The design gives the units along the front of the building legibility and a sense of autonomy.

Bedrooms Floor Plan (4th, 6th, and 8th Floors)

Living Areas Floor Plan (3rd, 5th, and 7th Floors)

Al-Kateb Hospital

Address: 17 Hendawi Street
GPS: 30.0424010, 31.2177210
Year: 1946
Architect: Abu Bakr Khairat

This L-shaped hospital is set back from the street, fronted by a large rectangular garden overlooked by the patient rooms. The short part of the L contains the entrance lobby, raised above ground by several steps, topped by the surgery room, with administration on the third floor. The entrance leads to a waiting room and reception, followed by the main staircase. The rest of the building houses all the hospital functions, including inpatient rooms along the north façade, with rooms oriented diagonally to the northwest in order to maximize natural light and air circulation.

All rooms are equipped with a small balcony protruding to one side, creating a sawtooth façade of rooms and balconies jutting out of the otherwise rectilinear structure. The windows and balcony doors of the rooms on the north side are placed at the corner of each room. Two secondary stairs are placed at either end of the rear of the building. Service rooms, storage, and mechanical rooms are in the basement, lit by clerestory windows above ground level. The hospital's exterior is cubic and minimal, with rounded balcony corners contrasting with the orthogonal nature of the remaining features. Simple metal railings further enhance the horizontality of the design.

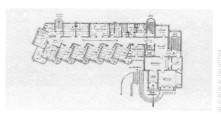

Bishara Building

Address: 118 Corniche al-Nil
GPS: 30.044871, 31.218332
Year: 1937
Architect: Charles Ayrout

The Bishara Building consists of a ground floor of two apartments entered from the street; a raised first floor with the entrance and a generously designed elevator lobby, flanked by two apartments; and five identical floors, each with three residences. All living spaces overlook the Nile. Built just before the start of the Second World War, the building includes a bomb shelter for residents. The U-shaped plan is divided into three sections, with the southern arm extending slightly longer than the northern, as it houses the stack of three-bedroom apartments. The central part includes the stairs to the rear, a hallway, and the stack of one-bedroom apartments. The north arm contains the stack of two-bedroom apartments. The elevation is designed asymmetrically, with emphasis on the north corner of the front façade. The glazed yellow-brick façade is articulated with two sets of long deep balconies running along the east and south faces, culminating in rounded extrusions outside the otherwise cubic volume of the building. Amenities included hot water, central heating, and radio connections to all apartments.[59]

Agouza Hospital

Address: 176 Corniche al-Nil
GPS: 30.053992, 31.215447
Year: 1939
Architect: Mustafa Fahmy

This sprawling hospital built on a 35,000m² Nile-side plot was founded by a charitable foundation to serve the general public. The three-story building is composed of a north–south central spine with three identical, equally spaced east–west wings; then a central administration building flanked by two additional smaller buildings extending to the east; and a final east–west block at the southern end of the spine. The façade is adorned by a mélange of elements quoting Fatimid and Mamluk architecture, such as keel arches painted to resemble *ablaq* (alternating colors), floral decorative panels around the arches, and *muqarnas* column capitals. The main entrance of the administration block is set in a portico on the first floor, reached by a double stair.

Shahrazad Hotel

Address: 182 Corniche al-Nil
GPS: 30.057163, 31.215323
Year: c.1982
Architect: Galal Momen

The massing of this hotel is broken into three main parts: a two-story podium covering the entire site, followed by a recessed block of twelve floors of rooms and an off-center, five-story, boxy volume crowning the structure. While the podium contains the reception areas and dining halls, the boxy structure above was designed to house the entertainment functions, such as restaurants, cabaret, and a nightclub. The exterior of the entertainment box is decorated with mosaic tiles with representations of dancing figures. The remaining floors largely share the same floor plan, with slight differences such as a narrow six-story section on the right side of the block of rooms, which leans diagonally outward.

MOHANDISEEN

Residential building overlooking Mustafa Mahmoud Square.

Mohandiseen

Cairo's population grew exponentially in the 1930s, yet the Second World War slowed or halted many of the city's urban and architectural projects, making the situation dire by the time the war ended. Some architects had already proposed plans for the westward urban expansion of the city; one such was Mahmoud Sabry Mahboub's 1930 plan for a series of avenues connecting circular squares with residential blocks, utilizing garden-city street patterns. Then in 1944 the Awqaf Administration announced its intention to plan a city on lands it managed on the west bank of the Nile. The plan was not popular, as Cairo had historically developed in a desert environment, preserving agricultural land. Starting in 1949, however, streets were laid out and various professional syndicates were offered land at lower than market prices. In 1955 the Engineers' Syndicate purchased the largest share of 8 hectares, and the area became known as Madinat al-Mohandiseen ('Engineers' City').

Mohandiseen adjoins Dokki and Agouza and encircles preexisting villages, notably Mit Uqba, which was subsequently urbanized following the organic street pattern inherited from the village. The first wave of construction in the area consisted of villas and low-rise apartment buildings, but Mohandiseen acquired its present look in the 1980s and 1990s, as higher-density, taller, and larger buildings filled the area and began to replace earlier structures. One of the earliest housing projects in the area was the set of the forty Awqaf housing blocks built in clusters of five in a belt running north–south across the busy 26 July Corridor, just north of the Zamalek Club.

Madinat al-Awqaf

Year: 1948
Architect: Mahmoud Riad

The Awqaf Administration managed a large consolidated plot of agricultural land between the Nile and the Upper Egypt rail line to the west. Influenced by garden-city town planning, Riad provided the urban plan to parcel the Awqaf land for development. The plan begins with a bridge to carry Fuad I (now 26 July) Street, the roadway extending diagonally from Downtown and cutting across Zamalek, across the Nile. Three major radial avenues define the main features of the plan; around them a series of secondary and tertiary streets create human-scale residential blocks. The largest of the three avenues is laid diagonally across the site (today's Gameat al-Diwal al-Arabiya Street); in its center is a traffic circle with three parallel semicircular streets. The semicircular street pattern is repeated at the western edge of the plan. A building code accompanied the plan in order to limit building heights, specify the percentage of buildable area, and require setbacks from the street. The Modernist street pattern contrasts with the spontaneous road layout of existing villages, which remained despite the plan.

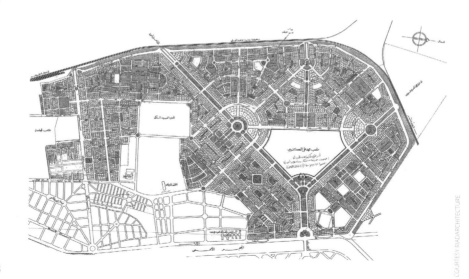

Media City Apartments

Address: 93 Ahmed Orabi Street
GPS: 30.063825, 31.203547
Year: 1959
Architect: Sayed Karim

Collective housing models developed by Sayed Karim in response to the state's investments in middle-income housing, largely implemented in Nasr City, found their way into this part of Cairo in a project originally intended to house employees of state media and broadcasting, namely the TV and Radio Administration located across the Nile in Bulaq. The original design for the large corner site included six twelve-story H-shaped blocks placed along the Nile and 26 July Street, each three blocks sharing a three-story podium with services and common spaces. The three blocks along the Nile were placed at a 45-degree angle to the river.

Three additional rectangular blocks, as well as a slender high-rise tower, were placed at the back of the site, with green space in between. The implementation of the project did not conform to the original design, however. Instead, the waterfront was given to al-Balloon Theater, the National Circus, and the Agouza district presidency. Only two blocks were built along 26 July Street, the third replaced by a cross-plan, revival-style mosque erected later. A total of eight blocks following two of Karim's housing typologies were implemented in a partial realization of the original placement. The project was expanded further west, with six additional blocks built along Ahmed Orabi Street. While the scheme was envisioned as a complete urban environment, its piecemeal implementation sacrificed its overall integrity.

Architecturally, the project transplants Nasr City models unmodified, with large-footprint high-rise blocks divided into multiple entrances, in some cases with two- to three-bedroom apartments arranged along the outer walls, with service spaces along the core ventilated by air shafts. Modular façade treatments of shifting rectangles articulate the buildings' skin. The planned podiums were never implemented.

National Center for Social and Criminological Research

Address: 4 Midan Ibn Khaldun
GPS: 30.065568, 31.208132
Year: 1959
Architect: Ali Raafat

The center was established in 1955 to conduct social research, and its new facility is a unique example of low-rise administrative architecture in the city that integrates indoor and outdoor space. The original program included meeting rooms for researchers, a library, an auditorium, a museum, a cafeteria, photography laboratories, criminology labs, and a psychology clinic. The design anticipated the future growth of the institution to allow for horizontal expansion of the psychology clinic, and vertical expansion of the labs and research spaces. The building occupies a 4,000m² plot, and incorporates terraces enclosed by breeze blocks and an open-air courtyard with seating for the cafeteria. The building is square in plan, with all public functions located on the raised ground floor, with two additional rectangular floors in the center of the block hosting the research facilities.

Different programmatic elements are architecturally expressed on the exterior, such as the museum, enclosed with a horizontal screen to the left of the main entrance, and the auditorium to the right of the entrance marked with concrete vaults that allow diffused light into the space.

Sphinx Cinema

Address: 1 Gameat al-Diwal al-Arabiya Street
GPS: 30.060410, 31.207194
Year: 1965
Architect: Ali Sabit

Cairo was dotted with a dozen outdoor cinemas built in the 1950s and 1960s in locations such as Bab al-Louq, Roda Island, Sakakini, Heliopolis, and Nasr City, all of which have been demolished or are disused. The outdoor Sphinx Cinema accommodated over one thousand seats and was a popular site for theater performance as well as film screenings. Located at the entrance of Mohandiseen, the large roofless structure is square in plan with a boxy, multistory, rectangular volume on the west edge for the stage/screen and dressing rooms. The screen is framed within a series of concrete recesses, the outer one articulated in a pattern achieved with rectangular tiles with a three-dimensional design.

The entrance pavilion on the east wall houses ticket windows and concession stands, utilizing outdoor materials such as brick cladding for walls and cement-tile floors. The main seating area is sunken in the center of the building and is accessible by wide steps. Seats are arranged in three zones (right, left, and middle). The north and south concrete walls were designed as enclosures utilizing a modular design of breeze blocks and brick cladding. The cinema has been damaged by fire, and at the time of writing it is at risk of demolition.

121
Residential Building

Address: 26 Gameat al-Diwal al-Arabiya Street
GPS: 30.056729, 31.205570
Year: 1986
Architect: Farouk al-Gohary

The Metabolistic façade of this building is composed of interlocking modules; each is shaped like a wireframe hollow cube, with an obtuse corner. The tops of the cubes form part of the floor of the balconies above, while the bottoms form part of the ceiling of the balconies below. The result is a mesmerizing geometric basket-weave of concrete forms that give the only elevation of the building a pixelated three-dimensional quality.

In plan, the floor plates zigzag to create the continuous balconies across the width of the building. The U-shaped structure with adjoining buildings on either side allows for light and air to enter spaces from the front elevation and from the rear of the building. Gohary realized a similar façade design in the cylindrical Ibrahimi Building in Abu Dhabi.

City Central Premium Offices

Address: 24 Gezirat al-Arab Street
GPS: 30.054222, 31.198889
Year: 2017
Architects: Amr al-Refaei and Muhammad al-Baradei

The architects of MAAP Consultants are filling a gap in Cairo's architectural practice, as they specialize in repurposing and refitting existing buildings and unfinished structures, contrasting with the pervasive approach of demolish-and-rebuild. City Central entailed the transformation of a 1960s residential building of a typical typology found across Mohandiseen into an office building with floors rentable to various businesses. The building consists of a slightly recessed ground and first floor occupied by a store, followed by eight levels of offices. Each floor was originally divided into two unequally sized apartments and is now redesigned a single open-plan space by removing all internal non-structural walls. The top floor gives access to the roof terrace, with additional enclosed space pushed to the back.

The most prominent feature of the redesign, which was implemented in seven months, is the façade treatment, composed of a modular screen of steel chassis clad with local Trieste-style marble. The deep grid pattern of the window screens and vertical fins make the dynamic façade sit comfortably within the immediate context, without demolition of the existing structure, and implementing an entirely new design.

Residential Building

Address: 16 Lebanon Street
GPS: 30.055827, 31.197779
Year: 1980s
Architect: Unknown

This Brutalist eighteen-story apartment building is distinguished by its bold modular façade design, composed of two adjoining stacks of bulging balconies. Due to the narrow, deep plot size the width of the façade allows for two adjacent balconies, one for each apartment. Rather than the typical flat façade treatment common in Mohandiseen, its balconies are designed as extruded volumes slanted at the top and the bottom, creating a sharp edge along the railing height.

The edge can be softened with plants if maintained by the residents. The flat, black-marble-clad, double-height base of the building is occupied by a commercial space and the entrance lobby, followed by the stacked floors. After the first ten levels the remaining floors shrink in size, as each is set back to accommodate building-height regulations. The overall visual effect from street level is disorienting, but the balconies are shaded and retain complete privacy due to the extruded design of each unit.

Villa Shawky

Address: 20 Muhammad Kamel Morsi Street
GPS: 30.0507360, 31.2077980
Year: 1968
Architects: Salah Zeitoun and Mustafa Shawky

In the 1950s and 1960s the still-developing Mohandiseen and Dokki, as well as the expanded frontiers of Heliopolis, witnessed the rise of this residential typology idiosyncratically called the 'villa.' Despite their popular naming these buildings were essentially small-scale apartment buildings, typically of three floors, occupied by a single family, and without a garden. In many cases a main family apartment (usually the largest) is located on the ground or first floors, followed by smaller apartments on the upper floors for members of the family (siblings, grown children, or grandparents). The apartments are either linked by a shared stair or, in some cases, the family apartment is entered separately, with a second entrance serving the upper apartments.

Architect Mustafa Shawky designed this apartment-house along with Salah Zeitoun (the pair had worked together repeatedly) to accommodate a double-car garage on the ground floor, followed by three equally sized apartments. A fourth floor was added later and does not belong to the original design. The frontage of each apartment is divided into two-thirds for the living room and one-third for one of the two bedrooms. The front rooms are lit with a continuous strip of windows, with two glass doors to the balcony.

Shared shaded balconies across the width of the façade articulate the exterior with three smooth, white, concrete balcony walls contrasting in texture and color with the rough concrete of the main body of the building. The compact living area is designed as a single open space, with the bedrooms, kitchen, and bathroom enclosed.

Villa Badran

Address: 2 Sudan Street
GPS: 30.058679, 31.190430
Year: 1971
Architect: Gamal Bakry

Villa Badran can be considered the pinnacle of experimentation in organic forms in Cairene architecture. It was designed for a middle-class family on a plot of land along Sudan Street that was purchased in 1968 on the still-undeveloped edge of Mohandiseen. The house is a rebellious statement by Gamal Bakry against the mass adoption of diluted Modernist design idioms across the city, particularly, indistinguishable rectilinear forms. Instead he created a modest house, designed from the inside out, avoiding straight lines entirely (seeing that rectilinear spaces cause stress to the inhabitants), opting instead for organic forms and curvilinear lines. In this approach, the formalistic composition on the outside is a direct result and reflection of the spatial arrangements of the interior. The result is a series of interlocking bulbous forms that are only occasionally interrupted by shaded window openings and planted terraces. Despite its proximity to the street the house is entirely private.

While the original idea was to build an adobe house, practical and structural needs required the use of reinforced concrete, which was left exposed and only tinted with an earthy reddish color. The first floor of the two-story house is arranged into a private section including the office near the entrance hall followed by two bedrooms sharing a terrace. The public section includes a free-flowing space that bends slightly to create a distinctive dining room, living area, and salon. A circular fireplace is the heart of the living room, and all rooms have access to terraces with planted edges. The elliptical stairwell is located in the center of the house directly opposite the entrance hall, giving quick access to the second floor with the master bedroom and additional living space and terraces. Throughout the building, spaces are demarcated by slight changes in the floor levels, with steps up or down. This subtle shift in the floor plane is mimicked along the roofline, creating clerestory windows that provide indirect sunlight into otherwise darkened spaces.

The house was sold by the original family and transformed into a currently poorly kept restaurant, which led to the demolition of the bedrooms on the ground floor, the addition of new boxy spaces to accommodate the new function of the building, and the defacement of the original exterior finish.

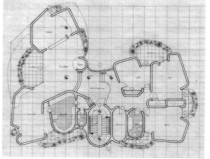

Mohandiseen

IMBABA

Façade detail of the original workers' housing in Imbaba, built in 1950.

Imbaba

Imbaba was a small village west of the Nile, whose accessible location near Cairo after the construction of the Imbaba Bridge in 1924 attracted industrialists to establish factories in the area. The Anglo-Egyptian Motor Company opened its industrial facility there in 1937, followed by others such as the Shurbagi Textiles factory. Imbaba also hosted a number of brick factories, supplying the city with the fundamental construction material. The outbreak of the Second World War stalled efforts to urbanize the area, but in 1947 a plan by Ali al-Meligi Masoud proposed transforming the entire area into housing blocks. Part of this plan was later implemented as the Workers' City: the increased number of workers, and their low wages, necessitated the establishment of worker-housing settlements for the area's first formal residents, and a first phase, begun on 1.4 km² of land in 1946, was completed in 1950. Egyptian architects had floated plans for workers' housing since the 1920s; for example, Muhammad Mahmud's 1929 plan for housing in Sayeda Zeinab proposed attached townhouses. The topic was hotly debated after the end of the Second World War, as architects such as Mahmoud Riad made the case that unless the state and factory owners invested in housing for employees, who were unable to afford standard rents, they would proceed to build informally, which would be seen as a detriment to the city.

A few industrial facilities remain in Imbaba, such as the Amiriya Printing Press (#127), and since the 1960s the area has densified and grown informally to the north and west, maintaining its identity as a working-class district.

Imbaba Bridge

GPS: 30.076113, 31.223035
Year: 1924
Architect: Baume-Marpent

The first Imbaba Bridge over the Nile was installed in 1890, with a single rail crossing. The current iteration of the bridge was completed in 1924 by the Belgian firm Baume-Marpent to allow train, vehicular, and pedestrian crossing. Construction started in 1913 but was halted due to the outbreak of the First World War. It is composed of seven equal-sized steel-truss sections resting on piers. The second truss section from the west was designed to swing, powered by electricity, in order to allow for boat passage, though this facility no longer functions. In section, the bridge allows for train passage in the center, flanked by the two directions of vehicular traffic, with two additional walkways above for pedestrian and bicycle traffic. Evenly spaced curved trusses carry the pedestrian platforms above the roadways, partially enclosing the road as a tunnel. Four steel stairs connect the pedestrian paths to street level, two on each side of the Nile. The design of the bridge combines purely structural elements with ornamental ones, particularly at the two ends.

New Amiriya Printing Press

Address: Corniche al-Nil
GPS: 30.077252, 31.223163
Year: 1973
Architects: Ahmed Charmi, Ali Labib Gabr

The successor of the historic Bulaq Printing Press, established in 1821, is the Amiriya Press, the largest print house in the Middle East. The mammoth building occupies a 35,000m² plot with a total of 70,000m² of building space. It was commissioned in 1956; however, due to several financial and technical setbacks it was not completed until 1973. Built along the Nile in Imbaba's industrial zone, the building is composed of two main elements: an L-shaped structure along the outer corner, landmarked with a soaring tower, and a two-story factory space occupying the remainder of the large rectangular plot. The L-shaped block is six stories high along the Nile side and five stories on the south side. The factory space is designed with a grid of columns supporting the sawtooth roof. In addition to printing facilities, the building houses offices for administration, editors, technicians, computer labs, scanning rooms, and other facilities, as well as loading docks, a cafeteria, and a mosque. The exterior is simply designed with strip windows, and the building's main vertical circulation is contained in the tower at the corner.

Workers' City

Address: Madinat al-Ummal
GPS: 30.079214, 31.217385
Year: 1950
Architect: Ali al-Meligi Masoud

The first phase of Masoud's plan was completed in 1950 and consisted of 1,106 units, rented to workers with lifelong contracts at a low rate of around LE2 per month paid only for the first twenty years. Wages for workers at the time ranged between LE7 and LE15 a month. The project was organized with a grid of numbered streets and blocks, dotted with green areas, with a service block in the center for schools, a market, and medical facilities. Each block consisted of two rows of housing with a strip of green space in between. Seventy-five percent of the units consisted of two attached single-family town houses, with living space on the ground floor (with access to a garden) and two bedrooms on the upper floor.

Another typology consisted of two-story horizontal blocks with six two-room apartments. The cubic concrete structures were faced with stone, and stairs were placed in a slightly protruding volume topped with a concrete gabled roof. Implementation of Masoud's plan for six thousand units was interrupted by the sudden change of government in 1952. Users modified most of the units over the years by adding floors, extending into the gardens, or replacing the units entirely. Few of the original units remain.

Imbaba

Tahrir City

Address: al-Tayar Fekry Zaher Street
GPS: 30.083563, 31.218392
Year: 1958
Architect: Unknown

Rather than continue building Masoud's Workers' City, in 1954 the state initiated a new housing project on the site of its unrealized second phase. The urban pattern of this new development was centered on Block 37, with schools and services. The new housing model was replicated in Helwan and Helmiyat al-Zatoun, with a total of four thousand units completed by 1958, catering to workers and low-wage government employees. The model, marketed by the state as "villas for workers," consisted of compact attached duplex units built in rows, with shared green areas. Each unit, entered directly from the street, consists of a small living space and kitchen on the ground floor, a compact stair leading to a bathroom on the intermediate level, and two bedrooms with balconies on the upper floor. The cubic concrete units were constructed economically with no embellishment and only essential finishes. The buildings were faced with red brick or stucco.

Giza Park

Address: al-Matar Street
GPS: 30.076003, 31.191556
Year: 2013
Architects: Sites International

The site of the former Imbaba pilot-training airport, closed in 2002 due to urban encroachment, was developed into housing blocks and a 15-hectare park. After the success of al-Azhar Park (2004, #7), its designers were given the tender to develop a green space here. The concept of a rural-themed park evolved to reflect the area's former agricultural landscape before its urbanization in the 1950s. Geometrically defined entrance plazas give way to meandering lines of landscaping. Features such as pigeon towers, waterwheels, footbridges, and traditional countryside seating, in place of typical benches, are placed throughout the park to assert the rural theme. Structures on the site are designed using vernacular vocabularies, materials, and finishes. Egypt's diverse ecological conditions are represented within the park: the flat site was given topographical variety with hills, valleys, and water features. A stream originating at the entrance represents the Nile. There is also a secluded oasis section with palm groves, as well as recreated agricultural fields.

ZAMALEK

Sculpture by artist Fathy Mahmoud on the façade of the Zamalek Tower, designed by architect Sayed Karim. The two collaborated on several buildings in the late 1940s and early 1950s.

Zamalek

By 1866 the construction of the Ismailiya Canal, along with embankment reinforcements in central Cairo, made Zamalek on the island of Gezira (formerly Bulaq Island) flood-free. Well into the nineteenth century the island was largely deserted, with the exception of the extant palace built in 1868 by Khedive Ismail (now the centerpiece of the Marriott Hotel) and a retreat built by Muhammad Ali in 1830 (now demolished). Early developments on the island include the construction of Qasr al-Nil Bridge in 1871, the founding of Gezira Sports Club in 1886, and the establishment of the Agricultural Exhibitions in 1898. In 1912, the completion of Bulaq Bridge, designed by William Scherzer and connecting Bulaq and Zamalek, accelerated the development of a residential district in the northern half of the island. Starting in the 1920s, a growing number of villas and apartment blocks built in a range of styles populated the area. Large apartment buildings increasingly crept into the nascent district, particularly during the building boom following the end of the Second World War.

Having stabilized as a leafy, elite district in the center of the city, Zamalek saw skyrocketing real-estate prices, which spelled disaster for many of its earlier small-scale residences. From the 1970s, many such houses, including that of the renowned Egyptian singer Umm Kulthoum (#146), were demolished as high-rise, high-end apartment blocks devoured large parts of the district.

Exhibition Grounds
(now the Opera Grounds)

Address: Tahrir Street, Gezira
GPS: 30.04237, 31.22436
Year: 1936–49
Architects: Mustafa Fahmy, Ahmed Charmi, Ali Labib Gabr, Hassan and Mustafa Shafie.

The main entrance to the site is the 1949 Neo-Moorish gate overlooking Saad Zaghloul Square. Another, Art Deco, circular gateway with a soaring tower and flagpoles from 1936 overlooks Galaa Square toward Dokki. The site is currently home to Cairo's Opera House and Museum of Modern Art, but before it was transformed into an arts and culture complex it was the city's fair grounds, with the first agricultural exhibition held here in 1898. From 1926 until the 1960s, when new fair grounds were built in Nasr City, the site hosted the country's agricultural–industrial exhibitions, held to showcase Egypt's economic development. During this period the site witnessed the construction of numerous short-lived buildings and gateways.

Major buildings that once stood here were the Cotton Palace and the Hall of Industries. Architect Mustafa Fahmy gave the site its current shape as part of a plan completed in time for the 1936 exhibition. Buildings such as the Grand Palais and Petit Palais at the western corner of the site were also completed in 1936. These two buildings are articulated with staggered towering elements facing the entrance to the site from this side. The design combines Modernist and Art Deco features with the addition of elements from Fahmy's repertoire of reinterpreted Islamic vocabularies. The Grand Palais, designed by Hassan and Mustafa Shafie, was briefly transformed into the Museum of Egyptian Civilization; the letters of that name still faintly appear on the tower. The Eastern Hall, designed by Ali Labib

Gabr and Ahmed Charmi, was refurbished as the Museum of Modern Art in 1991. This rectangular building consists of a double-height central hall flanked by two wings, with galleries on two floors. Other reused buildings include the Aboud Pasha Exhibition Hall, currently the Music Library. Notable losses include the Banque Misr Hall, a triangular industrial concrete-and-glass building that stood on the site of today's Palace of the Arts.[61]

Opera House

Address: Tahrir Street, Gezira
GPS: 30.04237, 31.22436
Year: 1988
Architect: Nikken Sekkei Ltd.

Cairo's original nineteenth-century opera house was engulfed in flames in 1971, devastating the city's musicians and performing artists. Envisioned as the centerpiece of an arts district in the city's former fair grounds, the new Opera was built by the Government of Japan as a development project. The building hosts three performing spaces aligned along a central axis: a large theater with 1,300 seats, a small theater with five hundred seats, and an open-air stage with a six-hundred-seat capacity. The symmetrical building is composed of a progression of cubic volumes culminating in the 43-meter-high dome above the large stage. The massing of the structure directly reflects the building's various functions and spaces. In addition to the large dome, a smaller one is positioned above the square entrance hall. The hall is entered through a forecourt enclosed with a series of arches, a motif repeating throughout the design. Other programmatic functions include rehearsal rooms, a museum, a music library, classrooms, and lounges. The aesthetics of the building partly mimic Mustafa Fahmy's existing structures on the site. The resulting simplified Islamic architecture is apparent in the domes, arches, cubic volumes, and geometric arrangements of the functions.

Mahmoud Mukhtar Museum

Address: 5 Tahrir Street, Hurriya Garden
GPS: 30.040511, 31.222995
Year: 1962
Architect: Ramses Wissa Wassef

Egyptian feminist Huda Shaarawi spearheaded the effort to create a museum dedicated to sculptor Mahmoud Mukhtar after his death in 1934, and a collection of his works was gathered. The eight-room museum was envisioned as a meditation on light, with spaces designed especially for certain sculptures to be illuminated naturally, but this aspect of the building has been eliminated, as subsequent renovations opted for artificial lighting in all galleries.

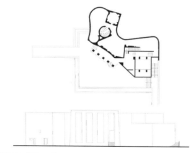
Plan and Elevation

The museum is reached by a footbridge, as the level of Hurriya Garden sinks below street level. The architect took advantage of the topography by creating a two-story building entered from the top floor. In plan the museum has two contrasting sides: the front, austere and rectilinear; the back, undulating with several curves. The building is fronted with a monumental portico of five square pillars, recalling ancient temples. The smooth marble cladding on the pillars contrasts with the textured cladding on the rest of the concrete structure. Rather than being centered, the entrance is placed between the first and second pillars on the right as one approaches the building. Inside, a double-height space gives way to a series of intimate rooms displaying works in bronze, marble, stone, and plaster. A small stair leads to the lower floor with additional display spaces as well as the grave of the artist, giving the museum a second function as a mausoleum.

1952 Revolution Museum

(unfinished)

Address: Montazah al-Giza
GPS: 30.039731, 31.225734
Year: 1951–2009
Architect: Ahmed Mito

It was from this building that the Free Officers broadcast the overthrow of the Egyptian monarchy in 1952. Originally built in 1951 by the palace to function as a rest house and a dock for the royal yacht, the building was never used for its original purpose, due to the abrupt end of the reign of King Farouk. Subsequently, the officers used it as their Revolutionary Command Center.

The original two-story building is square in plan with an open courtyard in the center. Asymmetry is achieved by incorporating an attached mosque with a minaret at the northeast corner. In 2003 construction work commenced to implement designs by Ahmed Mito to transform the building into a museum. The renovation saw the construction of steel ribs in the shape of a bird taking flight, representing the Eagle of the Republic, above the roof of the otherwise Neo-Classical edifice.

135

Cairo Tower

Address: al-Burg Street
GPS: 30.046008, 31.224286
Year: 1961
Architects: Naoum Shebib, Shams al-Din Ashraf

Rising 48 meters higher than the Great Pyramid, the 187-meter-tall Cairo Tower is the single most visible and recognizable architectural symbol of post-1952 Egypt. It was commissioned in 1954 as a monument to the new republic. Shebib's structural-engineering talents were unleashed, as he designed a building composed of three intricately connected parts: skin, skeleton, and core. A slender, soaring core with the elevator and stairs rises to the top, supported by a skeletal structure composed of four reinforced-concrete columns connected horizontally at intervals by concrete rings, forming the body of the building. The outer skin is a concrete latticework with diamond shapes that become larger as the pattern moves up, giving the structure the appearance of lightness and upward movement. A capsule at the top of the tower contains a restaurant, a café, and an observation deck. The latticework skin opens up at the base of the capsule, mimicking the appearance of the pointed petals of a blooming lotus flower.

Construction was halted due to the 1956 war and resumed in 1959, leading to the building's inauguration in 1961. The observation deck at the top provides panoramic views over Cairo. A revolving restaurant located below the deck is constructed with a floor plate that rotates slowly around the central core on steel wheels. A needle antenna designed as a single unit crowns the structure. The cylindrical tower rises above a cubic volume at the base, where the entry hall, elevator access, waiting room, and administration are located. A large brass sculpture of the Republican Eagle (with the two stars representing the brief union between Syria and Egypt) adorns the façade of the cubic volume. In the circular hall surrounding the elevator is a fine Modernist mosaic mural depicting folkloric representations of the various cultural groups within the Republic. The exterior of the building's latticework skin is covered with eight million yellow, brown, and white mosaic tiles. Between 2007 and 2014 the building was given a face-lift, including a new exterior lighting system, revamped entry hall, and the construction of additional service spaces and emergency stairs.

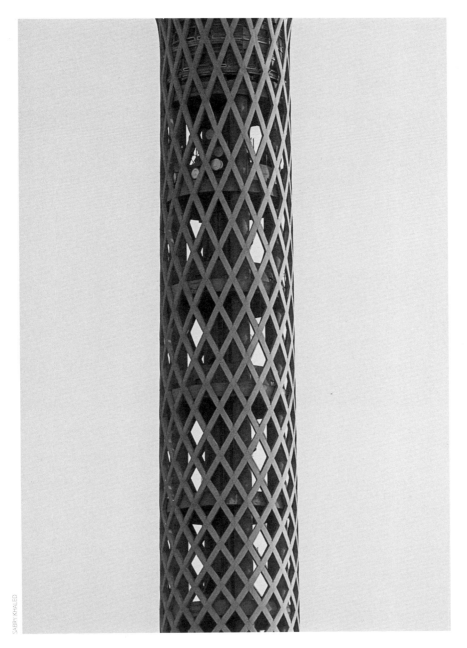

Zamalek

Nabil Amr Ibrahim Palace

Address: 16 Gezira Street
GPS: 30.056433, 31.223075
Year: 1923
Architect: Garo Balyan

This eclectic Neo-Islamic building was erected as a private residence for Prince Nabil Amr Ibrahim. The house is square in plan with an entrance portico to the south composed of four slender marble columns carrying three arches, topped by a wooden awning. The portal leads to a double-height rectangular hall with a balcony gallery around its perimeter and a dome above the center. Thematic rooms are arranged on two floors, including a Persian room. The house fuses Islamic architectural elements and decorative motifs from various periods and locations. The exterior of the building is decorated with Neo-Fatimid and Neo-Mamluk elements, such as the windows that flank the entrance. A crenellated parapet, usually found in historic religious architecture, crowns the house. In 1999 the palace was reopened as the Museum of Islamic Ceramics, with the basement transformed into a temporary exhibition space.

All Saints Cathedral

Address: 5 Michel Lutfallah Street
GPS: 30.057995, 31.223830
Year: 1988
Architects: Awad Kamel Fahmy, Selim Kamel Fahmy

The previous All Saints Cathedral, designed by British architect Adrian Gilbert Scott and completed in 1938 behind the Egyptian Museum, was demolished in 1978 to make way for the construction of the October Bridge. The Egyptian government donated a plot of land in Zamalek for the construction of the new church. The funnel-like cathedral sits on a podium and is organized around an axial cross-shaped plan, with an organ occupying the mezzanine above the main entrance. A portico composed of pilotis supporting diamond-shaped concrete shading modules distinguishes the front elevation. Folding walls on the four axes lead up to three diamonds above each of the four main walls of the church. The concrete diamond shapes are transitional elements between the folded walls below and the sculptural roof above.

The folded ceiling funnels up, with the highest point—directly over the center of the cross plan—culminating in a shallow dome. On the exterior the folds terminate in pointed shapes, making the entire roof structure resemble a lotus flower. A freestanding Brutalist tapering bell tower is built in the back, at the east corner of the building near the apse.

Forte Tower
(unfinished)

Address: 1 Hassan Sabry Street
GPS: 30.055853, 31.220121
Year: 1976
Architect: Gamal Bakry

At 166 meters, the unfinished Forte Tower is the tallest building in Egypt. The cylindrical 45-story structure was designed to include a 450-room hotel, stores, restaurants, and a nightclub. Circular hallways giving access to rooms arranged around the perimeter with views over the city surround a central circulation core. The tower does not express distinctive skyscraper elements such as base, shaft, and crown. A concrete cantilevered awning extends above the undersized entrance on the raised ground floor, which is reached by steps that lead to a double-height entrance lobby. The partially finished exterior is composed of modular window units. The uniformity of the exterior is broken by a floor halfway up the structure, possibly designed for a restaurant and marked by large semicircular arches.

During implementation the appearance of the tower departed from Bakry's original design. Political favoritism and corruption stalled the project after the transition from Sadat to Mubarak. Subsequent protest by Zamalek residents over the building's size, location, and its lack of sufficient parking put the project on hold indefinitely.

Islamic Congress Secretariat
(proposed)

Address: 11 Hasan Sabri Street
GPS: 30.058535, 31.221510
Year: 1957
Architect: Sayed Karim

The proposed secretariat building for the Islamic Congress had a footprint of 3,000m² situated in the garden of the villa that functioned as the organization's head office. The design was composed of three distinctive parts: a two-story podium for administration, reception, exhibition hall, and public areas; a six-story office block, placed above the podium along the main street; and a general-assembly 2,500-seat auditorium, located at the back of the site. The building's program would have included other facilities such as a public library and archives in the lower part of the structure and a social club with a restaurant for delegates, with a roof garden.⁶²

Rodrigue Flats

Address: al-Aziz Othman Street
GPS: 30.058424, 31.219875
Year: 1945
Architect: Henri Frisco

The construction contract for this building was signed on the eve of the outbreak of the Second World War, and work continued despite the rise in building-material costs during the conflict. The L-shaped corner building consists of a private residence on the entire first floor, followed by three identical floors, each with two apartments. The ground floor contains the entrance, garages, and service spaces. The corner of the building, where the entrance is located, is articulated as a cylindrical volume containing the circular main staircase, set within a solid concave volume giving way to the two side wings. The elevation of the building is symmetrically designed, with corner windows and long balconies with rounded corners accessed from living spaces, followed by a vertical arrangement of half-circular balconies for the bedrooms. The entry sequence starts with a double stair, with one elevator to the right. The owner's apartment on the first floor contains two separate sleeping wings at the extremities of the L-plan, with living spaces at the corner, including a living room and sitting room with access to a large terrace overlooking the large garden in the back, a dining room, breakfast room, and office, as well as a smoking room.[63]

Lebon Building

Address: 19 Gabalaya Street
GPS: 30.05831, 31.21725
Year: 1950
Architect: Antoine Selim Nahas

This large, twelve-story residential block is carved into two connected sections, with two separate entrances reached via a spacious outdoor passage on the raised ground floor. Wide steps from the street reach the lobby level, where the space between the two entrances to the right and left is supported by robust pilotis, leading toward the garden at the back of the building. The two sections that comprise the structure are unequal in size, the larger section containing four apartments of five to seven rooms per floor, the smaller section containing three apartments of four to five rooms per floor. Apartments begin at the third level, as the basement and first two stories form the base of the building, with service spaces, garage, and mechanical rooms. The recessed fourteenth floor contains three large apartments with roof gardens. The building's entry sequence is remarkable: the raised entrance level is entirely open yet separate from the street; from there the glazed portal walls lead to a circular marble-clad lobby, reached by a few steps, which leads to the rectangular elevator lobby and the stairs. The generously designed circulation system comprises spacious hallways and landing lobbies, in addition to the large stairwell. Four air shafts are evenly located in the core of the building to provide ventilation to all the service spaces and service stairs to the kitchens. All living spaces are arranged along the perimeter overlooking the Nile, with windows and balconies in all rooms. The concrete exterior is muted, with an emphasis on horizontality created by the long, shaded balconies carved out of the mass of the building.

Henri and Georges Boinet Building

Address: 5 Shagarat al-Durr Street
GPS: 30.05958, 31.21765
Year: 1934
Architect: Charles Ayrout

Charles Ayrout's bold and consistent style is exemplified in this residential block. The building occupies half the 2,000m^2 plot, with the remaining area dedicated to a lush garden. The building was originally divided into two sections: a five-story block along the street, each floor housing three apartments, ranging in size from three to five rooms; and a second, three-story, conjoined block containing a single large apartment on each floor. Two 'villas' with roof gardens are located at the top of the taller block. Servant rooms are unconventionally placed in the mezzanine level above the ground floor, to free the roof for the use of the villas. The roof of the lower section of the building was utilized as a playground for children.

Apartments are spaciously designed, with separate reception and private wings. Each apartment is exposed to three sides, maximizing natural light and ventilation. A notable feature is the main staircase, which functions as a link between the structure's lower and taller blocks. Typical of Ayrout's architecture, the building transforms depending on which part is being viewed. The main elevation is symmetrical, with deeply recessed balconies shielded behind a grid of sixteen equally-sized openings. The two corners of the block rise taller and are articulated with porthole windows and sharp corner windows. A series of arched openings punctuates the parapet containing the roof terraces of the villas. Industrial windows are utilized throughout the building.[64]

Ali Labib Gabr Building

Address: 22 Ibn Zinki Street
GPS: 30.06052, 31.21696
Year: 1951
Architect: Ali Labib Gabr

With a triangular footprint, this building consists of a ground floor followed by six identical floors of apartments, with a 'villa' and roof garden designed as the residence of the architect at the top. In addition to the general and service entrances, a third entrance along with a *porte cochere* is accessible only to the architect and his family to reach the villa. The ground floor hosts the garage, service rooms, and the spacious, marble-clad, circular elevator hall near the center. Typical floors include four apartments ranging in size between six and seven rooms. The villa on the seventh and eighth floors was originally designed with an office, sitting room, living room, and four bedrooms, but was later modified to add rooms. The design of the exterior is understated, with an emphasis on horizontality created by the long balconies. The two corners on the Nile side are chamfered. The architect's villa is located at the north corner of the building, with a view toward Gabr's earlier work, the villa of Umm Kulthoum, now demolished.

Zamalek Tower
(Wahbi Mousa Soliman Building)

Address: 18 Shagarat al-Durr Street
GPS: 30.061309, 31.218287
Year: 1953
Architect: Sayed Karim

Standing on a prominent 850m² corner site, this 65-meter-high Brutalist structure stood out in its low-rise, tree-lined context when it was built. The eighteen-story building contains thirty-six single-floor apartments and twenty duplexes, in addition to eight stores on the ground floor facing the thoroughfare of 26 July Street and a basement-level garage. Two high-speed elevators and one furniture elevator serve the residents, in addition to two service stairs leading directly to the kitchens. There are two typical floor plans, alternating for the first twelve floors of the building. The first, on the odd-numbered floors, contains three apartments, each with four rooms (for living spaces), as well as two bedrooms. In addition, these floors contain the living/lower floors of two duplexes. The second typical plan, on the even-numbered floors, contains three apartments similar to the ones on odd floors, as well as the upper floors of the two duplexes, with their bedrooms and private quarters. All kitchens and bathrooms are arranged around air shafts for ventilation and for service access, and to separate wet from dry areas in the building. Six setback floors at the top contain a total of seven duplexes and three apartments with terraces, roof gardens, and commanding views over the city.

Concrete is used extensively throughout, from the skeletal structure to external details and interior finishes. Other building materials include red brick and sandstone, used for walls. The tower's two prime elevations are treated according to sun exposure and function. *Brise soleil*, in the form of a concrete screen, fronts the windows on the east façade. A column of small balconies, designed with an extruded, slightly curved floor, are placed every other floor (corresponding with the duplexes) at the southern end of the east façade. Nearly all the fenestrations are designed in modular sections that fold on hinges, to open entirely with no obstruction, sliding on brass rails. Interior finishes include parquet floors, oak doors, and oak flooring on the concrete steps inside the duplexes. Marble floors cover the building's entrance hall and all hallways.

The entrance façade features a large sculpture by artist Fathy Mahmoud, one of several collaborations with architect Sayed Karim. The Art Deco winged muscular figure appears in midflight, with a soaring tower in the background.[65]

Zamalek

Dar al-Hana
(Madame Khayyat Building)

Address: 5 al-Malek al-Afdal
GPS: 30.063698, 31.217206
Year: 1938
Architect: Max Edrei

This three-story structure is entered at the corner, which is slightly concave. Above the entrance is an Art Deco relief sculpture of a reclining woman, and above that a vertical panel of windows illuminating the marble-clad staircase rising with the elevator in its core.

The verticality of this corner element, reflecting the vertical movement behind it, contrasts with the horizontality of the rest of the frontage. The building's three floors are articulated with three horizontal stripes matching the height of the uniformly sized windows punctuating the façade. The wafer-thin roofline cantilevers slightly, giving the structure its Modernist look. The floor slabs partially protrude from the flat façade to create narrow balconies lined with minimally designed railings of thin steel, further extenuating the horizontality of the design.

Every floor contains three apartments—right, left, and center—each designed with total separation between living and private quarters. Two additional sunken apartments are accessed directly from the street, each with a small outdoor area. All rooms are designed with generous, airy volumes. Amenities include storage spaces in the basement, laundry rooms on the roof, direct access to kitchens for service staff, central heating, and garages.[66]

Villa Umm Kulthoum

(demolished)

Address: 5 Abu al-Feda Street
GPS: 30.064404, 31.215880
Year: 1936
Architect: Ali Labib Gabr

Built on a triangular site surrounded by three streets and overlooking the Nile, the two-story villa featured a taller, rounded corner with ample balconies, outdoor space, and a large garden. Built for the famous diva, the house was modest in scale and modern in style. The plastered finish of the structure concealed the brick masonry and reinforced-concrete supports. Its design featured streamlined, modern curves and rounded corners. Deep balconies and cantilevered elements above windows shaded the interior and reduced the building's temperature.

The first floor housed the reception and public areas, while the second contained the private quarters, including a master bedroom suite, three additional bedrooms, and a sitting room. The architect designed the interior and carefully selected the furniture, combining Modernist, Art Deco, and traditional pieces. The floors of the public areas were covered with Carrara marble, leading to the main staircase. Service areas, including a separate service stair, were tucked away behind the main staircase. Parquet floors were used in all private areas.

The singer lived in the house until her death in 1975. Despite initial intentions to turn it into a museum, the building was demolished in 1982. An identical copy was built in Baghdad by an Iraqi businessman in the 1950s. Ironically, the Iraqi version withstood war and is still in use, while the Cairo original is long gone.[67]

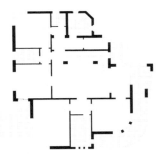

First Floor Plan

Virgin Mary Church
(al-Maraashli Church)

Address: 6 Muhammad al-Maraashli St.
GPS: 30.06685, 31.21891
Year: 1959
Architect: Ramses Wissa Wassef

This reinforced-concrete church is the crystallization of Wissa Wassef's approach to creating a Modernist vernacular language. The main façade is monumental, with two sets of steps leading to the entrance level. The seemingly simple elevation is designed as a composition of elements layered from back to front as follows: a flat, square plane the width of the church is fronted by a vertical, rectangular plane as tall as the church at the center; a narrow, pointed arch marks the blue mosaic interior of the semicircular niche at the top of the vertical plane; inserted into the niche is a square vestibule topped by a small dome; the vestibule is articulated with two columns supporting a pointed arch leading to the door.

The church is oriented east–west and is raised on a podium hosting service and activity rooms. The floor plan is an open rectangle, while the ceiling echoes elements of a classic church configuration: central nave, side aisles, and transept. The ceiling is highest in the center and steps down at the sides. Two tall, rounded protrusions against the east wall recall the transept. The shape of the roof is determined by the size and curvature of the five arched ribs that support the building, which are visible on the outside. The ribs, or pillars, are embedded into the church's north and south outer walls. Tall, rectangular stained-glass windows topped by small, arched windows are placed between the ribs. Additional light enters from the clerestory windows punctuating the taller central section of the church. A large dome, supported by the east wall and two pillars, marks the holiest part of the church, the semicircular apse. The square bell-tower placed south of the building is composed of three stepped-back sections, with tapered corners at each transition. A small pavilion connects the bell tower to the body of the church and contains the baptistery and administration offices.

Main Floor Plan

Sedky Pasha Building

Address: 17 Aziz Abaza Street
GPS: 30.062747, 31.223924
Year: 1947
Architect: Albert Zananiri

The Sedky Pasha Building is in a prestigious location on the east bank of Zamalek, overlooking the Nile to the east and a small square to the west. It has a footprint of 1,200m^2 and houses the office of Sedky Pasha (prime minister of Egypt 1930–33 and again in 1946), located on the ground floor. The main entrance is in the south façade, reached by a small set of steps, flanked by two sets of three pilotis. In terms of architectural form, the structure is austere, minimal, and marked by a slight curve on the west façade that corresponds with the curve of the street. Deep balconies on the building's typical six floors articulate the corners of the structure. Each floor contains four large apartments, ranging from five to seven rooms and including service quarters separated from the rest of the living space. Four 'villas' occupy the seventh and eighth floors. The reinforced-concrete structure was furnished with imported marbles and all amenities such as hot water and heating.[68]

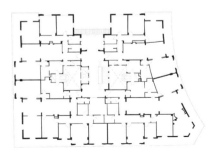

Typical Floor Plan

SHUBRA

Stairs at the Don Bosco Italian Technical Institute.

Shubra

Shubra is a legendary area in northern Cairo defined by the Nile to the west, the train tracks heading to the Delta to the east, the Ismailiya Canal to the north, and Bulaq to the south. In the nineteenth century, transformation of the area from a small village and agricultural hinterland to an urban settlement was spurred by the 1847 construction of the northward sycomore-lined Shubra road leading to the 1808 palace and gardens of Muhammad Ali Pasha. Development in the area increased with the establishment of Bulaq as an industrial center in the 1830s and the construction of the train station in 1856 at the start of the Shubra road. Shortly after 1900, tramlines were extended into Shubra, reaching four lines by 1912. Increased accessibility, in addition to the appearance of several tobacco factories, and the investment of private companies to develop the area quickly transformed this region in northern Cairo into a proper working-class suburb with pockets of elite presence in the form of mansions and large apartment blocks. Several communities concentrated in the area, including Italian immigrants, Greeks, and Armenians, as well as a sizable Jewish community. Shubra today boasts one of the largest concentrations of Coptic Christians in Cairo, with several important churches.

In terms of urban development, it exhibits a patchwork of patterns triggered by private companies, government housing, incremental sale and urbanization of previously agricultural land, and the demolition of mansions that were replaced by public schools or various forms of housing. Along Shubra Street are some large apartment blocks from the 1920s to the 1950s that match the grandeur of their Downtown counterparts.

149

Corniche al-Nil Towers

Address: 97 Corniche al-Nil
GPS: 30.078101, 31.230177
Year: 1992
Architect: Development and Popular Housing Company

This project was initially envisioned as a large dynamic volume composed of eleven attached recessing and protruding towers of varying heights rising above a three-story podium. Published elevation drawings show the tallest section of the building rising to twenty-four stories, while the staggering narrow tower sections share five circulation cores distributed across the site, and the shortest section of the block consistsing of eight residential floors above the podium, which in this section was designed to house a large cinema hall.

The current building, however, is a less ambitious version of the original design. The eighteen-story structure still follows the logic of the original design—with a three-story commercial podium giving way to an apartment tower divided into six blocks, each with a separate entrance and circulation core, with a maximum of fourteen floors of apartments. The podium includes commercial spaces, a parking garage, and office spaces. A total of 196 housing units, ranging between two and four bedrooms, comprise the complex. The apartments were developed as middle-income units within a much larger site that includes a dozen low-rise, low-income housing blocks behind Corniche al-Nil Towers. Due to the site's location along the Nile, the government-owned Development and Popular Housing Company decided to benefit from the vistas by building more profitable units in a high-rise structure, separate from the more affordable units at the back that are at the core of the company's mandate.

Rod al-Farag Market

Address: al-Khalifa al-Mutawakkel Street
GPS: 30.074000, 31.233895
Year: 1947
Architect: Unknown

Constructed in 1947 as Cairo's wholesale market, primarily for fruits and vegetables, the current building was only the gateway into a series of single-story rows of stalls in what is today Rod al-Farag Park. For five decades after its construction the market fulfilled its role, becoming a key feature in the city's commercial life and attracting farmers from around the Delta and Upper Egypt to sell their produce to Cairo's thrifty buyers and suppliers to the city's markets elsewhere. In 1996 the market was decommissioned and moved to Ubour on the outskirts of the capital, in an effort to gentrify the surrounding area and to reduce congestion. The rows of stalls were demolished and the main building was repurposed as a cultural facility for the district. The main building, which formed the entryway into the market beyond and housed its administration, is all that remains of the original complex. It is located on the corner of the site, and it arcs to follow the traffic circle it overlooks. The tripartite concrete and brick structure is composed of a triple-height gateway in the central section dominated by a large pointed arch, flanked by two equally sized, slightly shorter wings. The wings are each composed of a double-height ground floor topped by a single-story upper level. The ground floors of the wings are each articulated by four large pointed-arch windows, each topped by three small pointed windows on the upper floor. The exterior is clad in red brick, with a slightly protruding parapet further articulated with roof tiles. The central section of the building is extended further in height, with an added cornice along its roofline.

Don Bosco Italian Technical Institute

Address: 2 Abd al-Qader Taha Street
GPS: 30.082751, 31.237258
Year: 1926
Architect: Domenico Limongelli

Named after a nineteenth-century monk, Don Bosco is an Italian technical and vocational high school established in 1926, initially to educate lower-middle-class Italian youth. As the community dwindled in numbers the school continued to provide education to Egyptians. It grants graduates certificates recognized by the Italian government, the European Union, and the Egyptian Ministry of Education.

The 12,000m² rectangular site is occupied by a playing field surrounded by a three-story perimeter building on three sides, which includes an Italianate chapel on the south corner. The ground floor is slightly sunken below street level while the first floor, the school's main level, is reached by a set of steps from the street. The section of the building along Gisr al-Bahr Street is the longest at 142 meters, and is the most prominent part of the complex. The reinforced-concrete building is distinguished by its industrial red-brick exterior façade articulated by tall, evenly spaced shuttered windows that allow direct sunlight into the workshops on the ground floor and classrooms on the first and second floors. In contrast to the exterior façades, the interior ones overlooking the playing field are porous, with wide, shaded outdoor hallways leading to the various cross-ventilated educational spaces designed with high ceilings. The north part of the school was given a facelift in recent decades, which entailed adding a fourth floor as well as redesigning this section of the façade overlooking the playing field. The

redesigned facade is articulated with a concrete grid that results from the modular placement of pilotis intersecting with horizontal shading elements that drop below ceiling level. The corner structure connecting the 1926 building with the renovated section houses the main vertical circulation, with another spiraling stair placed in the center of the long section of the building.

Shubra

Khazindara Mosque

Address: Shubra Street
GPS: 30.082779, 31.245541
Year: 1927
Architect: Awqaf Administration

The name of this mosque is gendered female after its patron, whose identity is unconfirmed but is said to be Princess Khadiga Hanim, daughter of Muhammad Raghib Agha. The unusual building plan comprises three distinct functions (a school, a mosque, and a charitable fountain), each designed as a semi-independent structure connected by a façade envelope. At the center of the main elevation is a concave, semi-circular, outdoor space that acts as a transitional zone between the street and the interior. A single minaret is placed at the center of the concave elevation, to the right of which is the entrance to the mosque. The square, triple-height prayer hall is supported by sixteen marble columns arranged in a grid, topped by black-and-white *ablaq* arches with the four central pillars extended further up to support a dome in the center of the timber ceiling. The mosque is oriented diagonally in relation to Shubra Street so that the *mihrab* opposite the entrance faces Mecca. The double-height domed sabil is triangular in plan and is separated from the prayer hall by an irregularly shaped space. The sabil faces the corner of the site, where such fountains are traditionally found at the intersection of two streets. The L-shaped school to the north is nearly a stand-alone structure, attached to the overall composition only by the skin of the building. The façade is designed with a variety of Neo-Mamluk elements. There is a certain theatricality to the façade, particularly at the entrance plaza, where it stands as a thin surface articulated with a careful, almost classical composition of windows, sometimes with open air in-between spaces behind them, as the mosque's volume is pulled back from the street edge.

Saint Teresa Church

Address: Shubra Street
GPS: 30.084935, 31.246048
Year: 1931
Architect: Milan Freudenreich

Located away from the street and oriented southwest to northeast, this eclectic church is designed with a basilica plan, with a wide nave topped by a high gabled roof and flanked by side aisles with lower ceilings. A large dome near the center of the building rests on semicircular arches and robust cross-shaped pillars. Eight columns with Coptic capitals are positioned around each pillar, two on each side, to further support the structure. Half-domes articulate the transept and the apse. The decorative program of the interior is rich with colorful mosaics of floral and geometric patterns and figurative representations, such as the angels on the pendentives and an unusual ceiling with six muscular angels at the main portal.

The exterior of the church was originally left undecorated; however, it is architecturally articulated with three long, narrow arches, the middle of which is the tallest, reaching toward the pinnacle of the gabled roof. The arches are carried on two clusters of four columns in the center of the entrance portico. The main elevation is flanked by two protruding square towers housing the vertical circulation to the balcony. The towers are topped by shallow domes covered with roof tiles. A lattice pattern articulates the tops of the towers just below the domes. The exterior is decorated with pink, green, blue, and purple mosaic tiles arranged in geometric patterns and crosses. It is likely the exterior decoration was done incrementally after the interior was given its decorative program, with funds raised after the completion of the structure with pledges from the community to the church. Marble plates inside the church carry the names of patrons who made pledges, including notable celebrities such as Abd al-Halim Hafez, Muhammad Abd al-Wahab, and Umm Kulthoum, along with numerous intellectuals and ordinary citizens of various religious backgrounds.

DAHER & ABBASIYA

The Syndicate of Applied Arts Tower, part of the 23 July Development in Abbasiya Square.

Daher & Abbasiya

The northern districts of Daher and Abbasiya include several neighborhoods, such as Sakakini and Ghamra, that mostly developed from the second half of the nineteenth century onward. Khedive Abbas Helmi I established Abbasiya by surveying and parceling out the land, some of it gifted to various princes and elites to build private residences. Several palaces were erected in the area, most famously Zaafarana Palace (1870), currently used as the administration building for Ain Shams University. The building of barracks in 1851, followed by several military schools in the 1860s and the military engineering school in 1866, gave the area its identity. The strong military infrastructure made Abbasiya the base for British soldiers after the occupation of 1882. The establishment of the first Cairo–Alexandria rail line in 1856 and the construction of the current train station in 1892 directly impacted the development of surrounding areas.

Daher evolved into a middle-class district with a strong Christian presence, evidenced by the many churches in the area, while working-class Abbasiya had a significant Jewish population, with several synagogues and Jewish schools.

Proposals for economic housing in Abbasiya in 1920 remained unrealized. Medical facilities serving various communities in Cairo were established in the area, including the Greek, Italian, French, Coptic, and Jewish hospitals. The main arteries of Abbasiya and Ramses streets are lined with some of the district's most prominent buildings, like Saint Mark's Cathedral. Abbasiya Square was redesigned in 1960, with residential and administrative towers overlooking the new campus of Ain Shams University, home to several Modernist structures such as the new Faculty of Engineering and its two identical Brutalist lecture-hall buildings (#163).

Church of Collège De La Salle School

Address: 6 al-Beshnin Street
GPS: 30.061525, 31.258226
Year: 1955
Architects: Seddiq Shehab el-Din, Antoine Selim Nahas, D. Komides

Combining Gothic pointed arches with Modernist design, this reinforced-concrete church is a unique landmark in Cairo. The building was part of the 1950s expansion of the Collège De La Salle, originally founded in 1898. The main space of the church is raised on a podium. At ground level the entry hall leads to the double stair to the second story, where another entry hall transitions into the church. The floor plan of the church is rectangular, with no side aisles and no vertical side walls; instead, the striking roof forms the body of the structure. The roof is composed of a series of pointed ribs mediating between the large pointed arch forming the main elevation and the smaller arch of the same shape forming the apse wall. A balcony level with the church organ is placed above the entrance, which is the tallest part of the interior. Cross-ribs strengthen the roof and give the ceiling the appearance of latticework. A transept with two tall, narrow, pointed arches forms a cross along the roofline when it intersects with the centerline of the pointed arches over the nave. The concrete roof is perforated along the sides of the church with stained-glass panels. The same treatment is repeated on the front façade and in the ribbed semicircular apse. Doors along the sides of the church lead to a terrace that surrounds the building on three sides.

Al-Halabi Print House

Address: al-Halabi Square
GPS: 30.055788, 31.271098
Year: 1937
Architect: Unknown

Established in 1859 by an immigrant from Aleppo, the print house (also known as al-Maimuniya) specialized in printing and publishing historical Islamic texts, as well as the Qur'an. It was the largest print facility of its kind in the region, with international distribution reaching East Asia and West Africa, and a printing capacity in the 1940s of seven million books a year. The U-shaped, two-story, concrete building comprises open industrial spaces for printing machinery on the tall ground floor, followed by offices for administration and editors on the first level. Industrial windows maximize natural light in the work space. The most remarkable feature of the building is the entrance, marked by a vertical element with streamlined curves and custom-designed metalwork.

Residential Building

Address: 35 Sabil al-Khazindar Street
GPS: 30.0628010, 31.2698030
Year: 1931
Architect: Amin Abdel Qader

This six-story building takes the shape of its trapezoidal site, surrounded by streets on three sides and a narrow passageway on the fourth. Due to the large size of the plot, the center of the block is carved out as a courtyard, allowing light and air into spaces not overlooking the street. Apartments begin at ground level and are arranged with living space and bedrooms around the perimeter. The elevations are organized with three distinctive sections: the ground floor, four floors forming the body of the block, and the top floor articulated as a crowning level. Rooms are provided with abundant light through tripartite window units that consist of a wide window in the center flanked by two narrower ones. Art Deco details, such as the triangular balconies in the center of the two main elevations and the floral metalwork, are combined with small, semicircular balconies and dentil-like details. The building is prototypical of structures of the period built along the main avenues in districts such as Abbasiya and Shubra, echoing similar developments in Downtown and Zamalek.

École Alliance Israélite Universelle

Address: 13 Sabil al-Khazindar Street
GPS: 30.0621240, 31.2694940
Year: 1928
Architect: Unknown

Commissioned by the Alliance israélite universelle, the school was built to provide free education for one thousand underprivileged Jewish children, taught by 120 teachers. The concrete-and-brick building consists of a basement followed by two levels of classrooms and teacher offices. The scale is vast, as it stretches around the perimeter of the city block on which it is built. The design is uniform across the building's length except for the corners, which are articulated with a rounded first floor and a concave second floor. The main entrance is located at a prominent corner and is set within a raised circular portico with three equal-sized openings, each flanked by two columns. Steps at the middle opening of the portico reach the raised ground floor. The muscular brick exterior is sparsely adorned with carved-stone floral motifs, reminiscent of the palm-tree motifs found in Cairo synagogues. The building has seen the addition of a partial third floor on its roof, as it is currently rented to the Ministry of Education and is now known as al-Ahram Vocational High School.

Waqf Inji Zada

Address: 180 Ramses Street
GPS: 30.068542, 31.265435
Year: 1937
Architect: Antoine Selim Nahas

This twelve-story apartment building commissioned by Madame Inji Zada is a sleek, streamlined, white tower on a triangular corner site in Ghamra, halfway between the bustling Downtown and the suburban enclave of Heliopolis. The main features of the building's exterior are its clear order, minimal design, curved corners, and nautical bathroom windows. When it was completed, it stood in stark contrast to its low-rise surroundings and tree-lined streets. This was architect Antoine Nahas's clearest architectural expression of Futurist optimism.

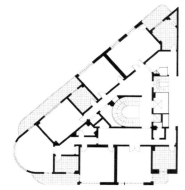

Ground Floor Plan

The apartment building consists of stores and a garage on street level, with two small apartments above followed by nine stories with identical floor plans, each consisting of two apartments (entry hall, living room, two bedrooms, kitchen, and bathroom). The top two floors are set back, with three additional apartments. The penthouse includes a small roof garden.

The building stands out for several technical reasons, including 9-meter-deep foundations and a sophisticated reinforced-concrete structure. A radio antenna to service the apartments, a first in Cairo, prominently topped the two-elevator building. Despite the compact building lot, the architect managed to include separate servant stairs with direct access to the kitchens.[69]

October Bridge

GPS: 30.069608, 31.264814
Year: 1969–99
Architect: Arab Contractors

Spanning 20.5 kilometers across central Cairo, the October Bridge is the city's main east–west corridor. The project was envisioned in the 1960s as the number of vehicles in the city continued to rise, causing traffic congestion along the inadequate street network. The highway was influenced by the American Robert Moses's ideas about urban renewal and planning, which favored private cars over public transport. The concrete structure consists of pillars rising 9 to 22 meters supporting 8-meter-wide highway sections. The tallest and widest spans of the bridge are at Ghamra, where suspension cables support the structure. Originally Ramses Bridge, it was renamed after the 1973 October War. The construction of the project required the demolition of buildings along its path, including the All Saints Cathedral that stood behind the Egyptian Museum in today's Abdel Munem Riyad Square.

Boutros Ghali Memorial Church

Address: 417 Ramses Street
GPS: 30.071826, 31.275201
Year: 1911
Architect: Antonio Lasciac

This church measuring 28 by 17 meters was built by the family of Boutros Ghali Pasha, who was prime minister of Egypt from 1908 to 1910, when he was assassinated following accusations of favoring the British in the Denshawai incident. Built as a memorial church with the family tomb in the crypt, the building's architecture is restrained, with simple lines and simplified Classical elements. With its high nave and two lower side aisles separated by two rows of granite columns, it reinterprets the Paleo-Christian basilica plan. Two monumental bell towers are built at the corners near the apse. The towers are austere, with minimally interpreted Classical elements such as columns and pediments, and are crowned with pyramidal forms.

The church is entered through a sequence of two colonnaded courtyards leading to the main elevation, which boasts a centrally positioned recess, with the door flanked by pilasters and topped by a flattened pediment in front of a large, semicircular window. The interior is decorated with frescos and mosaics depicting scenes from the life of Christ. Large, rounded arches carried by the columns lining the nave support the gabled timber roof[70]. In December 2016 the roof was heavily damaged in a bomb attack and it was subsequently rebuilt.

Saint Mark's Coptic Cathedral

Address: 417 Ramses Street
GPS: 30.072205, 31.275035
Year: 1968
Architects: Awad Kamel Fahmy, Selim Kamel Fahmy, Michel Bakhoum

Dedicated to Saint Mark, an apostle of Jesus and founder of the Coptic Church, the building was consecrated in 1968 to become the new seat of the Coptic Pope. (While the seat of the church is traditionally in Alexandria, it has been based in Cairo since 1800; until 1968 it was at Saint Mark's Cathedral in Azbakiya.) With a capacity for five thousand worshipers it was the largest cathedral in Africa and the Middle East. The form of the building, oriented east–west, is a Modernist interpretation of vernacular vaulted architecture. The cross-plan cathedral is lifted on a platform, underneath which are chapels and social-service facilities. The platform is reached by steps leading to the plaza in front of the monumental façade, flanked by two outdoor corridors extending like arms, covered by groin vaults. The main body of the reinforced-concrete cathedral takes the shape of a wide, pointed-barrel vault, with the transept adopting a similar form. At the intersection of the nave and transept is a dome resting on pendentives. A large, semicircular, half-domed niche forms the apse wall. Along the two sides of the body of the cathedral are aisles covered with a sloping, folded, concrete roof, with diamond shapes in front of each of the eight tall, pointed-arch windows, four on each side. The windows are filled with stained glass, the main decorative element of the otherwise plain interior. The façades on each of the four ends of the cross plan are articulated with three tall, narrow windows. The front elevation is designed with four pairs of columns carrying three pointed arches forming the entrance portico, which is topped by a terrace at the balcony level of the cathedral. Three tall openings with rounded arches complete the elevation. A soaring, freestanding bell tower is located south of the apse, designed with three staggered sections, the base larger than the top of the structure.

Marking the fiftieth anniversary of the Cathedral's construction, the building underwent a complete renovation in 2018, which involved extensive decorative painting on its previously austere exterior (on the bell tower, dome, and main body of the church), with additional redesign of the interior spaces to incorporate new decorative features and a new air-conditioning system.

23 July Development

Address: Abbasiya Square
GPS: 30.071340, 31.285456
Year: 1962
Architect: Nasr City Company

Part of the larger project of Nasr City was the insertion of blocks such as this in other parts of Cairo; this one was implemented in Abbasiya, with another in Mohandiseen. The Abbasiya Square development was meant to provide middle-income housing, as well as various government administrative buildings. The tallest structure is the Syndicate of Applied Arts Tower, consisting of twenty-three stories, with a five-story podium containing stores, banks, and offices, and the remaining eighteen floors occupied by eight apartments per floor. The glazed tower features protruding horizontal slabs at each floor, with the podium much wider than the body of the tower above. Other buildings included in the complex are three sixteen-story towers originally intended to accommodate three four-room apartments on each floor; they are now mostly occupied by government offices. The buildings consist of a central circulation core with three arms extended radially from its center; each arm is a stack of apartments. A large office block, the Misr Travel Tower, and several other office and mixed-use buildings feature architectural details similar to those employed in the design of the original Nasr City buildings.

Ain Shams University Lecture Halls

Address: Ain Shams University
GPS: 30.064141, 31.280174
Year: 1969
Architects: Farouk al-Gohary, Abdullah Abdel Aziz, Fuad Nassar, Emam Shelbi

Daher & Abbasiya

Four lecture halls of Ain Shams University are built into two identical buildings, each square in plan (25 x 25 meters) with two interlocking lecture halls stacked one above the other. The cubic volume of the structures is deconstructed, while the flat roof retains its pure square shape as it sits on the building like a lid. Each hall accommodates five hundred students, with seating arranged diagonally and the podium at one corner of the square room, a design that enhances acoustics without relying on microphones. Natural light is filtered through exterior zigzagging concrete screens doubling as sound insulation. The building is constructed of reinforced concrete, brick, and wood, all employed expressively inside and outside the structure.

Two exterior stairs give access to the top lecture hall, while the lower one is entered directly from the campus level.

Faculty of Engineering

Address: Ain Shams University
GPS: 30.065248, 31.278716
Year: 1933
Architect: Adolfo Brandani

In 1928 construction started on the massive, symmetrical, rectangular building designed to host an Arts and Crafts School of Ibrahim Pasha (now Ain Shams) University, with a focus on the decorative arts and craftsmanship. Between 1950 and 1961 the Law School used the building, before it became home to the Faculty of Engineering and Architecture. The three-story structure includes classrooms, workshops, a library, and offices placed along the outer perimeter and overlooking the four courtyards in the center, separated by bilateral hallways connecting the two longest sides of the building. The architecture matches the popular direction at the time for public commissions, incorporating modern construction materials with Beaux-Arts plan and dressed in a reinterpreted Classical façade with Neo-Islamic elements. The main elevation is defined by the large, protruding, central section, composed of three bays with a double-height portico on the second level above the portal in the center, further highlighted with a large dome above. The distinctive ribbed dome sits on four flat triangular pendentives, referencing *muqarnas*, with clerestory windows around the drum. The remainder of the external façades is punctuated by a regular order of windows in three rows, with a different design for the windows on each floor. Interior spaces were originally bare, with an airy, industrial feel. Over the years the building has witnessed alterations and additions.

Gamal Abdel Nasser Mosque

Address: al-Khalifa al-Ma'moun Street
GPS: 30.083440, 31.294290
Year: 1966
Architect: Galal Momen

This mosque was commissioned by a community organization from the Kubri al-Qubba neighborhood, and construction started in 1962. Due to shortage of funds construction was halted, and in 1965 it resumed with state funding. Due to its proximity to his residence, President Gamal Abdel Nasser regularly performed prayers in the mosque during the final years of his life. The site was chosen for his burial following his death in 1970. Part of the building was modified to fulfill its new dual functions, as a mosque and as a mausoleum for the president.

The structure consists of a large, rectangular prayer hall, with bays of various depths protruding from all four sides. Each bay consists of five attached tall arches. The arches are glazed and fronted by ornamental precast screens with Moorish patterns. The bay on the northeast façade functions as the mosque's vestibule, with five doors, one under each arch, leading to the interior. The *mihrab* is along the southeast wall, with a door leading to the protruding bay along this wall, which is used for the imam's office. The triple-height prayer hall is lit from clerestory windows that line the entire perimeter of the structure, giving the flat roof the appearance of lightness. Part of this effect was lost after modifications to the mosque required the partitioning of the rear area to become the memorial tomb. The deep bay along the back of the building, opposite the *mihrab* wall, is where the tombs of Nasser and his wife are located. A hallway separates this area from the rest of the mosque. A second level was added within this section to accommodate a reception area for official events associated with the memory of the president.

The exterior of the building is articulated with the ribbed arches of the protruding bays, and an exaggerated decorative parapet crowning the rectangular volume of the mosque. A slender, square minaret is situated at the east corner of the building, near the entrance. The distinctive minaret is topped by an oversized *muqarnas*-like element beneath a balcony. A delicate roof shades the balcony and gives way to the elegant pinnacle of the structure, making the minaret appear as if it hangs from the sky. The shaft is decorated with Moorish patterns, as well as clocks on each side.

HELIOPOLIS

Residential building by architect Max Balassiano, featuring a fusion of Streamline Moderne and Art Deco.

Heliopolis

Heliopolis is Cairo's first suburban desert city of the twentieth century, built beyond Abbasiya, northeast of the capital. The area comes second to Downtown in terms of the density of architecturally significant modern buildings, covering a wide range of styles. The Cairo Electric Railways and Heliopolis Oases Company was established in 1906 by a Belgian–Egyptian partnership between Édouard Empain and Boghos Nubar Pasha. In order to attract residents, particularly after the 1907 slump in the Egyptian economy, the company erected its first set of buildings, designed by Belgian architect Ernest Jaspar and forming the core of the area, today's Korba. The Basilique and the Hindu-style palace for Empain gave Heliopolis its first landmarks. The electric tram link, services such as schools and a market, and a set of recreational facilities such as Luna Park, a hotel (now the presidential palace), and a racecourse attracted residents. The area's population, which reached 6,800 by 1919, counted among them large numbers from Egypt's minorities (Syrians, Lebanese, and Armenians), as well as Europeans. Private constructions on land sold by the company grew exponentially in the 1920s and 1930s in areas such as today's Ismailiya and Safir squares. This wave added new buildings to the suburb, some adhering to fixed styles such as Art Deco, others eclectic, combining Modernist, Art Deco, and Neo-Oriental elements.

Another wave of growth took place in the 1950s and 1960s, including the buildings around Triumph Square, and Merryland Park (#183), as the area stabilized as an upper-middle-class enclave in Greater Cairo. Beginning in the 1960s, commercial spaces were created on the ground floors of many of the existing residential buildings in areas such as Roxy, as Heliopolis developed into its own commercial center. Because buildings in Heliopolis are under one hundred years old and mostly residential, they are rarely considered for heritage status or protection. The rise of land value since the 1990s has led to countless demolitions of low-rise buildings occupying 50 percent of their plots to give way to taller residential buildings with decorative pastiche façades covering 100 percent of the plots. The tram system that was the raison d'être of Heliopolis was decommissioned in 2016.

Waqf Asmaa Hanem Halim

Address: Salim al-Awal Street, Helmiyat al-Zeitoun
GPS: 30.111443, 31.316164
Year: 1948
Architect: Tawfiq Abdel Gawad

This building was originally designed as a charitable endowment comprising a vocational boarding school for fifty children up to the age of sixteen and a hostel for the long-term boarding of fifty elderly women. Accommodated within the hostel was also a safe house for six women temporarily in dispute with their families. The project was conceived in 1944 and was built in Helmiyat al-Zeitoun, then a suburb north of Cairo already home to several charitable organizations. The founder, Asmaa Halim, demanded the functions of the building be managed separately. The architect created an E-shaped plan that allowed the building's two main functions to be independent, each with an enclosed garden and separate entrance. The middle section of the building, linking the two, is three stories tall and includes service spaces, kitchens, and communal dining rooms. The streamlined structure features rounded corners, strip windows, clerestory windows, a glazed stairwell, and a long ramp making the second level wheelchair-accessible.

On the first floor are two classrooms and a large workshop on the school side, and on the hostel side are administration, storage, and service areas, as well as the sleeping room of the safe house. On the second floor are the shared sleeping rooms, with beds arranged in large open spaces, located on both the school and hostel sides of the building. The third floor in the middle section of the building houses offices and common rooms for the social workers and teachers. The roofs of the building's two side wings are accessible as terraces. Other spaces included in the facility are a library, common rooms, and a prayer room.

The architect paid particular attention to building materials and cost-reducing techniques and finishes. The entire project cost LE20,000 (Egyptian pounds) at the time of construction. The building has seen numerous renovations over the years and has lost its original character.[71]

Heliopolis

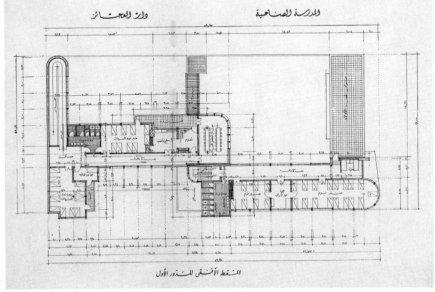

المدرسة الصناعية   دائرة العمائر

المسقط الأفقي للدور الأول

Heliopolis Hospital
(Ferial Hospital)

Address: Heliopolis Square
GPS: 30.106842, 31.337090
Year: 1955
Architects: Mustafa Shawky, Salah Zeitoun

In 1940 the first clinic opened in this part of Heliopolis, which later expanded into a twenty-bed hospital in a villa donated by Princess Ferial until the required funds were raised to construct a purpose-built hospital to serve the middle-income residents of the area. Construction started in 1949, with several setbacks that delayed the project's completion to 1955. The overthrow of the monarchy in 1953 led to the name of the hospital being changed from Ferial to Heliopolis. The building, occupying a 20,000m^2 plot, consists of a ground floor and three upper floors, with a capacity for 175 beds. When it opened, hospital beds were segregated by class, including first- and second-class rooms, a section for workers treated at lower prices, and a free section. The plan is organized into several parts: an arced entrance pavilion along Hegaz Street, the main spine of the hospital perpendicular to the arc, and a side wing for the inpatient section to the east. The outpatient section, extending to the west of the main spine, is designed as a square with a large courtyard in the center. An extension was later built at the southern end of the spine.

on the first floor of the arc, reached by a semicircular car ramp. Offices for administration are located in this section on the first and second floors. The ground floor of the spine contains service spaces, kitchens, storage, and mechanical systems. Examination rooms are on the first floor, and surgery rooms are on the second floor. Services such as X-ray rooms shared by the inpatient and outpatient sections are placed between them. Beds are located on the second floor of the inpatient and outpatient sections. The third floor was initially designed with additional beds for patients, as well as boarding rooms for doctors and nurses.

The hospital's overall design is driven by the separate but connected programmatic components of functionality and easy circulation. Stairs are added within each section to facilitate movement. Rooms flank hallways in order to maximize natural light and ventilation in all spaces. The spine of the building includes additional external hallways, accentuating the horizontality of the architecture.[72]

Heliopolis

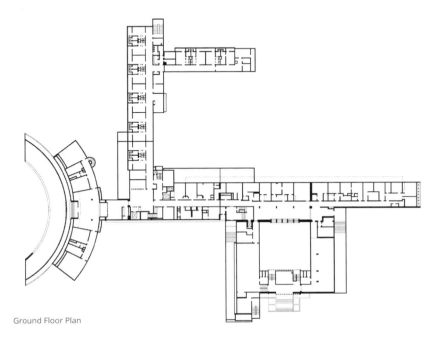

Ground Floor Plan

Saint Catherine's Church

Address: 10 Muhammad Shafiq Street
GPS: 30.102326, 31.339562
Year: 1950
Architect: Naoum Shebib

After experimenting with reinforced-concrete, thin-shell construction in his design for Saint Thérèse Church in Port Said (1948), Shebib utilized the same technique for the construction of Saint Catherine's Church, commissioned by the Syrian community in Heliopolis. Typical of Shebib's approach, the design combines form with structure. In the context of Cairo, the building reimagines what a church building can be, without entirely doing away with established typologies. The church still relies on the central-nave model terminating at an apse, but the sculptural roof, the expression of building material, and the interior's minimalist iconographic program make it unorthodox.

PRIVATE COLLECTION

Oriented parallel to the street, the church consists of a single ribbed vault interrupted in its center by three identical parabolic narrower cross-vaults, or ribs. The overall effect resembles three creases or folds in the otherwise smooth surface of the main vault. The three forms are in reference to the Holy Trinity, and each is topped with a cross. Each of the cross-vaults terminates at both ends with a long, narrow, elliptical stained-glass window, giving the main church space six windows. The ribs of the cross-vaults rest on six slender, visible pilotis. Two side aisles are added beyond these pilotis, and are enclosed by folding external walls with clerestory windows, making the heavy, sculptural roof appear to hover above the space.

Le Méridien Hotel

Address: 51 al-Uruba Road
GPS: 30.091272, 31.336333
Year: 1987
Architect: William Taylor

This hotel consists of a basement and three floors for services, lobby, bar, restaurants, public areas, and conference and banquet halls, followed by five identical U-shaped floors with 318 guest rooms. A centrally located circular staircase connects the functions of the podium from the basement to the roof of the third story, where a large terrace with a swimming pool is located. The exterior of the relatively solid podium contrasts with the punctuated façades of the upper floors. A set of semicircular arches defines the ground floor, two of which are extruded to form a canopy over the entrance in the center. The top floor protrudes slightly and is articulated with arched windows to form the building's crown. Translucent alabaster panels conceal the two stairs at the front of the building.

Society for Culture and Development

Address: 42 al-Thawra Street, Ard al-Golf
GPS: 30.085443, 31.335966
Year: 1997
Architect: Magd Masarra

Founded in 1977, this NGO's activities in the three governorates of Greater Cairo, in addition to Fayoum, encompass cultural and educational development and the provision of services to special needs children. The headquarters of the organization has a circular footprint, with a two-story base topped by a four-story crescent-shaped block toward the back of the site. The building's spiral form is achieved by a series of concave and convex lines in its plan, creating a complex volume of curves, cylinder, circular drum, and the crescent block with two setbacks at the top. Fenestration is defined by a set of narrow horizontal slits, functioning as screens to control direct sunlight, which reinforce the building's horizontality.

Heliopolis War Cemetery

Address: Nabil al-Waqqad St., Ard al-Golf
GPS: 30.079875, 31.329667
Year: 1941
Architect: Hubert Worthington

Cairo was an important hospital center in the Middle East during the Second World War, with wounded soldiers arriving here from the war front. There are 1,742 British and Commonwealth casualties buried or commemorated in the Heliopolis War Cemetery, in addition to eighty-three war graves of other nationalities. The site also includes replacements for First World War memorials in Aden and Port Tawfiq, which were destroyed in 1967 and the 1970s respectively.

The symmetrical entrance is composed of eight robust rusticated columns supporting a trellis, flanked by two identical stone pavilions with pediment roofs. At the center, beyond the entrance, is the War Stone, a monolithic memorial block behind which are the rows of graves separated by a central path leading to the 'Cross of Sacrifice' in the center of the cemetery.

Baron Empain Palace

Address: al-Uruba Road
GPS: 30.086688, 31.330238
Year: 1911
Architect: Alexandre Marcel

Situated on higher ground with views over Heliopolis is the iconic mansion of Édouard Empain. The silhouette of the building is divided into two elements, a rectangular volume containing the main functions of the house, and a *prang*, a tower-like spire in Khmer Hindu architecture, which houses a dramatic timber staircase. The mansion is built on a terraced podium with steps, containing the basement and lifting the building above street level. It consists of a double-height first floor for reception areas, a second floor for private quarters, and a roof terrace. On the first floor, the building's Beaux-Arts general layout consists of a large central hall flanked by two equal-sized rectangular rooms. Terraces are at the back of the mansion, where a secondary entrance is located, while the kitchen and connection to the grand staircase are at the west side. The second floor consists of two living spaces located above the large central hall, flanked by a master bedroom to the east and two additional bedrooms to the west, separated by a hallway linking the stair with the living space.

The reinforced-concrete building's most remarkable feature is its ornate exterior, with numerous quotations from ancient Hindu architecture, starting with the *chaitya* arch, a barrel-vault archway functioning as an entrance niche. The decorative program includes reinterpreted Hindu classical elements such as the columns and entablatures with elephant heads, and relief sculptures of deities and mythical figures such as a set of *Naga* statues—the seven-headed serpent protector of Buddha—adorning the podium. The rooftop terrace features *torana*s, freestanding ornamental gateways. The building also includes *mashrabiya*-like screens and other wooden features, most notably the spiraling timber stairs occupying the tower. The garden of the palace was landscaped with terraces and dotted with Classical statues, most of which have disappeared over the years.

Cathedral of Our Lady of Heliopolis (Basilique)

Address: Al-Ahram Street
GPS: 30.093639, 31.325100
Year: 1910
Architect: Alexandre Marcel

Known as the Basilique, this church was constructed at the same time as the Baron Empain Palace (#172), with a street connecting the two structures. The cathedral consists of a cubic volume topped by a large dome resting on four large, semicircular arches. The front and rear arches are extruded outward to create the coffered entrance niche at the front and the apse at the back. The two side arches are slightly extruded to create the two side galleries. Tower-like forms topped by domes articulate the four corners of the building. Three coffered barrel vaults carried on four pairs of red-granite columns, all set within the large, semicircular niche, mark the entrance. Stairs to the organ mezzanine flank the main portal. The mezzanine, supported on each side by three semicircular arches resting on wide red-granite columns, runs around three sides of the church, overlooking the main space. The stark interior of the church is adorned only by paintings of Jesus flanked by two angels above the apse. Light enters the space from three sides through glass-and-concrete screens set within the large arches on all sides but the apse. The semicircular, half-domed apse wall is articulated with seven blind niches separated by red-granite columns, topped by a row of clerestory windows. The church is the final resting place of Édouard Empain, who is buried in the crypt.

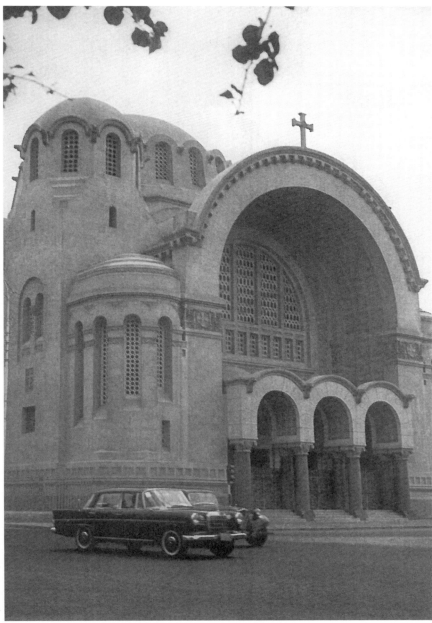

Heliopolis

Fayza Hanem Owais Building

Address: Nazih Khalifa Street
GPS: 30.092869, 31.324936
Year: 1949
Architect: Muhammad Sherif Nouman

This building occupies a 1,540m² corner plot facing the monumental Basilique. The basement houses a garage for thirty vehicles, while the ground floor, with a marble-clad entrance hall leading to the main stair, includes six two-bedroom apartments, two of which have private entrances, the remaining four being entered from the hall near the stairs. The plan of the building is organized around the central circulation core of the stair and two elevators, where apartment entrances are located. The five identical floors each contain four apartments with five rooms each and one apartment of four rooms. Apartments are divided into public and private wings, with parquet floors and built-in closets. The two apartments on the outer corner of the fifth floor are duplexes, each with an internal stair leading to additional space on the sixth floor, as well as roof gardens. The main feature of the exterior are the 2.5-meter-deep balconies along the north and west façades. The rooms along these balconies are arranged in a sawtooth diagonal order that gives each of them two corner windows for added ventilation, rather than a single window had the rooms been arranged parallel to the façade.[73]

175
Mahallawy Building

Address: Nazih Khalifa Street
GPS: 30.094001, 31.324139
Year: 1949
Architect: Tawfiq Abdel Gawad

This corner building is striking for its overall minimalist rectilinear aesthetic. The design is fairly straightforward, with a rectangular building occupying 50 percent of the 950m² plot, following the building code set in place by the Heliopolis Company. The entrance is placed away from the corner, along the side street, which gives access to the raised ground floor immediately, with entrances to three apartments. The stair with an elevator at its center forms the main vertical circulation. The hallway repeats on each of the seven floors, with three two-bedroom apartments on each. Foldable partition walls separate the living room and sitting areas of the apartments, making it possible to create one large open space. An air shaft at the center of the block ventilates wet rooms and provides service access to kitchens. A stack of 5-meter-deep balconies, intended as outdoor rooms, is attached to the structure's north façade, most have been enclosed by residents. Despite the even grid visually created by the horizontal lines of the floor plates intersecting with five round pillars rising to the sixth floor, balcony spaces are not evenly distributed across all units. Only the two front apartments access the balcony, with the corner apartments having three balcony bays, and the second apartment along the front having access to one bay.[74] The building has been substantially altered.

176

Residential Building

Address: Sesostris/Mamoun Streets, Korba
GPS: 30.090119, 31.324394
Year: 1911
Architect: Camille Robida

One of the early Heliopolis typologies, this concrete-and-brick construction consists of three floors, each with two large apartments. The symmetrical plan is rectangular, with a generously sized stairway placed in the center at the front of the building. Each of the apartments is designed with a series of spacious rectangular rooms positioned around a reception area placed immediately at the entrance. Ceiling heights exceed 4 meters, giving the interior an airy feel while helping maintain cool temperatures. Large, shaded balconies are attached to all sides of the building except the back, functioning as oversized shading devices, reducing direct sunlight from the interior while providing ample outdoor space, with balcony access from nearly every room. The balconies are designed with an independent structural system of slender, square, reinforced-concrete columns and beams, with cast-concrete screens for railings. The cantilevered roofs of the balconies at the top floor are slightly slanted.

Large windows with wooden shutters allow residents to further control light. The buildings were decorated with colorful glazed tiles in place of cornices, cement-tile floors, muted ironwork, and solid woodwork for the main doors and railings, as well as floral wallpaper or Art Nouveau murals for apartment interiors, according to the tastes of residents.

Cinema Farouk
(Cinema Palace)

Address: 6 al-Ahram Street
GPS: 30.089834, 31.318426
Year: 1949
Architect: Max Balassiano

The cinema's footprint occupies about one-third of the plot, following regulations at the time from the Heliopolis Company. The remainder of the land was later transformed into an open-air cinema. The original Art Deco structure stands on 1,000m² at the corner of the site. The whitewashed exterior features rounded corners and an extruded central bay with a deep niche for the main entrance marked by two slender pilotis. The single-hall cinema has a capacity of 1,200, on the ground and balcony levels. Marble steps lead to the raised ground floor. The elliptical ticket hall was decorated with neon lights in various patterns, with ticket windows at opposite ends of the space.

Two entrances lead to the main theater space, and a stair to the balcony, with an additional stair leading to offices and the projection room. The interior was richly decorated with an underwater theme, including frescoes representing marine life, plaster ceilings shaped like seashells, and blue cement tiles.[75]

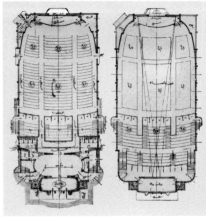

178

Heliopolis Company Buildings

Address: Ibrahim al-Laqqani Street, Baghdad Street
GPS: 30.091519, 31.319021
Year: 1908
Architect: Ernest Jaspar

Heliopolis was a new kind of urban development, and it required a new kind of architecture. The Belgian architect Ernest Jaspar moved to Cairo in 1905 to design many of the landmark buildings that gave Heliopolis its distinctive style. The large blocks lining today's Ibrahim al-Laqqani and Baghdad streets are a harmonious synthesis of concrete, brick, and stone construction, with wooden shading devices and details. These are brought together in a pseudo-Islamic style that, unlike the historicism of the period, does not take direct quotes from specific historic buildings or styles. Instead, the features that appear to be Islamic are largely invented, and mixed together in a playful manner. The architectural style Jaspar created is an example of successful place-making *ex nihilo* in early-twentieth-century Cairo.

Large granite columns along the street distinguish the three- to four-story buildings, creating shaded sidewalks with stores, a necessary architectural solution to the hot desert environment when these blocks were first constructed. The colonnades give way to spacious porticos on the second floor, articulated with rows of identical columns, or with large arches resting on the columns below. Wooden awnings carried on slender stumps shade the large balconies of the top floor. Occasional tower elements, for vertical circulation, rise an additional floor to create rhythm across the long façades. Domes or square porticos crown these towers, or in some cases they resemble minarets. The architect created a set of architectural elements of arches, column capitals, and geometric decorative friezes and borders to adorn the exteriors. The overall composition of the elevations is ordered and visually interesting, innovative yet historically anchored. The elevations create deep screens that shade interior spaces from the hot sun, creating more livable temperatures in the tall interiors of the generously designed apartments. Entrances to the buildings are set between the storefronts and are simply designed with a long hallway leading to the main stair.

Heliopolis

Elias Bey Rizq Building

Address: Boutros Ghali Street
GPS: 30.092891, 31.320825
Year: 1948
Architect: Milad Greiss

This five-story building has a 300m² footprint, with apartments ranging in size from one to three bedrooms. Its typology represents a smaller scale of development typical in suburban districts at the time. Such developments were often commissioned by a family, for various members of the family to occupy different apartments in the same building, or as an investment as a rental property. Despite its small scale, finishes found in luxury Downtown buildings are included, such as oak parquet floors in apartments, marble-clad entry halls, and service stairs in the air shafts connecting kitchens. In this particular block the floor plans are arranged with living spaces along the street-facing side and bedrooms along the back. The stripped-down front façade is symmetrical, with two apartments on each floor having access to a balcony that runs the entire width of the building.

Regine Khoury Building

Address: Aflaton/Ibn Sina Streets
GPS: 30.095197, 31.339817
Year: 1934
Architect: Ezra Chamass

The design of this symmetrical, three-story Art Deco building focuses on the corner, where the entrance and vertical circulation are placed. The main portal is framed by two robust columns carrying a pediment-like awning with roof tiles. This is followed by vertical windows set within a slight recess lighting the stairs. The stairwell is crowned with a flat square roof that appears to hover above it. Hinge-like articulations at the top of this vertical section give the building the overall appearance of an open book. From this spine, two side wings extend along the side streets, each housing a stack of three apartments. Terraces for the raised ground-floor apartments, accessed by outdoor marble stairs flanking the entrance, and deep balconies for the following two levels add to the building's muscular massing. With incorporated arches in the terraces and rounded corners throughout, the building combines Streamline Moderne lines with Art Deco details. The symmetrical, corner-focused design is mirrored in the ironwork of the main gate.

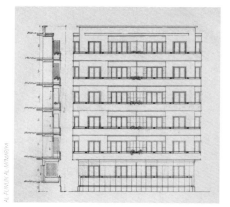

Fattouh Bey Guinenah Building

Address: al-Ismailiya Square
GPS: 30.096610, 31.333867
Year: 1941
Architect: Albert Khoury

With a footprint of 700m², this four-story structure was erected on part of the garden of Fattouh Bey. The symmetrical corner building contains three apartments on each floor, one on the corner and two at the sides. It is entered from the corner, leading to an elliptical lobby, followed by the main stairs in the back. The entire length of the stair is backed by glass, with operable windows to improve light and ventilation. The elliptical space is repeated on each floor, leading to the apartment entrances. The design of the two side apartments includes two separate wings for sleeping, each with two bedrooms, while the corner apartments contain a total of two bedrooms, along with a large living and dining area. Four smaller apartments are located on the ground floor.

The design incorporates several elements to maximize ventilation, such as windows from multiple directions in each apartment. Deep balconies along the exterior façade provide shade and reduce indoor temperatures. The exterior features curved corners, rounded edges, corner windows, and a perforated concrete canopy along the roofline. The structure is built of a reinforced-concrete frame filled with limestone blocks.[76]

Merryland Apartments

Address: Shehab al-Din Khafaga Street
GPS: 30.100858, 31.322247
Year: 1958
Architect: Sayed Karim

Commissioned by the Heliopolis Development Company to redesign the former racecourse, Sayed Karim produced an ambitious proposal for an urban community comprising three towers overlooking Merryland Park. The project was geared toward middle-income housing for five hundred households in typologies ranging from three-bedroom apartments to duplexes, referred to in Karim's writing as "villas." The entire complex was envisioned as a vertical "neighborhood."

The project was partially realized twice, first in Heliopolis and again in Maadi. At the Heliopolis site, the unbuilt cylindrical block would have included eight three-bedroom apartments per floor. This block was implemented in the Maadi iteration of the project. The long, slightly curved middle block contains thirty duplexes every two floors, and the twenty-story tower houses twelve three-bedroom apartments per floor. The tower was not implemented in the Maadi version.

The two built blocks are not connected, and each displays its own architectural characteristics, with little resemblance between them. The façade of the slightly curved block of duplexes is organized as a grid, with interplay between balconies and window panels. The building has three entrances, each with its own circulation core consisting of an indoor main stair, outdoor service stair, and an elevator. The twenty-story tower block is massive in scale and sits on a grid of robust polished black-cement pilotis. In plan the building is shaped like an elongated hexagon, making the front and rear elevations bulge along their centerlines. With the exception of a column of windows in the center of the two main elevations, the rest of the façade is composed of equally sized, equally spaced, square balconies cantilevered from the façade. The balconies appear like staggered open drawers from a monolithic mass, enhancing the architectonic quality of the building.

In the original design the three buildings would have shared a podium containing daycare facilities, stores, a cinema, a clinic, and other services. A sculptural roof garden above the middle block with views over the park is a nod to Le Corbusier; however, neither podium nor roof garden was implemented.

Heliopolis

183
Merryland Park

Address: al-Hegaz Street
GPS: 30.098041, 31.318742
Year: 1963
Architect: Sayed Karim

The creation of Cairo's first Modernist public park was part of the project to reuse the former racecourse. The complete plan put together by Sayed Karim proposed a series of Modernist housing blocks around the park on three sides, but this was scrapped. Instead, he created a dynamic landscape design that utilizes irregular geometry and avoids symmetry, and which incorporates various activities such as a bandstand, a children's area, and service facilities such as restrooms and snack stands. At the center of the park is a curved pavilion for the main cafeteria, with a cantilevered roof overlooking the paddling pond. Concrete is utilized expressively in details, pavilions, and most notably in the north gate facing the Merryland Apartments.

The park was designed with access on all four sides. The main gate, located on Hegaz Street, is composed of a long, slightly curved brick wall with a canopy supported by two rows of mosaic-covered pilotis. A second sculptural gate (now disused) near Karim's Merryland Apartments (#182) is composed of a double triangular concrete frame. In 2018 the park's design was altered in a renovation, and the cafeteria was expanded into a food court, though some of the original architectural features remain.

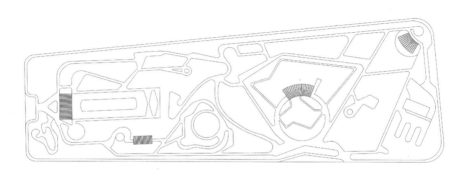

Master Plan

Heliopolis

Madinat Ghernata

Address: Hegaz Street
GPS: 30.094871, 31.318334
Year: 1928
Architect: Unknown

The racecourse stands known as Madinat Ghernata (Granada, previously named Alhambra) were part of an entertainment complex that also included a casino, now demolished. Currently, three buildings stand on the site: the stands, a lookout tower, and a domed pavilion. The stands consist of two connected parts, a rectangular, two-story block with square towers at the front corner, and the steps for seating at the back, shaded with a cantilevered concrete roof. The ground floor consists of a large double-height space, while the second level is shallow in comparison. At the center of the ground-floor elevation is the entrance, designed with five 'oriental' arches, once entirely open, which were later filled with colored-glass doors. Three small windows top each of the arches. Vertical circulation was placed in the two square towers, rising two additional floors in height, each topped with a balcony and a cupola. The building is also adorned with *ablaq* and *mashrabiya*s.

Next to the stands is the lookout tower, a concrete structure with three slender columns intersecting with a sculptural spiral stair leading to a small enclosed viewing platform, with a single triangular balcony at the fourth floor. The floors below are exposed, with only a simple railing at each landing. With few architectural elements, this small structure combines Modernist, Art Deco, and Neo-Oriental design. The pavilion was once a restaurant named Andalusia, designed as a rectangular hall, with an onion dome toward the entrance. Iterations have been made to the site repeatedly, including adding side stairs and reconfiguring interiors. In 2018 the site underwent a complete renovation as part of an adaptive reuse project.

185
Debbane Bey Building

Address: Roxy Square
GPS: 30.092113, 31.314459
Year: 1940
Architect: Raymond Antonius

This symmetrical cubic building is entered through a raised ground-floor level, where the spacious lobby stretches the entire depth of the structure, leading to a circulation core containing the grand staircase and service stair. Two mirrored apartments are located on this floor, each with two bedrooms located at the rear of the building, away from the street. The following three floors each contain a single large apartment, with two sleeping wings, each with two bedrooms placed at the back, in addition to four living spaces and a spacious shaded balcony at the front. A penthouse with a private roof terrace is located at the top of the building. The exterior is distinguished by the deep recesses of the balconies at the center of the main elevation. A grid of concrete pillars and beams defines the balconies, the floors of which protrude slightly in semicircular shapes. Long rectilinear balconies and corner windows seen on the two side façades provide the living and sleeping rooms with sunlight and air.[77]

Gamal Abdel Nasser Museum

Address: 6 al-Khalifa al-Ma'moun Street
GPS: 30.086572, 31.309227
Year: 2017
Architect: Karim Shaboury

The former residence of President Nasser remained vacant after the passing of his wife in 1990. The original 1940s house on the site was much smaller, and it was expanded and modified several times when Nasser chose it for his private home. Alterations done in the 1950s included a U-shaped wing at the rear, to accommodate more rooms and to create a courtyard, as well as an entrance portico added to the front façade. Shaboury's design transformed a building that was intended for private use into one fit for a public museum, with the necessary display spaces. The house became the main object within the museum: the architect maintained this separation by locking the preserved entrance of the house while creating a new entrance pavilion to the side. The solid volumetric intervention on the east side of the building clearly marks the entrance and borrows the architectural language of the Nasser period. The courtyard was transformed into an atrium, functioning as a distribution point to three visitor itineraries: the house, the president, and the revolution. Extensive research was carried out to retain the original feeling of the interior spaces of the house during the president's lifetime, seen particularly in the living spaces, the bedroom, and Nasser's two offices.

187
Villa Kamel Bek Abdel Halim
(demolished)

Year: 1932
Architect: Charles Ayrout

This villa consisted of a single cubic volume with various articulations, recesses, and extrusions. The symmetrical, two-story structure included various sitting rooms, a dining room, office, and service areas on the first floor, and four bedrooms, nursery, and nanny's room on the upper floor. Both floors were organized as a series of rooms around the perimeter of the structure, with a large central hall with the grand staircase. While the plan is Beaux-Arts in essence, the elevations are Streamline Moderne. Floating semicircular balconies contrasted with linear ledges shading the tops of window openings. Steps led to the shaded entrance portico, highlighted architecturally with four concrete ribs rising above it. Reinforced concrete was the main structural element, infilled with sandstone masonry. The exterior was plastered over with stucco.[78]

188
Villa Mrs. Valadji
(demolished)

Year: 1933
Architect: Charles Ayrout

This structure consisted of two conjoined, separate villas for two sisters, interlocking within the building's three floors. With a footprint of only 135m^2, this was an exercise in compact design. The lower villa was entered on the east side, with living space on the ground level and an internal stair to the first level of bedrooms. The top villa was accessed from the west side, with a stairway leading to the first level with bedrooms and the second level with living space and additional bedrooms. Typical of Ayrout's style, the building featured rounded balconies and a clear geometry. A notable feature was the large expanse of industrial glass, in the form of a strip window, placed across three rooms on the top floor.[79]

Heliopolis

NASR CITY

Masjid Dar al-Arqam, completed 1994, is designed with a flat roof supported by four piers in the center of the building and an envelope of slender arches. The focal point of the mosque is the freestanding black marble *mihrab* wall, which is pulled away from the façade.

Nasr City

The idea for a Modernist desert city was already in place by 1953. In 1959 Nasr City was established by presidential decree and was promoted as "City of the Revolution." The original plan was provided by Sayed Karim, but due to a dispute with the state the project was implemented after the first phase of construction without the participation of its architect. The project was envisioned as a model for desert expansion that included government buildings and a wide variety of housing typologies to counter the country's housing crisis. Organized as a grid of superblocks, each with green spaces and social services at the center, the implementation of the scheme was slow and costly. Nasr City's original housing options ranged from large, high-density high-rises to small, low-rise units and individual villas.

Apartments originally built for rent remained empty, and by the 1970s the entire economic model of the project was oriented toward home ownership, abandoning the façade of socialist development propped up for the first decade of its life. The liberalization of the economic structure governing the project allowed investors to enter the scene by buying plots of land for private developments. The original plans and building models were abandoned, and caps on building heights were overlooked. Today, Nasr City is a district of Greater Cairo with little autonomy, most of its buildings erected after the 1980s, many smaller buildings completed in the 1960s and 1970s having been replaced one or more times in the few short decades since the district was founded, as the value of real estate continues to rise. It is now largely a middle- and upper-middle-class area, with a plethora of shopping malls and a high rate of car ownership. Electric trams, whose network was expanded from Heliopolis to Nasr City in the 1960s to facilitate connectivity, were taken out of service entirely in 2014.

Nasr City Plan

Year: 1953
Architect: Sayed Karim

The Nasr City plan created by Sayed Karim bore the hallmarks of a Functionalist city and a 'rationalized' Modernist utopia. It comprised nine zones: the Olympic zone; the international-exhibition zone; the athlete-housing zone (which connected the Olympic zone and a commercial zone); the university area (which included an expansion of Ain Shams University and a new campus for al-Azhar University); the governmental zone (with new headquarters for various state institutions and ministries); the military zone (including a military parade ground and a monument to the Unknown Soldier); the touristic zone (located on higher ground, with parks and views over the city); the medical zone; and the residential areas (consisting of independent residential superblocks with their own commercial, medical, and cultural services). Initially the city was planned with its districts, sectors, and blocks all numbered, as in Brasília and Chandigarh, as an organizational principle. However, this numbering system was never implemented, and streets were given familiar names.

The development was meant to be low-density, with 250 to 500 persons per hectare. Green areas and schools were designed within walking distance of all residential blocks. A strict code of building heights governed the logic of the plan, composed of freestanding residential blocks surrounded by trees and oriented to maximize air circulation and reduce direct sun exposure. Nodes were created throughout the plan as places of gathering, such as the casino, commercial area, cinema, and post office. Models of residential buildings ranged from small individual houses to apartment buildings of four to six apartments, to large-scale blocks with tens of apartments and duplexes. Some traces of the original designs remain in Nasr City, but much of Karim's plan was never fully implemented or has been significantly altered.

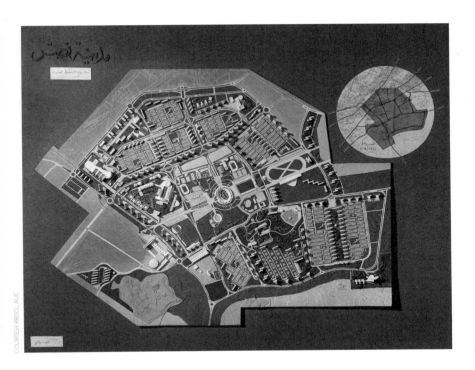

Nasr City

Al-Azhar University Campus

Address: al-Nasr Road
GPS: 30.058991, 31.313825
Year: 1962–65
Architect: Tawfiq Abdel Gawad

Building a new, Modernist campus for the ancient al-Azhar University was an ambitious task but a necessary one for President Nasser's control of religious authorities in the country. The new campus was given a 300-hectare plot of land in the new development of Nasr City. The sprawling campus was designed with numerous blocks housing various faculties, arranged orthogonally along a central spine. According to the original plan, the campus was organized by function. With the main entrance on Salah Salem Road, the first buildings to be encountered were the central library and the university administration. Religious faculties were placed near the entrance of the campus, to reflect the origins of the university in Islamic studies. Scientific and technical faculties were placed next, most notably the Faculty of Medicine, a sprawling building with multiple wings and lecture halls connected to a central spine. Farther into the campus were the athletic and recreational areas to the east and the residential areas to the west, including housing for faculty, workers, and students. A university hospital was planned with direct access to the public in the vicinity of the Faculty of Medicine.

Architecturally the campus was designed with contemporary language, with flat roofs, strip windows, and cubic volumes containing classrooms and offices. No explicit references were made to historical elements of Islamic architecture, as Tawfiq Abdel Gawad strongly opposed historicism and believed in the honest expression of building materials. Ornamentation comes occasionally in the form of patterned cement breeze blocks.

The Faculty of Medicine is the most complete realization of Abdel Gawad's approach to designing the university, entirely driven by function and the organization of activities. While the architect makes no explicit reference to architectural style or aesthetics in his description of the project, he goes into minute details with regard to function and plan-making. For example, in the Faculty of Medicine the main concerns include the creation of quiet, acoustically sound lecture halls and the design of special entrances for cadavers to be delivered to the dissection labs.

While most of the buildings in the initial plan were implemented, some, such as the university stadium, were not built; others, such as the university hospital, were built later, following different designs. Over the years the original buildings have suffered many alterations and some new buildings have been added.[80]

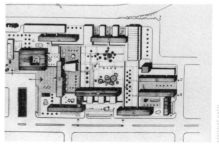

Nasr City

Cairo International Stadium

Address: al-Estad
GPS: 30.069444, 31.312884
Year: 1960
Architects: Werner March

Werner March designed the Berlin Olympic Stadium for the occasion of the 1936 Games. He was invited to Cairo in the 1950s to draw up plans for a stadium, and partnered with Egyptian structural engineer Michel Bakhoum to realize the project. The stadium, the first major construction in Nasr City, is sunk 12 meters into the ground and comprises two tiers, with seating capacity for forty-five thousand in the lower level and thirty-five thousand in the upper level. The earth structurally supports the lower tier, which starts at ground level and slopes down. Ramps encircling three sides of the structure were created, using earth dug from the center of the stadium, to bring spectators to the second tier, lifted above ground level by 20 meters at the highest point. Reinforced-concrete ribs support the weight of the upper level, which cantilevers over the lower.

A five-story structure along the west side of the stadium hosts a variety of functions: VIP lounge and viewing box, locker rooms for players, physical therapy facilities, bathrooms, a canteen for spectators, concession stands, a press room, and television studios. Along the west side, the narrow, slightly curving, boxy structure with its concrete exoskeleton of eighteen ribs marks the largest of the four entrances; three others are located on the east, north, and south sides. The design takes into account the need for thousands of people to move safely at one time, with main entryways ranging in width from 10 to 24 meters, in addition to fifty-two secondary passageways and fourteen tunnels to the lower tier. The design makes it possible to empty the stadium in just fifteen minutes.

Expo City
(proposed)

Address: Salah Salem Road
GPS: 30.0719345, 31.2981002
Year: 2009
Architect: Zaha Hadid

The result of a two-phase competition, the proposed Expo City includes various programmatic elements such as exhibition halls, a conference center, a business hotel, two thirty-story office towers, a shopping center, and gardens. The plan is organized in clusters arranged around a 'river,' or main circulation artery, running north–south across the site. Building masses and in-between spaces are integrated harmoniously with fluid forms and smooth gestural curves. The overall plan holds a topographic quality, recalling masses of land carved over time. The design features several building-skin treatments, such as perforated and ribbed façades, that aim to control natural light and reduce building temperatures. The design is driven by circulation, easing the movement of crowds of people during major events.

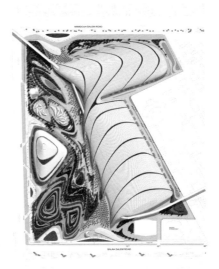

Nasr City

Unknown Soldier Memorial

Address: al-Nasr Road
GPS: 30.065306, 31.313856
Year: 1975
Architect: Samy Rafea

Monuments to the Unknown Soldier are an invented tradition that started only after the First World War. The commission for Egypt's memorial was given after the 1973 October War to artist Samy Rafea, who was later responsible for the tile murals on the walls of Cairo's Metro stations. Rafea worked to develop popular art, or art for the people, and his works utilized recognizable signs and symbols in order to reach the masses. The ancient Egyptian monuments eternally commemorating kings inspired the pyramidal shape of the 32-meter-tall memorial. The structure is an abstraction of the ancient form and is composed of two interlocking perpendicular triangular concrete frames, creating the silhouette of a pyramid, with its center left hollow. An eternal flame is placed at the center. The pyramidal form is covered in stone cladding, carved with rows of soldiers' names written in Kufic script. The secular memorial refers to both Islamic and ancient Egyptian art without relying heavily on historicism or direct quotations from particular historic monuments. After his assassination just across the road at the parade stands (#194), President Anwar Sadat was buried at the memorial.

Military Parade Stands

Address: al-Nasr Road
GPS: 30.064136, 31.314682
Year: 1960
Architect: Abd al-Hadi Hosny

Military parades were held at Nasr City shortly after it was established. At the time of their construction the parade stands stood in an empty desert site, with only a strip of tarmac in front and the stadium in the distance. The symmetrical reinforced-concrete structure is composed of three semi-independent sections. The wider middle section is attached to a two-story building at the rear with indoor viewing boxes and a waiting area for important guests. The center of the indoor facility is adorned with the Republican Eagle on the façade, which is flanked by two sets of outdoor stands. The cantilevered concrete roof of the middle section of the stands is larger and taller than those on the two side sections, which are designed with triangular folds. From the back of the parade stands the skeletal structure of the evenly placed pillars and cantilevered beams is visible. A sculptural, curved tower element pierces the folded roof at the east end to support a capsule space that functions as an exclusive higher observation point. President Sadat was assassinated at this site in 1981.

Government Sector

Address: Salah Salem Road
GPS: 30.078383, 31.315750
Year: 1960
Architect: Sayed Karim

Occupying one of the large city blocks planned by Sayed Karim, the Government Sector is an assemblage of administrative buildings forming a cohesive whole. Part of the logic of the new city was to provide new government buildings to absorb the expanding state bureaucracy. Office buildings for nine governmental institutions were built, including the Accountability State Authority, the Central Agency for Public Mobilization and Statistics, and the National Planning Institute.

Architecturally, the office buildings are consistently designed, with similar features such as strip windows, clean lines, and sun breakers. The reinforced-concrete structures share a basic typology consisting of two parts, a podium at the base with the office-tower slab above. The exteriors of the slab blocks are painted white, with dark mullions for windows and sun-reflective glass. Most of the buildings are designed as slender rectangular slabs, with a central hallway in each of the identical floors, flanked by brightly lit offices arranged along the front and rear façades. Other programmatic functions such as auditoriums and large meeting halls are designed with distinct architectural form at the bases of the office blocks. The auditorium in the back of the Accountability State Authority is an example of this approach.

Nasr City Company for Housing and Development

Address: Yusef Abbas Street
GPS: 30.075728, 31.314978
Year: 1959
Architect: Sayed Karim

The architecture of the original Nasr City buildings showcases repetition and modular design. The building designed to house the authority undertaking the construction of Nasr City exemplifies the architectural logic of the entire development. The structure consists of a two-story podium followed by seven identical floors of offices and a recessed top floor, originally used as the cafeteria, with a roof terrace. A recessed 'lost floor' between the base and the main body of the building creates a gap, making the top part of the structure appear to hover above the base.

The various functions of the building are expressed architecturally in distinctive forms. For example, the equally sized office spaces are distinguished on the north and south façades by a grid of alternating protruding rectangles forming shallow balconies. The meeting rooms and administrator offices on each floor are stacked along the west façade, appearing as a distinct volume, with a solid concrete wall and different fenestration than the rest of the building. Part of the podium, facing the street, is lifted on pilotis, which creates a recess at the base where the main entrance is located. Publicly accessible services and the building's reception are in the double-height base and mezzanine. The building was modified significantly over the years.

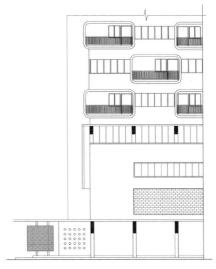

Partial Front Elevation

Housing Model 20

Address: al-Tayaran Street
GPS: 30.076221, 31.320888
Year: 1959
Architects: Ali Labib Gabr, Ahmed Charmi

This ten-story building model has two entrances, each leading to four apartments on each floor, with a total of eight apartments per floor. The repeated floor plan is symmetrical along both axes and consists of three long sections: two along the longer elevations, lined with apartments, and one in the center, containing two vertical circulation shafts and three air shafts for ventilation. Each apartment consists of an entry hall, a living room, and one to three additional rooms. Kitchens and back rooms are located along the inner core. The elevation is marked by floating square concrete shapes, one for each of the balconies on levels two through nine.

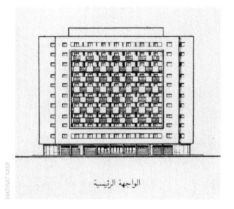

الواجهة الرئيسية

مسقط الدور المتكرر

Housing Model 10

Address: 15 al-Nasr Road
GPS: 30.067801, 31.324264
Year: 1959
Architects: Mohamed Sherif Nouman, Sayed Karim

Designed for middle-income residents, this building model consists of a ground floor plus ten identical floors of apartments for up to five hundred individuals. The modestly sized two-bedroom apartments are arranged with living and sleeping rooms along the outside, and kitchens and bathrooms along the core of the building, ventilated by eight air shafts. The exterior of the structure consists of a grid of equally sized balconies for all rooms. The original set of Model 10 buildings was built along al-Nasr Road, opposite the Rabaa al-Adawiya Mosque. Six of the identical blocks were situated diagonally to the street grid, creating small front gardens for each.

The buildings belong to District 1 of Nasr City, which covers 57 hectares, with twenty-one buildings of the high-density models such as Model 10, Model 15, and Model 6 for a total capacity of around ten thousand inhabitants. The center of the plot was designed for a park and low-rise buildings such as stores, schools, a police station, and a telephone and telegraph office.

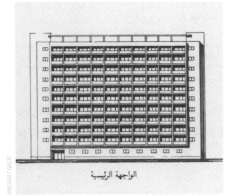

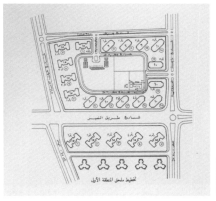

Housing Model 15

Address: 9 Yusef Abbas Street
GPS: 30.068425, 31.320284
Year: 1959
Architect: Sayed Karim

One of the more distinctive Nasr City typologies is the H-shaped, eleven-story Model 15. Each building contains forty three-room apartments and sixty-six four-room apartments. In order to avoid creating a large monolithic structure, it is divided into three parts, composed together in an H with a central block and two side wings. In plan, the floors are symmetrically arranged, with two circulation cores and corresponding entrances placed at the opposite ends of the central block as it connects with the side wings. The circulation cores consist of a stair and two elevators, with five apartment entrances at each floor landing. The shape of the building maximizes the external wall surfaces, thus providing all rooms with windows along the exterior. Air shafts, two small ones in each of the side wings and one large one in the central block, ensure all service spaces are properly ventilated. The main elevations of the two side wings consist of alternating vertical arrangements of floating concrete planes, demarcating the balconies and windows. The two elevations of the central block consist of a modular design of alternating solids and voids for windows and balconies.

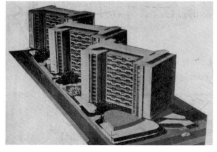

Nasr City Cinema
(Demolished)

Address: Yusef Abbas Street
GPS: 30.062898, 31.322690
Year: 1962
Architect: Sayed Karim

Entertainment facilities, such as a cinema and a casino, were envisioned as integral parts of Nasr City to attract potential residents. The open-air Nasr City Cinema had a seating capacity of 1,200 persons. The cinema also included a stage for live performances, with actors' rooms behind the stage and projection wall. The design consists of four independent structures, one on each side of the rectangular cinema hall, with the central space between them given over to rows of seating as the ground gently slopes down toward the screen/stage. The building was entered from Yusef Abbas Street under a raised rectangular volume containing the administration. Along the exterior wall, next to the entrance, were five stores. Another small structure along the southern wall contained the kitchen, bathrooms, and stairs to the projection room on the second level. The design maintained the feeling of openness with the use of materials such as breeze block and screens. The various walls and pavilions that make up the cinema are cubic in form, with the occasional slanted wall or surface. All floors were clad with mosaic cement tiles, suitable for the outdoors.

Al-Rahma Mosque

Address: 74 Ali Amin Street
GPS: 30.053726, 31.333113
Year: 1982
Architects: Hassan Rashdan, Hassan Metwalli

Cairo offers few examples of experimental mosque architecture that does not rely on historical forms or decorative motifs. Al-Rahma Mosque, commissioned by a charitable organization, is a rare example of unconventional mosque design in the city. The massing of the building takes an octagonal pyramid shape, topped with a dome. There are three stacked sections in the design: a sunken service area, with space for ablution and other purposes, the main prayer room contained within the octagonal pyramid, and the dome crowning the structure. The unusual roof structure defines the interior, which is raised above street level. Four narrow slit windows punctuate every other wall, allowing diffused light into the space.

Additional light enters from the clerestory windows below the dome, making it appear to hover above them. The main entrance, defined by a protruding hollow box, is located to the side and is reached by a set of steps. This leads to the main prayer hall but also to the women's area on a partial mezzanine level above the entrance, overlooking the main space. Four monumental freestanding minarets complete the composition of the building and add to its Brutalist aesthetic. The two front minarets are shorter than the two placed behind the mosque, which have a wider spacing between them. The minarets soar with vertical ribs crowned by octagonal balconies, reached by spiral stairs within the structure.

Housing Model 22

Address: Abbas al-Aqqad Street / Zaker Hussein Street
GPS: 30.045897, 31.339171
Year: 1959
Architect: Sayed Karim

Model 22 buildings, found at the southeast corner of District 7, consist of six apartments, two per floor, each with two bedrooms, a sitting room, living room, and dining room. The nine identical buildings are arranged parallel to one another, with alternating front and back gardens for each block. The design is compact and efficient; for example, in order to avoid the need for air shafts, bathrooms and kitchens were designed along the outer wall as part of the core of the building, consisting of the main stair and hallway. The ground floor is freed up by lifting the apartments on pilotis. The entrance leads directly to the stairs and to tightly designed hallways giving access to the apartments. Each apartment comes with two balconies, and windows in all rooms, placed to allow for cross-ventilation. The exterior is simply designed with horizontal articulations. The balconies on the narrow sides are stacked to one side, creating a contrast of solid and void. The building design is an example of Karim's attempt to cater for middle-class lifestyles in an affordable, compact form.

Housing Model 33

Address: 74 Ali Amin Street
GPS: 30.052956, 31.336063
Year: 1959
Architect: Sayed Karim

Perhaps the most fully realized example of Sayed Karim's ideas about mass housing and his interest in high-rise construction, five Model 33 buildings are located side by side in District 7 of Nasr City. Set back from the street, green areas envisioned as gardens surround the buildings, though they currently suffer from poor maintenance and several plots have been reused as plant nurseries. Each building consists of three connected sections. In plan the design displays characteristics of Metabolism, the Japanese architectural movement that created megastructures with modular elements connected in a fashion inspired by organic biological growth. The three sections that compose the building are each shaped like a three-pointed star, with three arms extending from a central circulation core. While the ten-story Model 33 is made up of three of these sections, in theory more can be added, creating a meandering vertical city.

The building is lifted on pilotis, freeing the ground floor to maintain visual and spatial continuity with the garden. Users have modified this feature, as stores currently enclose some of these areas under the blocks. Each of the building entrances leads to a spacious, hexagonal hall with a main stair enclosed with breeze blocks, an emergency stair, and two elevators. A hexagonal atrium rises the entire height of the building in the center of the circulation core. Each floor gives access to six apartments, arranged in three pairs. With six apartments in each of the building's three sections, the total number of units per floor is eighteen, and each building houses 180 apartments. The apartments are carefully designed, with little wasted space, and they are available in two-bedroom and three-bedroom options. Living and sleeping rooms are placed along the building's outer walls, with windows or balconies, while service rooms are located along the inner core of the building, ventilated by air shafts.

The exterior of the building is designed with crisp lines, ribbon-like surfaces, rectilinear articulations, alternating window placement, and stacks of deep corner balconies. A thin concrete shading element supported by slender columns traces the perimeter of the structure along the roof, which was designed to function as a rooftop garden shared by the community.

Nasr City

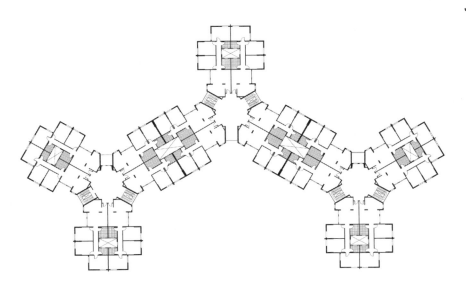

Typical Floor Plan

MAADI

Concrete screen façade of a residential building on Road 256.

Maadi

The construction of the rail link between Cairo and Helwan in 1904 led Elie and Victor Mosseri to purchase land near the railway south of the capital, which would become Maadi, named after a nearby village. The Delta Land and Investment Company was created to develop the land-speculation project, and retired Canadian officer Alexander James Adams produced the plan. Since Maadi was envisioned as a leafy garden city, the company enforced strict zoning regulations and building codes. The area is designed with a grid of streets overlaid with diagonal streets connecting traffic circles. By 1911 there were twenty-nine occupied houses in the area. During the First and Second world wars Maadi hosted military bases for British and Commonwealth troops, resulting in the area becoming populated with expatriates, who built houses in a variety of styles often linked to their home country.

Nationalization policies transformed the area's demographics and led to the establishment of the Maadi Development Company, as the suburb expanded eastward and westward. Demolitions of houses began in the 1970s, making room for some higher-density apartment blocks dotting the area, and later some of the city's tallest residential towers were built along the Nile near Maadi.

204

Residential Building

Address: Road 256
GPS: 29.967896, 31.270802
Year: 1962
Architects: Samir Fikry and Ragai Riad

Originally designed as a four-story building, this residential block belongs to a typology that was widespread in the 1960s and 1970s in Maadi, Heliopolis, and Mohandiseen. These family-commissioned concrete apartment buildings often incorporated a large family apartment on the entire ground or first floor, followed by additional floors, usually with two apartments per floor, for other members of the family. The building is set back from the street, with pilotis lifting it and creating a shaded space leading to the entrance. Building features commonly found in this typology include the use of brick cladding, particularly in the entrance and lobby areas, the inclusion of *brise soleil*, in the form of breeze-block screens, on the façade, and built-in planters on the balconies.t

Saint Thérèse Church
(proposed)

Year: 1950s
Architect: Sayed Karim

This funnel-shaped building is designed around two rounded arches placed parallel to one another. The smaller arch forms the altar wall and the larger one forms the entrance elevation at the front. The curvaceous, thin, concrete-shell structure contrasts with the sharp edges and straight lines of the bell tower and a floating horizontal plane cantilevered above the entrance along the main façade. The front and rear elevations are glazed, allowing for direct sight lines through the building. Two hyperbolic arches are also cut through the sides of the funnel to add to the building's structural integrity and to bring more light into the space. The church featured a large, stylized, relief sculpture of Christ, and a reflecting pool at the center of the main elevation. The design echoes Oscar Niemeyer's Church of Saint Francis of Assisi at Pampulha, Brazil.

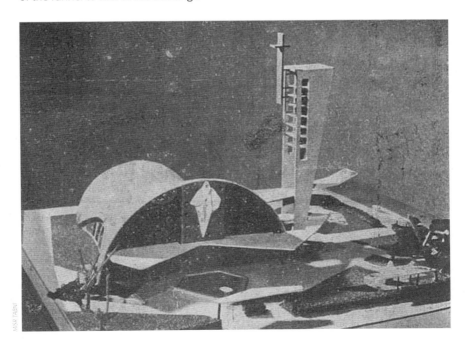

Maadi Mosque

Address: al-Farouq Square
GPS: 29.957603, 31.256507
Year: 1938
Architects: Awqaf Administration, Ahmed Bey Helmy

This building embodies the efforts made by the architects at the Awqaf Administration to create prototypes for modern mosques in Egypt. In form, it consists of two attached volumes: the prayer space is contained within a 10-meter-tall crenelated volume, while the ablution room is in a 6-meter-tall unarticulated block. Soaring at 24 meters, the square minaret is placed at the meeting point between the building's two volumes, near the main entrance. The mosque has no dome, retaining an overall cubic massing. The prayer hall is entered via a series of steps leading to a minimal interpretation of Islamic archways set in an extruded volume. A grid of reinforced-concrete columns in the prayer hall supports the timber of the roof, leaving a rectangular opening in the center. The *mihrab* is located aligned with the entrance on the opposite side. The entire structure is clad in stone.[81]

207
Villa Sayed Karim

Address: Road 11 / Road 79
GPS: 29.961206, 31.260012
Year: 1948
Architect: Sayed Karim

Building regulations in Maadi at the time specified an unbuilt buffer area along the perimeter of each plot ranging from 3 to 5 meters, depending on what neighbored the site on each side. The shape of this villa was largely determined by this reduction of buildable area on this 800m² plot, in addition to the existence of an ancient tree at the corner of the site. The L-shaped house bends around the tree, and part of the structure leading to the main entrance is lifted on pilotis in order to maximize the garden.

In terms of floor area, the ground floor is the smallest, containing a garden room and service areas as well as the entrance hall and main stairs. The garden room's main wall was designed as a set of glass folding doors that allow it to be entirely open to the outside. The materials of the walls and floors seamlessly continue from the outside to the inside of the room. At 235m², the second floor is the largest, divided into a public wing, composed of the living areas, kitchen, and dining room, and a private wing occupied by the master bedroom. The children's rooms and the architect's studio are located on the third floor.

One of the main features of the house is the spacious spiraling stair with sleek, minimal railings and a glass-block wall, topped by a shallow dome. A neon lighting fixture, now removed, spiraled around a metal rod suspended from the dome, dramatically illuminating the entire height of the stairs. Karim's attention to detail is best appreciated in the main living space, entered through large oak sliding doors that disappear into the walls when opened. The spacious room is organized by function: a music corner with a piano, three seating areas, and an elevated dining room reached by three steps. The wall separating the kitchen from the dining area is elaborately designed to conceal the air-conditioning duct above and heating radiator below, as well as some storage areas accessed through the kitchen. What appears to be a black-and-gold lacquered-wood decorative piece inset into the wall is a sliding door that allows open access into the kitchen.

From the choices in timber, stone, and textiles, Karim's attention to detail is exemplified in this house. Another notable feature is the planted window ledge, forming a natural treatment of cactus plants lining the strip windows running across the width of the dining area. Fluorescent lights are discreetly placed along the windows above the planters. Karim also designed the furniture of the house, using oak, leather, and a variety of textiles.[82]

Illustrations overleaf

Maadi

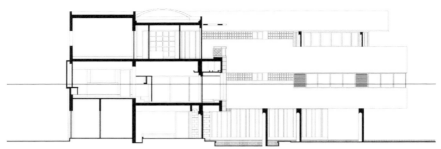

Cross Section

Maadi

Maadi Garden Villas

Address: Road 9
GPS: 29.961336, 31.257764
Year: 1949
Architect: Sayed Karim

Sayed Karim favored the duplex, or villa as he called it, as an ideal form of dwelling. He often integrated duplexes into his designs for large residential buildings. The Maadi Garden Villas is a collection of eight duplexes, four of which have two bedrooms, the others have three. The ground floor is dedicated to the car garages and service rooms. Levels two and four are identical, with the living spaces of the duplexes, while levels three and five contain the bedrooms. Each duplex is equipped with a stair that connects its two levels. An elliptical stairwell along the street brings residents to the apartment entrances on the second and fourth levels. The building turns its back on the street and faces the

small side garden, where all apartments have access to balconies. The side façade is the most dynamic, with levels two and four protruding slightly out of the main body of the building. The sleeping floors are rectilinear and are recessed slightly, giving them shaded balcony spaces.

Maadi Palace Building

Address: 9 Mustafa Kamel Street
GPS: 29.960094, 31.259608
Year: 1996
Architect: Ashraf Salah Abu Seif

This corner building consists of a base with stores and a mezzanine level, followed by seven additional floors. There are two entrances for the building: the apartments are accessed from Mustafa Kamel Street, the offices and commercial spaces from al-Nahda Street. The residential section, mostly containing three-bedroom apartments, is entered via a flight of steps to the mezzanine level, where the elevator lobby is located. The exterior reflects the two separate functions of the building. The commercial side is designed with a flat façade, a grid of windows, and a large, double-height portal in the center, while the residential side is deconstructed into a series of cubic volumes and recesses, with a discrete entrance reached by a flight of steps. The residential elevation appears to have been carved with the deepest recesses and highest concentration of terraces placed along a diagonal line across the façade. The interplay of volumes creates private terraces and balconies for all apartments, further accentuated by additional details such as windows with eyebrow arches, concrete planter boxes, and wooden pergolas.

Supreme Constitutional Court

Address: Corniche al-Nil
GPS: 29.968636, 31.239415
Year: 1999
Architect: Ahmed Mito

In 1994, the head of the Supreme Constitutional Court, Awad al-Murr, instigated the construction of a purpose-built structure to house it. It was previously accommodated in the High Court (#51), located Downtown. An architectural competition was held, which led to the selection of Ahmed Mito as the project architect. Al-Murr was a vocal opponent of Modernist and contemporary architecture, and required in the competition that entries reflect Egypt's ancient civilization. While Mito's first submission did not include direct visual references to ancient monuments, the implemented design was a compromise, as the jury from the court favored a classical design that directly quoted from ancient sources. Mito's solution was to incorporate simulacra of historical elements, composed unconventionally, forming a semicircular leaning colonnade with a curtain-wall backdrop. The main level of the court is elevated above street level, reached by two symmetrical ceremonial stairs. A domed central hall functions as the main distribution point for the internal spaces of courtrooms, meeting rooms, and offices. There is irony in incorporating in a modern court building references to ancient elements that are associated with funerary architecture, making the building reluctantly Postmodern.

Maadi Towers

Address: 7–66 Corniche al-Nil
GPS: 29.963475, 31.246334
Year: 1987
Architect: Arab Contractors

Also known as Abrag Osman, the Maadi Towers were envisioned as a 'towers-in-the-park,' high-Modernist, middle- and upper-bracket housing project. The complex, built on a Nile-side 160,000m² plot, consists of eighteen cast-in-place concrete towers. Together, these Brutalist structures contain 1,044 apartments, ranging in size between 125m² and 405m². They are arranged in two clusters, with different typologies. The first typology is seen in the five forty-two-story towers, at 140 meters high, with a square footprint placed closer to the Nile. These buildings consist of a concrete-grid exterior within which windows and balconies are set. The circulation cores are at the center of the towers, with living spaces arranged along the perimeter of their plan. At the bottom of each of the five towers is a four-story base, with a recessed, glazed entrance hall set behind the concrete columns carrying the structure, and apartments begin at the fifth floor. The second typology is seen in the twenty-six-story rectangular towers arranged parallel to the Nile in the southern part of the site and perpendicular to it in the north. The first four floors of these towers are terraced at a 45-degree angle at the front of the buildings. The slender, concrete ribs that support the terraced floors create a colonnade at the ground level. Like the other typology, the exterior consists of a concrete grid of windows. Green areas and leisure and commercial spaces are placed between the towers.

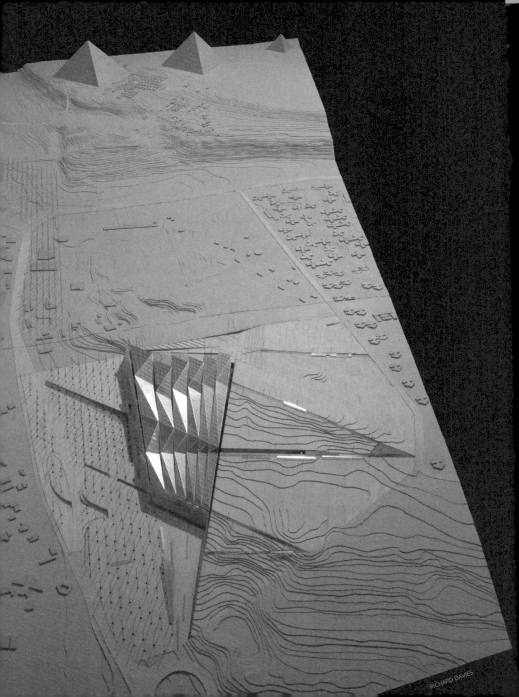
RICHARD DAVIES

OUTSKIRTS

Site model of the Grand Egyptian Museum.

Outskirts

Since 1900, Cairo's boundaries have been constantly expanded, often by private companies seeking real-estate development, as was the case with Maadi, Heliopolis, Manial, Agouza, and other districts. This direction has only been exponential since the establishment of Nasr City, and later the many desert cities initiated by the state. Poor infrastructure and upkeep, and the lack of enforced building codes and preservation policies toward modern constructions, have left Cairo's twentieth-century districts in a state of perpetual neglect, leading to an exodus of large sectors of private capital investing in real estate. The looming Administrative Capital comes after moves of other major institutions to the outskirts of Cairo, from the American University to the Egyptian Museum, leaving behind their Downtown buildings for new twenty-first-century facilities. The desert frontier of Cairo includes some of its newest buildings, such as the Crédit Agricole head office (#214). The periphery of the city has received disproportionate government spending in terms of infrastructure, given its relatively low population numbers; however, it lacks state services such as schools and hospitals, and public housing is limited and often grouped in small plots of land amid massive areas of privately owned developments, suburbs, and entire towns such as Rehab. Building codes and urban-planning rules within these private enclaves are largely up to their developers, and they vary greatly from one to the next. In addition to buildings that are part of these new developments, this section includes several older structures that were built in locations that were relatively secluded at the time of their construction.

The American University in Cairo

Address: AUC Avenue, New Cairo
GPS: 30.017235, 31.500810
Year: 2008
Architects: Abdelhalim Community Design Collaborative, Sasaki Associates

The purpose-built 260-acre university campus in New Cairo radically transformed the nature of the American University in Cairo since its founding in 1919. The new suburban campus master plan is centered on a main spine connecting a series of courtyards and plazas meant for community gathering. In-between spaces for gathering and reflection dot the campus. Faculty buildings, classrooms, administration, and the central library are reached via the central spine. Abdelhalim CDC and Sasaki designed the university's six schools, and other architects were commissioned to carry out the design for single buildings: Hardy Holzman Pfeiffer Associates for the Library, Ricardo Legorreta for the Campus Center and student residences, and Ellerbe Beckett for the indoor and outdoor athletic complex.

The campus is surrounded by gardens and landscaped areas designed by Carol R. Johnson and Associates in collaboration with Sites International. Despite the involvement of several architectural offices in the overall design, harmony is achieved by the use of certain geometric forms, consistent use of materials—sandstone is employed throughout—and the commitment to environmentally conscious design that reduces building temperatures and controls sunlight with a variety of shading devices. Traditional architectural elements such as *malqaf*s (windcatchers), *shukhshaykha*s (vented domes), and *mashrabiya*s (wooden screens) are implemented throughout, sometimes in a modernized, minimal form, at other times as direct quotations from traditional architecture.

The Library's striking exterior is composed of a double façade with a concrete-grid screen protecting the glazed, five-story structure from the sun. A monumental stone-clad gateway marks the entrance.

Outskirts

Bank ABC

Address: North 90 Road, New Cairo
GPS: 30.020612, 31.416151
Year: 2018
Architect: Engineering Consultants Group

A six-story, concrete, skeletal structure already stood on this site before it was purchased by ABC Bank to be transformed into its head office. The project included the integration of the bank's building program into the existing structure, making the necessary alterations to interiors and designing a skin system. The building sits above a two-level basement that houses mechanical rooms and a 260-car garage. An entry lobby on the ground level gives access to lounges and a cafeteria for employees. The following six identical floors house offices.

The structure has a glazed curtain wall, with a second, perforated, outer wall functioning as a sunscreen. The concrete outer shell is stone-clad, with openings are of varying sizes depending on sun exposure and direction. The north and south façades are marked with narrow, small openings corresponding with the building's six office levels, while two rows of larger, wider openings expose the curtain wall on the east and west façades. The cladded concrete outer façade hovers above the ground floor giving it the appearance of lightness.

Unity Building
(Crédit Agricole Head Office)

Address: Ring Road, Qattamiya
GPS: 30.006280, 31.402043
Year: 2015
Architect: Engineering Consultants Group

One year after its completion the Unity Building gained LEED Platinum certification, the highest level of the US Green Building Council rating system to evaluate the environmental performance of a building. The building's design ensures efficiency in its use of water and energy and use of environmentally friendly materials, as well as creating high-quality indoor environments. The structure, with a footprint of 5,100m², houses offices for up to 1,500 employees, with facilities such as a restaurant, gym, training rooms, and meeting rooms, as well as a three-hundred-seat auditorium.

The U-shaped building consists of two basement levels, garden level, ground floor, and three typical floors for administration. Open office spaces are modularly designed, with workstations that can be adjusted to clusters of four or six, in addition to individual offices, boardrooms, and meeting rooms placed around the internal core overlooking the atrium

Internally, the building is organized around this atrium space and courtyard overlooked by office windows, thus minimizing the surface of externally exposed façades. A large floating roof cantilevers to create deep shadowed areas on the façade's most exposed surfaces. The floor-to-ceiling fenestration is carefully designed with varying widths to control and minimize direct sunlight. A system of double walls protects the building's exterior to reduce temperatures.

Cairo International Airport
(Terminal 1)

Address: North 90 Road, New Cairo
GPS: 30.127223, 31.401968
Year: 1963
Architect: Mustafa Shawky, Salah Zeitoun

Cairo's first airport was today's Almaza Airport, opened in 1932. The current facility stands on the location of a Second World War British–American airbase that was handed to the Egyptian authorities after the war and was transitioned into use as a civilian airport. With the expansion of commercial aviation and the growing tourism industry, a new terminal building was commissioned in 1955. At the time of its completion it was the largest and most modern airport in the region, handling one million passengers in its first year.

The 75,000m² building consists of several overlapping boxy volumes containing the main components of the airport: arrival hall, departure hall, services, and administration block. The freestanding 50-meter-tall air-traffic-control tower is located at the front of the building. One of the most striking features was the spacious departure hall, designed with a wide expanse uninterrupted by columns. A row of rectangular pillars marks off the large entrance hall, with the area of airline desks. The dropped ceiling with its brightly lit grid of light boxes was a nod to American corporate architecture and gave the interior a contemporary feel. Wall and floor surfaces were clad in a variety of Egyptian stones. The building was designed with seventeen elevators, two escalators, and twenty-five sets of stairs. The administration block, located overlooking the runway, consists of six stories, partially lifted on pilotis. Its façade comprised a grid of small windows arranged in strips corresponding with the floors. Vertical concrete sun-breakers gave the block architectural definition.

The building (now known as Terminal 1) underwent subsequent renovations. The 1963 concrete exterior is no longer visible today, as the structure is presently covered with paneling and some parts were demolished or severely altered. The main departure hall has been redesigned for current security standards, though it retains the feeling of openness in its original design.

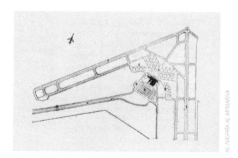

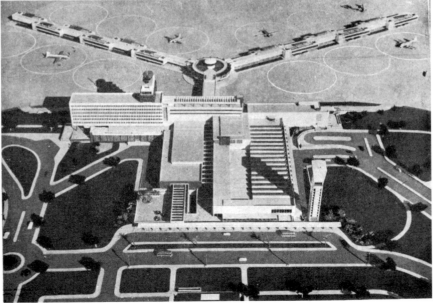

Outskirts

Abusir House 2

Address: Abusir, al-Badrashin
GPS: 29.900657, 31.205962
Year: 2003
Architect: Tarek Labib

The residence and studio of architect Tarek Labib is located in a village on the edge of the agricultural land facing the pyramids at Abusir. The house reinterprets vernacular forms and constructs them in unusual combinations of materials: concrete block, red brick, and translucent salt bricks from Siwa. The dwelling is contained in three sculptural volumes that emerge from the ground, with additional rectilinear forms protruding from them to create the various rooms. The volumes are not equal in size but they echo one another in terms of their forms, with a wave-like, sweeping curve on one side cut off by a straight line at an angle on the other. All the curved lines in the building are generated from the traditional Coptic cross-vault reinterpreted as a parabolic arch.

The house is entered through a portico under one of the two-story sculptural forms. The red-brick vaulted entertainment room is the focal point of the slightly raised ground floor. The 6-meter-wide parabolic arches on either end of the space govern the shape of the room in section. A smaller red-brick vaulted archway is set within the larger arch separating the dining room from the kitchen. The wall space between the two inset arches is filled with translucent salt brick. The office space is located on the mezzanine level. The first floor is centered on a living room flanked by the master bedroom wing to one side and a smaller guest bedroom to the other. A courtyard placed among the three main volumes of the house acts as a circulation core and ventilation shaft.

Outskirts

217

Harraniya Arts Center

Address: Harraniya Village
GPS: 29.969003, 31.176389
Year: 1951–72
Architect: Ramses Wissa Wassef

The Harraniya complex of buildings was implemented over two decades to include tapestry workshops, an exhibition hall, dwellings for resident weavers, farm buildings, a museum for artist Habib Gorgi, and several houses such as that for artist Adam Henein. Envisioned as a utopian, self-contained weaving village, its design integrates with its agricultural and natural surroundings. The mud-brick architecture further draws the connection with the land. The arrangement of volumes, rooms, and circulation is rational yet free from fixed grids, making the village feel spontaneous. Cubic volumes topped by domes with openings for cross-ventilation reduce indoor temperature and create comfortable spaces. Light plays an important role in the design, giving it a sculptural quality. A set of architectural elements appears throughout the complex, such as wide pointed arches, tapered buttresses, timber ceilings, and turned-wood details. The project received the Aga Khan Award for Architecture in 1983.

Farouk Resthouse

Address: Giza Pyramids
GPS: 29.980351, 31.135957
Year: 1946
Architect: Mustafa Fahmy

This 513m² ancient-Egypt–inspired structure built as a resthouse at the Pyramids for King Farouk is symmetrical in plan, and its interior spaces are modern in spirit, but its decorative program is pastiche. The rectangular building is located at the foot of the Great Pyramid, surrounded by 3-meter-high walls on three sides and the edge of the Giza Plateau to the north. Two elaborate gateways are located in the western wall. The main façade is tapered at both ends, topped with a cornice mimicking that of an ancient Egyptian pylon. In the center is the entrance, set within an Egyptian-themed gate flanked by two large replica statues of Thutmose III and eight tall, narrow, slit openings. A long strip of alternating windows and statuettes of King Tutankhamun running almost the entire width of the façade defines the second level. The staircase is located in the center of the rear of the building and is expressed architecturally with two smaller pylon forms perpendicular to the façade.

The ground floor contains a central hall leading to the stair in the rear, flanked by a reception space and an office. The top floor contains a bedroom wing and living, dining, and smoking rooms. Constructed of stone-clad brick masonry, the structure's interior was lavishly finished with marble and parquet floors, with notable features such as hollow alabaster pharaonic-style lotus columns lit from inside. Wall paintings depict ancient Egyptian hunting and war scenes. The furniture ranged in style from Arabesque for the public reception areas, to Louis XIV for the bedroom, and Art Deco for the office furniture. There were several replicas of hand-picked ancient pieces from the Egyptian Museum chosen by the king, such as Tutankhamun's throne.

After 1952 the house was opened to the public as a museum for a brief period, then it was transformed into a cafeteria. It has been unused since the 1960s and shows significant damage today.

Grand Egyptian Museum

Address: Alexandria Desert Road
GPS: 29.994913, 31.119365
Year: Projected 2022
Architect: Heneghan Peng

This design for a new museum of Egyptian antiquities to be located on a 50-meter-high plateau overlooking the Pyramids of Giza two kilometers away was the winning entry of an international competition that ended in 2003. It takes the shape of a chamfered triangle positioned with visual axes from the site to the three Pyramids, which are visible from within the museum. The 100,000m² complex sits on a 50-hectare site that includes 24,000m² of permanent exhibition space, a conference center, a conservation center, a children's museum, and gardens. The main galleries are organized as a series of long, layered spaces, each with a focal point on the Pyramids outside. Visitors approach the museum across an open plaza flanked by landscaped areas with vegetation inspired by ancient Egyptian gardens. The monumental outer façade was initially designed of translucent stone installed in triangular panels of varying sizes, but this was changed during implementation to a glass curtain-wall with triangular panels. Triangles are a consistent motif throughout the project in form, ornamentation, and details. Pyramidal forms marking the main entrance are extruded from the otherwise flat façade. Once behind the edge of the façade, visitors are met with a grand atrium space, the building's most public area, functioning as the main distribution point to the various spaces and galleries via a monumental stair lined with Egyptian sculpture.

Pyramid House

Address: New Giza
GPS: 30.017953, 31.071316
Year: 2009–19
Architect: Shahira Fahmy

This concrete-and-glass house located on a hill overlooks the Pyramids of Giza. The house is organized into two interweaving volumes, connecting in different points that become shared spaces. The building's form results from the interior arrangement of functions divided into four loosely defined quadrants of the house: the formal living space for social gatherings located on the upper floor, afforded the best view from the site; the indoor pool and related activities underneath; the family room, kitchen, and bathroom on the ground floor to have a better connectivity with the garden; and the three bedrooms on the upper floor. One of the volumes, containing the family room, clings to the ground facing the surrounding palm groves, creating a horizontal axis. The other volume detaches itself from the ground toward a better view of the Pyramids, creating a vertical axis. By lifting the vertical-axis volume off the ground, the architect createds a space underneath for a covered terrace and indoor pool. A ramp connects the entrance lobby to the formal living space on the second level, bypassing the more private parts of the house.

Ground Floor Plan

221
National Cancer Institute

Address: al-Bustan, Sheikh Zayed
GPS: 30.029841, 31.015113
Year: Projected 2019
Architect: Skidmore, Owings, & Merrill

The design of the largest cancer center in Europe, the Middle East, and Africa consists of several modules connected by circulation spines that facilitate movement between various program elements of the 836,000m² campus. While general access spines allow all users to reach common spaces and service facilities such as lounges and cafeteria, staff-only spines are designed for efficient movement across the vast site. The program includes a thousand-bed hospital, in- and outpatient facilities, research laboratories, and a nursing institute, as well as facilities for training and conferences. Six modules compose the inpatient facility, and four additional volumes constitute the outpatient hospital. The complex is punctuated by several landscaped courtyards and a system of building-skin treatments that reduce temperatures while maximizing indirect sunlight. The building, largely funded by donations and subscriptions, is designed for implementation in phases that will create a comprehensive whole when completed.

Dar al-Handasa Office Building

Address: Smart Village, Alexandria Desert Road
GPS: 30.074512, 31.024109
Year: 2013
Architect: Perkins+Will

This six-story building houses the offices of Dar al-Handasa, an architecture and construction company. Situated in the Smart Village, an office park located along the Cairo–Alexandria Desert Road, the LEED Gold-certified headquarters has a triangular footprint, with a triangular glass-roofed atrium. Energy-saving features include a solar hot-water system, photovoltaic panels on the roof, an energy-recovery dehumidification system, a heliostat solar tube, a six-story water wall that cools the space through evapotranspiration, and a glazed building envelope that reduces indoor temperatures. The office spaces are designed with an open plan and extensive use of glass for maximum sight lines. Horizontal and vertical circulation facilitate movement, such as footbridges along the main façade, overlooking the atrium, that connect the different wings of the building. A screen with diamond-shaped ribs articulates the center of the building's glazed elevations. The same shapes are repeated in the atrium, as petal forms attached to the walls to reflect light. The main staircase climbs the height of the building, with an elaborate lighting feature in the center.

223
Designopolis

Address: Sheikh Zayed, Alexandria Desert Road
GPS: 30.077986, 30.952306
Year: 2012
Architect: Shahira Fahmy

With the rapid growth of suburban developments west of Cairo, Designopolis was envisioned as a retail park with a focus on design shops and showrooms catering to the furnishing needs of the area's new residents. Situated on the edge of Sheikh Zayed, the project stretches for 850 meters along the Cairo–Alexandria Desert Road, covering an area of 116,000m², with two hundred outlets comprising 60,000m² of retail space.

The architect created an outdoor pedestrian shopping experience, with the cubic volumes of the showrooms connected by a network of walkways, ramps, landscaped terraces, and steps. Parking and mechanical spaces are located below ground. The landscaping incorporates trees and plants suitable for the dry environment, such as olive trees.

Japanese Garden

Address: Muhammad Mustafa al-Maraghi Street, Helwan
GPS: 29.848821, 31.340454
Year: 1917
Architect: Muhammad Zulfaqar Pasha

With the opening of the first sulfurous baths in 1888, Helwan established its place as a therapeutic escape from Cairo. It evolved in the first half of the twentieth century as a leafy suburb, built on a grid of gardens and private dwellings. Landmarks in the area include the Khedivial Astronomical Observatory, built 1904, and Egypt's largest, now abandoned, private psychiatric hospital, completed in 1939 and overlooking the Japanese Garden.

The garden was the brainchild of statesman Muhammad Zulfaqar Pasha, prime minister 1910–14 and father to Modernist painter Mahmoud Said. He dedicated the garden to Sultan Hussein, ruler of Egypt at the time. Zulfaqar designed several thematic gardens, including al-Andalus in Zamalek. The Japanese Garden features a series of fish ponds, canals, hills, and a diverse array of trees. It is home to tens of cement-cast identical pink Buddhas, in addition to several larger individual statues, including two larger, seated Buddhas and a 3-meter Buddha head. A fountain features a seated Buddha over a lotus flower surrounded by three elephants. The park also featured a tall pagoda, a Japanese gate, and a large gazebo where bands performed. Cement-cast pink lanterns flank the park's central promenade, which divides it into two equal halves.

225
Studios Misr

Address: Marioutiya Corridor
GPS: 30.095197, 31.339817
Year: 1935
Architect: Abu Bakr Khairat

In 1925 Banque Misr established its film-production company in an effort to create a national cinema with local expertise. The studios, constructed in one year and completed in 1935, were established on a 7-hectare plot along Marioutiya Canal near the Pyramids. They comprised three filming studios in warehouse-like structures, the largest measuring 28 x 18 x 12 meters and the smallest 15 x 9 x 6 meters. The complex included spaces for all the necessary stages of film production, such as film-processing laboratories, printing facilities, editing studio, film-set workshops, actors' rooms, and make-up and costume rooms, in addition to outdoor film sets. The primary architectural focus of the site is the main pavilion comprising reception and waiting rooms as well as administration. The white, two-level Streamline Moderne building consists of a sweeping curve with large square windows on the ground floor and a strip window across the façade on the first level. To the south of the curved section a boxy, rectangular volume adjoins the structure, where the main entrance is located on the corner, marked by a soaring flagpole above the door and the name of the studio in Latin letters sitting on a cantilevered concrete awning. An entrance terrace reached by three steps is overlooked by a balcony from the director's office. A large sign in a stylized Arabic script crowns the curved façade with the words 'Studio Misr' appearing to hover above the structure. The first film produced in the new studios was *Wedad* (1936) starring Umm Kulthoum. The studio declined severely after 1960, when it was nationalized and became state-run. Although the building would be a logical site for a cinema museum, it currently lies unused and in poor condition.

Skyline

Address: Qattamiya Road
GPS: 29.966022, 31.350484
Year: Projected 2022
Architects: Raef Fahmi, Van Der Pas, Muhammad Hadid

Envisioned as the largest building in the world in terms of usable space, Skyline is a multipurpose development encompassing residential, entertainment, commercial, and office spaces in a single structure measuring 500 meters square. In order to bring light and air to all spaces in the fourteen-story building, a series of circular courtyards of varying sizes are carved out of the volume. These open-air, atrium-like spaces function as internal façades for residential units, most of which have views only toward the interior. The double-height ground floor and two additional levels form the commercial base of the building, rendered on the exterior with a modular design of triangular concrete supports. The exterior of the ten residential floors is glazed, with a strong emphasis on clean, horizontal lines that soften and curve at the center of each elevation. The building also features a fully landscaped roof garden, with recreational facilities such as a swimming pool.

Following Pages
Relief sculpture by artist Fathy Mahmoud on the exterior of the Chamber of Commerce designed by Sayed Karim (#26, built 1955) with figurative representations of Africa, the Mediterranean Sea, and Europe.

A pharaonic boat was discovered in a pit on this site in 1954, and the Brutalist museum that was built in 1964 directly over the pit reflects the Modernist attitudes of the time of its construction, refraining from pharaonic historicism despite its location at the base of the Great Pyramid. Private Collection.

Notes

1. Abd al-Gawwad 1989.
2. The northern part of Cairo alone, according to Janet Abu-Lughod, "doubled in population over the 1947–60 period to reach 1.6 million inhabitants, over one-third of Cairo's population." The overall population of the city nearly doubled over the same time span, and entire swaths of formally agricultural land (800 hectares in total) were developed as new residential districts (Mohandiseen and Agouza), in addition to the planning of Nasr City, a vast new urban expansion in the desert to the east (Abu-Lughod 1971, 179).
3. Sims 2010, 83.
4. Abu-Lughod 1971, 231.
5. As David Sims (2010) notes, "In 1950 virtually the whole of Cairo could be considered as formal" (p. 46). By 2009 a conservative estimate of 63 percent of the city's inhabitants lived in areas developed informally (p. 91). Architects are entirely absent from those areas.
6. Volait 2005.
7. Architectural Modernism in Egypt emerged in tandem with the development of Egyptian social sciences, the emergence of a newly fashioned urban middle class, and increasing national industrialization and consumerism in the interwar period (El Shakry 2007, 115).
8. Sayed Karim, "If Cairo were destroyed," *al-Ithnayn wa-l-dunya*, #586 (1945), 12–13.
9. Reynolds 2012.
10. Berman 1982.
11. Reynolds 2012.
12. Elshahed 2016a.
13. Wright 2008, 224, citing Ghannam 2002, 2.
14. For example, see Bozdogan 2001 and Cardinal 2012.
15. Modernist attitudes took shape in different national and cultural environments (Mercer 2005, 7).
16. Volait 1988.
17. Editors, "Architecture—Not Style," *Progressive Architecture* (December 1948), 49.
18. Sayed Karim, "A Year Onward," *Al Emara* 2/1–2 (1940), 2–4.
19. El Shakry, 2006.
20. Ormos 2009, 430–56.
21. Williams 2008, 76.
22. Steele 1997.
23. Bianca and Jodido 2004.
24. Wharton 2001, 52–54.
25. *Al Emara* #10 (1939), 510–17.
26. *Al Emara* #2 (1941), 68–70.
27. Capresi and Pampe 2015, 143–45.
28. *Al Emara* #10 (1939), 500–501.
29. *Al Emara* #3–4 (1940), 203.
30. *Al Emara* #3–4 (1940), 218.
31. *Al Emara* #3–4 (1953), 5–32.
32. *Al Emara* #7–8 (1940), 336–91.
33. El-Wakil 2016.
34. *Al Emara* #2 (1939), 72–82.
35. *Al Emara* #1 (1939), 18–22.
36. Taraga 2009.
37. *Al Emara* #6 (1939), 279–307.
38. *Al Emara* #7–8 (1941), 274–85.
39. *Al Emara* #3–4 (1952), 4–20.
40. *'Alam al-bina'* #9 (April 1981), 20–23.
41. *Al Emara* #3 (1949), 5–16

42 *Al-Nashra al-mi'mariya* (March 1968), 71–77.
43 *Al Emara* #2 (1941), 65–67.
44 *Al Emara* #7–8 (1947), 18–21.
45 *Al Emara* #3 (1948), 5–12.
46 *Al Emara* #1–2 (1949), 9–28.
47 Loeffler 1998, 250.
48 *Al Emara* #5 (1940), 304–309.
49 *Al Emara* #3–4 (1940), 198–99.
50 *Al Emara* #5 (1940), 281–87.
51 *Al Emara* #3–4 (1940), 186–87.
52 *Al Emara* #3–4 (1939), 142–45.
53 *Al Emara* #3–4 (1939), 148–49.
54 *Al Emara* #3–4 (1940), 159–65.
55 *Al Emara* #1–3 (1950), 84–85.
56 *Al Emara* #1–3 (1950), 31–34.
57 *Al Emara* #2 (1940), 86–89.
58 Bodenstein 2010.
59 *Al Emara* #3–4 (1940), 178–83.
60 *'Alam al-bina'* (May 1984), 17–18.
61 Elshahed 2016b.
62 *Al Emara* #3 (1957), 5–24.
63 *Al Emara* #7–8 (1948), 5–12.
64 *Al Emara* #1 (1940), 9–15.
65 *Al Emara* #1 (1957), 6–17.
66 *Al Emara* #2 (1939), 70–71.
67 *Al Emara* #3–4 (1939), 127–31.
68 *Al Emara* #4 (1948), 5–12.
69 *Al Emara* #1 (1939), 15–17.
70 Ciranna 2001.
71 *Al Emara* #4–5 (1949), 11–20.
72 *Al Emara* #6 (1957), 5–13.
73 *Al Emara* #8–10 (1950), 21–26.
74 *Al Emara* #9–10 (1949), 15–20.
75 *Al-Funun al-mi'mariya* #1 (1950), 35–40.
76 *Al Emara* #5–6 (1941), 220–23.
77 *Al Emara* #3–4 (1940), 193–95.
78 *Al Emara* #1 (1940), 24–25.
79 *Al Emara* #2 (1940), 82–83.
80 *Al-Nashra al-mi'mariya* (March 1968), 25–34.
81 *Al Emara* #10 (1939), 502–503.
82 *Al Emara* #1–3 (1950), 49–68.

Bibliography

ARCHIVES
al-Ahram Archives
Rare Books and Special Collections Library, American University in Cairo (RBSCL, AUC)
    Sayed Karim Collection
    Postcard Collection
    Ramses Wissa Wassef Collection
    Gamal Bakry Collection
    Hassan Fathy Collection
    Van Leo Collection
Mahmoud Riad Collection at RiadArchitecture

PERIODICALS
'Alam al-bina'
Bina' al-watan
Egypt Travel Magazine
Al Emara
al-Funun al-takhtitiya wa-l-mi'mariya
al-Funun al-mi'mariya
Al Hadika wal Manzil
Magallat al-muhandisin
Magallat al-shu'un al-baladiya wa-l-qarawiya
al-Musawwar
al-Nashra al-mi'mariya: li-gam'iyat al-muhandisin al-mi'mariyin al-misriyin

BOOKS AND ARTICLES
al-Qahira fi alf 'am, 969–1969. 1969. Cairo: Dar al-Katib al-'Arabi li-l-Tiba'a wa-l-Nashr.
Abd al-Gawwad, Tawfiq Ahmad. 1989. *Misr: al-'imara fi-l-qarn al-'ishrin*. Cairo: Anglo-Egyptian Bookshop.
Abu-Lughod, Janet. 1965. "Tale of Two Cities: The Origins of Modern Cairo," in *Comparative Studies in Society and History* 8/4 (July 1965), 429–57.
———.1971.*Cairo: 1001 Years of the City Victorious*. Princeton, NJ: Princeton University Press.
———. 1973. "Cairo: Perspective and Prospectus," in L. Carl Brown, ed., *From Madina to Metropolis*, 95–113. Princeton: Darwin Press.
Arbid, George, ed. 2014. *Fundamentalists and Other Arab Modernisms*. Beirut: Arab Center for Architecture.
Arnaud, Jean-Luc. 1998. *Le Caire, mise en place d'une ville moderne, 1867–1907*. Arles: Sindbad Actes Sud.
Avermaete, Tom, Serhat Karakayali, Marion von Osten. 2010. *Colonial Modern: Aesthetics of the Past, Rebellions for the Future*. London: Black Dog Publishing.

Avermaete, Tom, Mark Swenarton, Dirk Van Den Heuvel, eds. 2015. *Architecture and the Welfare State*. New York: Routledge.

Baron, Beth. 2009. "The Formation of National Culture in Egypt in the Interwar Period: Cultural Trajectories," in *History Compass* 7/1 (2009), 155–80.

Berman, Marshall. 1982. *All That Is Solid Melts into Air: The Experience of Modernity*. New York: Simon and Schuster.

Bianca, Stefano and Philip Jodido, eds. 2004. *Cairo: Revitalising a Historic Metropolis*. Turin: Umberto Allemandi & Co. for the Aga Khan Trust for Culture.

Bodenstein, Ralph. 2010. "Industrial Architecture in Egypt from Muhammad 'Ali to Sadat: A Field Survey," in Mohammad al-Asad, ed., *Workplaces: The Transformation of Places of Production: Industrialization and the Built Environment in the Islamic World*. Istanbul: Bilgi University Press.

Bozdogan, Sibel. 2001. *Modernism and Nation Building: Turkish Architectural Culture in the Early Republic*. Seattle, WA: University of Washington Press.

Capresi, Vittoria and Barbara Pampe, eds. 2015. *Discovering Downtown Cairo: Architecture and Stories*. Berlin: Jovis.

Cardinal, Silvia Arango. 2012. *Ciudad y arquitectura: Seis generaciones que construyeron la América Latina moderna*. Mexico City: Fondo de Cultura Económica/Consejo Nacional para la Cultura y las Artes.

Ciranna, Simonetta. 2001. "Italian Architects and Holy Space in Egypt," in Mercedes Volait, ed., *Le Caire—Alexandrie: Architectures européennes, 1850–1950*. Cairo: Institut français d'archéologie orientale.

Cohen, Jean-Louis. 2011. *Architecture in Uniform: Designing and Building for the Second World War*. New Haven, CT: Yale University Press.

Cohen, Jean-Louis and Monique Eleb. 2002. *Casablanca: Colonial Myths and Architectural Ventures*. New York: Monacelli Press.

Colla, Elliott. 2007. *Conflicted Antiquities: Egyptology, Egyptomania, Egyptian Modernity*. Durham, NC: Duke University Press.

Crinson, Mark. 2012. "The Building without a Shadow: National Identity and the International Style," in Raymond Quek, Darren Deane, and Sarah Butler, eds., *Nationalism and Architecture*, 115–34. Burlington, VT: Ashgate Publishing Company.

Curtis, W.L.1996. *Modern Architecture since 1900*. London: Phaidon Press.

Development and Popular Housing Company 1954–1974, 1989. 1990. Cairo: al-Ahram.

Elshahed, Mohamed. 2016a. "Cairo after the Second World War and the Rise of Arab Engineering Professionals," in Amale Andraos and Nora Akawi, eds., *The Arab City: Architecture and Representation*, 79–91. New York: Columbia University Press.

———. 2016b. "Egypt Here and There: The Architectures and Images of National Exhibitions and Pavilions, 1926–1964," *Annales islamologiques* #50, 107–43.

———. 2019. "Workers' and Popular Housing in Mid-Twentieth-Century Egypt," in Kivanc Kilinc and Mohammad Gharipour, eds., *Social Housing in the Middle East: Architecture, Urban Development, and Transformational Modernity*, 64–87. Indiana: Indiana University Press.

Fabri, Roberto, Sara Saragoca, and Ricardo Camacho, eds. 2015. *Modern Architecture Kuwait 1949–1989*. Zurich: Niggli.

Fahmi, Gamal al-Din. 1972. *Madinat Nasr: 1959–1971*. Cairo: Madinat Nasr for Housing & Development.

al-Gawhari, Mahmud Muhammad. 1954. *Qusur wa tuhaf: min Muhammad 'Ali ila Faruq*. Cairo: Dar al-Ma'arif.

Ghannam, Farha. 2002. *Remaking the Modern*. Berkeley, CA: University of California Press.

Hammad, Muhammad. 1963. *Misr tabni*. Cairo.

Isenstadt, Sandy and Kishwar Rizvi. 2008. *Modernism and the Middle East: Architecture and Politics in the Twentieth Century*. Seattle, WA: University of Washington Press.

Karim, Sayed. N.d. *Ishtirakiyat al-villa*. Cairo: al-Nahda al-Misriya Publishers.

Loeffler, Jane C. 1998. *The Architecture of Diplomacy: Building America's Embassies*. New York: Princeton Architectural Press.

Mercer, Kobena. 2005. "Introduction," in Kobena Mercer, ed., *Cosmopolitan Modernisms*. Cambridge: The MIT Press.

Ormos, Istvan. 2009. *Max Herz Pasha (1856–1919): His Life and Career*. Cairo: Institut français d'archéologie orientale.

Owen, Roger. N.d. "The Cairo Building Industry and the Building Boom of 1897–1907," in Ministry of Culture, ed., *Colloque Internationale sur l'Histoire du Caire 1969*, 337–50. Cairo: Ministry of Culture/General Book Organization.

Reynolds, Nancy. 2012. *A City Consumed: Urban Commerce, the Cairo Fire, and the Politics of Decolonization in Egypt*. Stanford, CA: Stanford University Press.

Sakr, Tarek Mohammed Refaat. 1993. *Early Twentieth-Century Islamic Architecture in Cairo*. Cairo: The American University in Cairo Press.

Scharabi, Mohamed. 1989. *Kairo: Stadt und Architektur im Zeitalter des europäischen Kolonialismus*. Tübingen: Ernst Wasmuth Verlag.

El Shakry, Omnia. 2006. "Cairo as Capital of Socialist Revolution?" in Diane Singerman and Paul Amar, eds., *Cairo Cosmopolitan: Politics, Culture, and Urban Space in the New Globalized Middle East*, 73–98. Cairo: The American University in Cairo Press.

———. 2007. *The Great Social Laboratory: Subjects of Knowledge in Colonial and Postcolonial Egypt*. Stanford, CA: Stanford University Press.

Sims, David. 2010. *Understanding Cairo: The Logic of a City out of Control*. Cairo: The American University in Cairo Press.

Steele, James. 1997. *An Architecture for People: The Complete Works of Hassan Fathy*. London: Thames and Hudson.

Taraga, Hana. 2009. "The 'Gate of Heaven' (Sha'ar Hashamayim) Synagogue in Cairo (1898–1905): On the Contextualization of Jewish Communal Architecture," in *Journal of Jewish Identities* 2(1), 31–53.

Volait, Mercedes. 1988. *L'architecture moderne en Egypte et la revue al-'Imara (1939–1959)*. Cairo: CEDEJ.

———. 2001. "Town Planning Schemes for Cairo Conceived by Egyptian Planners in the 'Liberal Experiment' Period," in H.C.K. Nielsen and J. Skovgaard-Petersen, eds., *Middle Eastern Cities 1900–1950: Public Spaces and Public Spheres in Transformation*, 44–71. Aarhus: Aarhus University Press.

———. 2005. *Architectes et architectures de l'Egypte moderne (1830–1950): genèse et essor d'une expertise locale*. Paris: Maisonneuve et Larose.

El-Wakil, Leïla. 2016. *La Banque Misr du Caire: Antonio Lasciac, les décorateurs italiens et le "style arabe."* Bern: Peter Lang.

Wharton, Annabel Jane. 2001. *Building the Cold War: Hilton International Hotels and Modern Architecture*. Chicago: The University of Chicago Press.

Williams, Caroline. 2008. *Islamic Monuments in Cairo*. Cairo: The American University in Cairo Press.

Wright, Gwendolyn. 2008. "Global Ambition and Local Knowledge," in Sandy Isenstadt and Kishwar Rizvi, eds., *Modernism and the Middle East: Architecture and Politics in the Twentieth Century*. Seattle, WA: University of Washington Press.

Index of Architects

Abdel Aziz, Abdullah 305
Abdel Gawad, Tawfiq 23–24, 36, 312, 323, 344
Abdelhalim Community Design Collaborative 378
Abdelhalim, Abdelhalim Ibrahim 41, 42
Abdel Hamid, Maher 194
Abdel Qader, Amin 298
Abu Seif, Ashraf Salah 371
ACE Consulting Engineers 147
Antonius, Raymond 97, 178, 213, 335
Arab Contractors 147, 301, 373
Arup, Ove 121
Ashraf, Shams al-Din 266
Awqaf Administration 91, 109, 202, 236, 238, 290, 366
Ayrout, Charles 35, 118, 187, 208, 231, 274, 337
Ayrout, Habib 133
Azema, Léon 134
Bakhoum, Michel 303, 346
Bakry, Gamal 20, 228, 246, 270
Balassiano, Max 309, 325
Balyan, Garo 268
al-Baradei, Muhammad 243
Baume-Marpent 252
Bayoumi, Abdel Fattah 194
Becket, Welton 88
Brandani, Adolfo 306
Brocher, Gustave 128
Cattaui, Maurice Youssef 125
Chamass, Ezra 328
Charmi, Ahmed 35, 72, 73, 78, 189, 204, 253, 262, 352
Dar al-Handasa 103
Development and Popular Housing Company 222, 286
Dixon, John Edward 195
Dorman Long & Co. Ltd. 90
Dourgnon, Marcel 33, 86
Edrei, Max 37, 114, 278
Engineering Consultants Group 42, 380, 381

Erlanger, Victor 134
Fabricius, Dimitri 116
Fahmi, Hussein 76
Fahmi, Raef 395
Fahmy, Awad Kamel 269, 303
Fahmy, Mahmoud 110
Fahmy, Mustafa 32, 35, 37, 132, 164, 189, 232, 262, 263, 387
Fahmy, Selim Kamel 269, 303
Fahmy, Shahira 389, 392
Fathy, Hassan 31, 40, 79
Fikry, Samir 364
Filsak, Karel 225
Foster + Partners 154
Frisco, Henri 272
Freudenreich, Milan 291
Fuad, Ahmad 96
Gabr, Ali Labib 32, 102, 129, 162, 210, 227, 253, 262, 275, 279, 352
al-Gohary, Farouk 242, 305
Graham, Bruce 150
Greiss, Milad 328
Hadid, Muhammad 395
Hadid, Zaha 148, 347
Hafez, Islam 221
Hardy, Jacques 134
Helmy, Ahmed Bey 366
Heneghan Peng 388
Herz, Max 34, 74, 76, 124,
Horowitz, Oscar 126
Hosny, Abd al-Hadi 349
Ismail, Muhammad Kamal 92, 137
Jacobsen, Hugh 104
Jaspar, Ernest 34, 310, 326
Karim, Sayed 10, 23, 28, 30, 36, 37, 38, 39, 43, 48, 101, 107, 112, 123, 133, 138, 144, 151, 174, 215, 229, 239, 259, 271, 276, 330, 332, 340, 342, 350, 351, 353, 354, 355, 357, 358, 365, 367, 370, 395
Khairat, Abu Bakr 181, 203, 230, 394
Khoury, Albert 24, 329
Komides, D. 296
Kosseiba, El Ghazali 169

Labib, Tarek 42, 384
Lasciac, Antonio 35, 84, 121, 128,
    173, 302
Leonori, Aristide 120
Leonori, Pio 120
Limongelli, Domenico 288
Mahboub, Mahmoud Sabry 143, 236,
Manescalco Bey, Alfonso 74
Marcel, Alexandre 319, 320
March, Werner 346
Masarra, Magd 318
Masoud, Ali al-Meligi 250, 254, 256
Matasek, Eduard 124, 125
Mazza, Youssef 183
Metcalf and Associates 177
Metwalli, Hassan 356
Michael Graves Architecture & Design
    149
Mito, Ahmed 42, 74, 372
Momen, Galal 92, 146, 233, 307
Nafilyan, Leon 98
Nahas, Antoine Selim 35, 95, 122, 220,
    273, 296, 300
Nassar, Ali Nour al-Din 145, 150, 214
Nassar, Fuad 305
Nasr City Company 304
Newnum, Eric 204
Nicholas, Charles 195
Nikken Sekkei Ltd. 263
Nouman, Muhammad Sherif 191, 198,
    322, 353
Omar, Muhammad Ramzy 139, 176, 180
Parcq, Georges 127, 128
Perkins+Will 391
Prampolini, Carlo 34, 182
Qinawi, Abdel Salam 117
Raafat, Ali 240
Raafat, Muhammad 106
Rafea, Samy 348
Rashdan, Hassan 356
al-Refaei, Amr 243
Riad, Mahmoud 10, 20, 38, 87, 88, 89,
    100, 101, 130, 166, 238, 251
Riad, Ragai 364
Robida, Camille 324
Rossi, Gaston 37, 114
Rossi, Mario 91, 109, 110

Sabit, Ali 241
Sabri, Saber 110
Sabry, Kamal 117
Said, Ezzat 224
Said, Salah Zaki 153
Sasaki Associates 42, 80, 378
Serageldin, Anis 36, 211
Serjeant, J.P. 116
Shaboury, Karim 336
Shafie, Hassan 206, 262
Shafie, Mustafa 206, 262
Shaheen, Medhat Hassan 94
Shawky, Mustafa 108, 117, 157, 245,
    314, 382
Shebib, Naoum 38, 119, 152, 185,
    266, 316
Shehab el-Din, Seddiq 296
Shelbi, Emam 305
Sidki, Ahmad 96
Silvagni, Carlo Virgilio 76
Sites International 42, 80, 257, 378
Skidmore, Owings, & Merrill 150, 390
Tawfiq, Prince Muhammad Ali 196
Taylor, William 317
Toms, Vladimir 225
Van Der Pas 395
Verrucci, Ernesto 131
Warner, Burns, Toan, and Lunde 145
Wassef, Ramses Wissa 20, 40, 264,
    280, 386
Worschech Architekten 217, 223
Worthington, Hubert 318
Zananiri, Albert 35, 163, 212, 281
Zarb, Arnold 123
Zeitoun, Salah 108, 117, 157, 245,
    314, 382
Zollikofer, Max 116, 136
Zulfaqar Pasha, Muhammad 393